Politics

"Well-chosen primary sources abound in *Hollywood and Politics: A Sourcebook*, and I eagerly read document after document. Critchlow and Raymond provide valuable introductions, putting each one into context, then wisely step back and let the original material speak for itself."
—Valerie Yaros, Screen Actors Guild Historian

"A much-needed volume of primary source readings on the politics of Hollywood and American filmmaking. Ranging from the Depression of the 1930s through the culture wars of the recent past, the book offers a balanced, wide-ranging array of materials that speak to how the movies—and the people that made them—have confronted and interpreted a variety of political issues. Thought provoking and engaging."
—Steven Watts, author of *The Magic Kingdom: Walt Disney and the American Way of Life* and *Mr. Playboy: Hugh Hefner and the American Dream*

Money, power, and celebrity—the stuff of Hollywood is also the substance of politics. While Hollywood celebrities such as Susan Sarandon, George Clooney, and Ed Begley Jr. continue to attract attention from the media for their involvement in politics, Hollywood has been involved in politics since its earliest days.

Hollywood and Politics: A Sourcebook documents the entertainment industry's participation in American politics on both the Left and the Right. From the 1920s through today, this volume provides scholars of history, politics, and film with the controversial history of Hollywood's involvement in American politics. Through twenty-four chapters that begin with Upton Sinclair and take us all the way to the satire of "South Park," readers are guided through elections, trials, speeches, and memorandums, many of which have never before been published, providing rare insight into the history of Hollywood activism.

From WWII to Iraq, and from Walt Disney to Charlton Heston, *Hollywood and Politics* lays a historical foundation for anyone interested in how celebrities helped shape our country's policies and culture.

Donald T. Critchlow is Professor of History at Saint Louis University in St. Louis, Missouri. He is the editor of the *Journal of Policy History*, and author of *The Conservative Ascendancy: How the GOP Right Made Political History*.

Emilie Raymond is Assistant Professor of History at Virginia Commonwealth University in Richmond, Virginia. She is the author of *From My Cold, Dead Hands: Charlton Heston and American Politics*.

Hollywood and Politics

A Sourcebook

Edited by
Donald T. Critchlow and
Emilie Raymond

Routledge
Taylor & Francis Group

NEW YORK AND LONDON

First published 2009
by Routledge
270 Madison Ave, New York, NY 10016

Simultaneously published in the UK
by Routledge
2 Park Square, Milton Park, Abingdon, Oxon OX14 4RN

*Routledge is an imprint of the Taylor & Francis Group,
an informa business*

© 2009 Taylor & Francis

Typeset in Sabon by
RefineCatch Limited, Bungay, Suffolk
Printed and bound in the United States of America on acid-free paper by
Edwards Brothers, Inc.

Library of Congress Cataloging-in-Publication Data
Hollywood and politics : a sourcebook / edited by Donald T. Critchlow
and Emilie Raymond.
    p. cm.
  Includes index.
  1. Politics and culture—United States—History—20th century—
Sources. 2. Motion picture industry—Political aspects—United States—
History—20th century—sources. 3. Motion picture actors and
actresses—United States—Political activity—Sources. 4. Motion picture
producers and directors—United States—Political activity—Sources.
5. Celebrities—United States—Political activity—Sources. I. Critchlow,
Donald T., 1948– II. Raymond, Emilie, 1973-
  E743.H6335 2009
  306.20973—dc22   2009011170

ISBN10: 0–415–96535–7 (hbk)
ISBN10: 0–415–96536–5 (pbk)

ISBN13: 978–0–415–96535–4 (hbk)
ISBN13: 978–0–415–96536–1 (pbk)

CONTENTS

Introduction

Money, power, and celebrity—the stuff of Hollywood is also the substance of politics. It's little wonder, therefore, that Hollywood and American politics have become so closely related. Celebrities campaign and contribute to candidates and political causes, while politicians and activists seek celebrity endorsements and donations to further their agendas. The relationship of Hollywood and politics is more than celebrity involvement, however. Because of the importance of movies in American popular culture, Hollywood has attracted intense scrutiny from critics who have found cultural and political bias in the film industry. At the same time, Hollywood involvement in political and social causes from anti-Communism in the 1950s, the civil rights movement and the anti-Vietnam War movement in the 1960s, feminism in the 1970s, the nuclear freeze movement in the 1980s, among many others, reveals a rich meaning to the term "Hollywood politics" in American politics.

This volume of primary documents seeks to engage readers interested in the multiple meanings of Hollywood and politics by using a topic approach. Specifically, this volume is organized into five parts: Electoral Politics, Public Policy, War and Patriotism, Social Movements, and Cultural Values. Each part includes chapters that allow readers to look at Hollywood politics through specific debates over a range of issues.

Hollywood involvement in electoral politics is examined through a series of elections, beginning with the California gubernatorial election in 1934. When Upton Sinclair, a socialist, won the Democratic Party nomination for governor in 1934 running on a program called "End Poverty in California" (EPIC), Hollywood studio moguls led by Louis B. Mayer, head of Metro–Goldwyn–Mayer (MGM), mobilized one of the most expensive campaigns at the time in the state's history to defeat Sinclair. The studios insisted that actors, directors, producers, and technicians contribute to the anti-Sinclair campaign. This massive fundraising effort allowed the studios to launch a massive media attack on Sinclair using pamphlets, editorials, and faked newsreels. Although Sinclair was defeated for election, many in Hollywood disliked this arm twisting by the studios. By the late 1930s, many in Hollywood had begun to shift to the left politically.

Other chapters in this part discuss celebrity involvement in the 1952, 1960, and 1964 presidential elections, and the California gubernatorial election in 1966. This election brought Ronald Reagan, running as an avowed conservative, to office. With this election, it appeared that Hollywood politics had come full circle. The defeat of Sinclair in 1934 was a conservative triumph, as was Reagan's election to the governor's mansion in 1966. Both elections show the power that Hollywood could exert on politics. More importantly, Reagan's election to the governorship, and later the presidency in 1980, reveal that celebrity and politics had become intricately linked.

Part II addresses Hollywood's involvement in debates over gun control, the nuclear buildup under Ronald Reagan, the HIV–AIDS research, and the environment. These issues mobilized Hollywood celebrities, although they often took different sides. Actors including Charlton Heston and Tom Selleck became spokespersons for the National Rifle Association, while comedian Rosie O'Donnell and actor Beau Bridges supported gun control legislation. The nuclear arms buildup under the Reagan administration in the 1980s elicited equally passionate debate when Hollywood celebrities Ed Asner, Martin Sheen, and Harry Belafonte joined peace demonstrations calling for a nuclear freeze on weapons development. Beginning in the 1980s, many in Hollywood also became involved in supporting HIV–AIDS research and awareness. In the 1990s, many in Hollywood expressed concern about the environment. Environmental activist organizations such as the Environmental Media Association enlisted Hollywood celebrities to promote their cause.

Part III explores Hollywood activism in World War II, the Cold War, the Vietnam War, the Persian Gulf War, the Iraq War, and the War on Terror. World War II and the Cold War involve America's struggle against totalitarian regimes, fascism in the 1930s and communism in the post-1940s era. The collapse of the Soviet Union in the late 1980s created a post-Cold War era dominated by politics of rogue nations, oil, humanitarian interventions, and terrorism. The uncertainty of this new post-Cold War international world created sharp dissent in Hollywood, but at the same time aroused fervent defenders of American military intervention in Iraq and Afghanistan.

Part IV examines debates over the social issues that have dominated post-World War II America, including the film industry. The emergence of the black civil rights movement in the 1960s aroused many Hollywood celebrities including Charlton Heston, Marlon Brando, and Harry Belafonte to become activists. Hollywood celebrities became involved in other civil rights struggles involving American Indians and women. At the same time, the film industry became increasingly sensitive to how racial and ethnic minorities were portrayed in films. This concern over racial and ethnic stereotyping came to include the depiction of Italian–Americans as gangsters involved in organized crime. Director Martin Scorsese and actor Robert DeNiro came under heavy criticism for their portraits of Italian–Americans as criminals.

The final part of this volume, Cultural Values, focuses on fierce debates over the film industry's involvement and obligation to shape American cultural values. These documents reveal that the culture war over Hollywood dates to its beginnings. Pressure from religious and veterans groups such as the American Legion led in the 1930s to the imposition of the Hays Code, a self-censoring guideline that prohibited violent and sexual content in films. Although the Hays Code remained in force until the late 1960s, the break-up of the studio system and the rise of independent film producers had already subverted the code. An even more far-reaching influence in changing culture, however, was the rise of pornography. A series of Supreme Court decisions beginning in the 1950s addressed definitions of obscenity and free speech, but the emergence of a large and hugely profitable pornographic film industry in the 1970s led directly to a culture war in American society. The debate over Hollywood culture extended beyond issues of free speech, artistic freedom, and definitions of obscenity and pornography. Involved in the culture war were basic questions over social responsibility, profit, and entertainment in the film industry.

In this culture war, critics of contemporary Hollywood charged that the film industry is a hotbed of liberal activism and that it has promoted a liberal cultural agenda. The West Coast has been deemed by these critics as "The Left Coast." Certainly many high-profile celebrities are enthusiastic supporters of progressive candidates and causes. However, history reveals that conservatives have long been active in Hollywood. Most of the founders of the old Hollywood studios were Republicans. The list of conservative celebrities is immense, including John Wayne, Jimmy Stewart, Ginger Rogers, and Ronald Reagan.

Throughout these documents, certain celebrities—John Wayne, Charlton Heston, Sidney Poitier, Harry Belafonte—appear and reappear.

These actors gained special media attention because they were stars and activists, but hundreds of others in Hollywood contributed and supported political campaigns and social causes. Movie stars, however, take on particular importance in politics because of their celebrity status. Politicians and social activists encourage celebrity involvement because it brings media attention. Inevitably in a mass culture, politicians and activists compete for the public's attention, so celebrity participation invites the media coverage.

Hollywood celebrity involvement in American politics is a fairly recent phenomenon given that the film industry emerged only in the early twentieth century. Celebrity itself is not new, however. Military heroes, famed authors, nationally known stage actors gained celebrity status in pre-modern American culture and politics. Military heroes such as George Washington, Andrew Jackson, William Harrison, Zachary Taylor, Ulysses S. Grant, and Theodore Roosevelt translated their national fame into political power. While America still has its military heroes who win political office, the influence of Hollywood celebrity on American politics reveals the power film has on the American imagination. In film, the audience's sense of heroism is reified into a movie image. Hollywood celebrity brings obvious name recognition, but it also introduces to voters a complex mixture of projected image, charismatic appearance, and actual personality.

In selecting the documents in this volume, the editors sought to capture the power that Hollywood celebrity plays in American politics. At the same time, the editors wanted to encourage readers to impart their own meaning to Hollywood and politics through these representative documents. Choosing which documents to include and what time periods to cover was not an easy task given the rich history of Hollywood's involvement and role in American politics. The editors prioritized issues and documents that agitated debate or created change. The editors realize that much has been excluded in this volume, but what has been included should introduce readers to the central and important role Hollywood has played in American politics. The selected documents are intended to provide intellectual engagement and entertainment. If this intention is fulfilled, we believe this volume should encourage readers to undertake further exploration of their own.

Donald T. Critchlow
Emilie Raymond

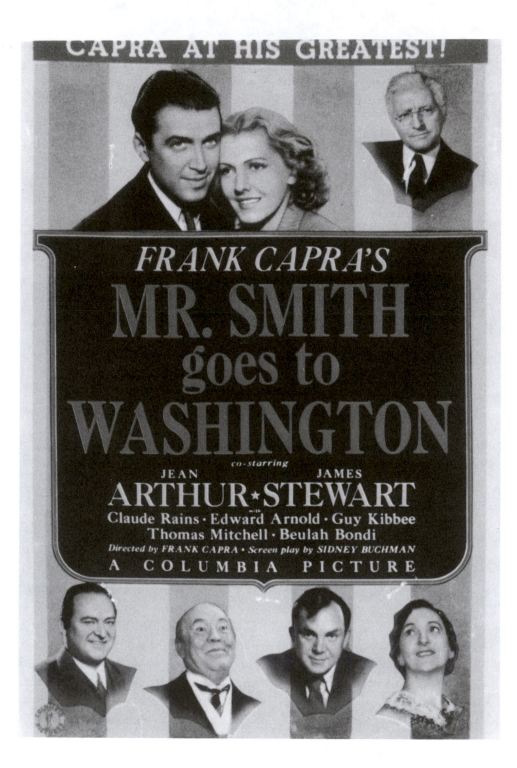

PART I

Electoral Politics

Hollywood's involvement in American politics is longstanding. Contrary to contemporary perceptions, this involvement has not always been on behalf of liberals. Indeed, there is a long tradition of support for Republican candidates.

In the 1920s and early 1930s, Hollywood studio moguls aligned generally with Republicans. One of the most notorious episodes of direct intervention in an election campaign came in 1934 when the major studios organized a massive and well-coordinated campaign to defeat Upton Sinclair, a socialist, health faddist, and well-known novelist who unexpectedly won the Democratic Party nomination for governor in California. Running on a program called "End Poverty in California" (EPIC) that called for the state to take over declining businesses and to form workers cooperatives, Sinclair organized a grassroots movement across the state. Never before had the California business establishment been so shocked and frightened. Sinclair made no bones about being a socialist. To make matters worse, Sinclair declared that he would even consider establishing a movie-making cooperative to challenge the Hollywood film monopoly.

The studio heads moved quickly to ensure Sinclair's defeat in the election. Louis B. Mayer, head of MGM, a conservative Republican, and a good friend of Herbert Hoover, joined his studio colleague Irving Thalberg in this anti-Sinclar campaign. Others studios joined the anti-Sinclair effort including RKO, Paramount, and Warner Brothers. These studios undertook a massive fundraising campaign to launch a huge media attack on Sinclair. The attack included pamphlets, place editorials, and news stories. Documentaries and faked newsreels were produced portraying Sinclair as a radical who would open the flood gates to tramps, the unemployed, and the Dust Bowl Okies to migrate to California to get on the Sinclair dole. One of the speakers hired to attack Sinclair was a young district attorney from Oakland named Earl Warren. The studio monguls did not forget Warren's service. He won election to the Lieutenant Governor's office in 1938 and then the governorship in 1942.

Although director Cecil B. DeMille had not been terribly active in politics until the stock market crash of 1929 (he voted for Franklin Roosevelt in 1932), he joined the campaign against Sinclair in 1934. DeMille's involvement in the '34 campaign led to increased activity within the Republican Party and in 1938 he explored running for the U.S. Senate in California.

The campaign against Sinclair was the most expensive race in the state's history, setting a record for state elections nation-wide. The studios tapped their employees to contribute to the anti-Sinclair war chest. Studio technicians, screen writers, directors, and actors were pressured—even forced—to contribute to the cause, and many did not like it. Sinclair's correspondence reveals that he did not enjoy great support in Hollywood, but many people, especially screen writers such as Dorothy Parker and actors such as Katherine Hepburn, resented this studio pressure. Sinclair overwhelmingly lost the election, but feelings lingered that the studio heads had gone too far. Nonetheless, the studio heads had learned an invaluable lesson on how to mobilize public opinion in an election and they would reemploy these methods in the 1950s when they set out to rebuild the Grand Old Party (GOP).

Actors, script writers, directors, and technicians channeled their resentment toward the arrogant studio chiefs when they began to organize in the mid-1930s unions. Within these newly formed unions, Communist Party (CP) members assumed leading roles and, while most Communists did not identify themselves as such, their opponents suspected them of being members of the CP.

Hollywood involvement in politics continued in the early years of the Cold War. Even as many actors and film directors continued their alliance with the Democratic Party that had developed during the decade of the Great Depression in the 1930s and World War II (1941–5), there were notable exceptions in Hollywood who declared themselves Republicans. Many of these actors have been forgotten by the movie-going public today but they included such notable screen stars as John Wayne, Gary Cooper, Cary Grant, Robert Taylor, Robert Montgomery, Barbara Stanwyck, Ginger Rogers, Randolph Scott, among others. Song-and-dance man George Murphy joined the state GOP central committee in the early 1950s, and actively campaigned for Dwight D. Eisenhower in the 1952 election.

The Democrat John F. Kennedy attracted strong support in Hollywood, as stars such as Frank Sinatra, Peter Lawford, Sammy Davis, Jr., Gregory

Peck, and Burt Lancaster campaigned for Kennedy. When Barry Goldwater won the Republican presidential nomination in 1964, the Hollywood Right was elated. Prominent conservatives such as Wayne and Reagan had campaigned for Goldwater during the primaries, but other stars had joined the crusade as well, including Jimmy Stewart, Glenn Ford, and television actor Walter Brennan.

Reagan headed up the Goldwater campaign in California. His speeches on behalf of Goldwater drew large audiences and won praise for their eloquence. The Goldwater campaign finally decided to air Reagan on the eve of the election. Money for this broadcast came from John Wayne who tapped former fraternity brothers at the University of Southern California to finance the event. On October 27, Reagan spoke on national television. He told his audience that they had two choices, "up or down, up to a man's old dream, the ultimate in individual freedom consistent with law and order—or down to the ant heap of totalitarianism." Within days after the speech, the Goldwater campaign raised eight million dollars.

One of the few successes for Republicans in 1964 was the election of George Murphy to the U.S. Senate. But, the greatest success came two years later when Ronald Reagan—backed by donors such as Justin Dart and Henry Salvatori—won the governor's race in 1966, placing him on the national political stage.

In a mass culture in which celebrity is important for selling products, politicians running for office inevitably seek the endorsement of Hollywood actors. Hollywood celebrities can help draw crowds to campaign events, and their endorsement can add a kind of lustre to a political campaign. Whether these endorsements help in enlisting votes on Election Day is another matter, however. It remains doubtful that Frank Sinatra's endorsement of Kennedy helped win voters. Still there is no doubt that politicians seek the involvement of Hollywood celebrities in their campaigns. Celebrities provide glamor to a campaign, and, equally important, Hollywood offers a reservoir of funds. In this way, money and celebrity prove essential for winning political power.

CHAPTER 1

The Contender: 1934 California Gubernatorial Election

1.1 "DEMILLE BACKS MERRIAM, SAYING FILMS THREATENED"

During the 1934 California gubernatorial campaign, the acclaimed director Cecil B. DeMille, along with a bevy of Hollywood moguls, supported the Republican candidate Frank C. Merriam over the Democratic hopeful, Upton Sinclair. In this article from the *Los Angeles Times*, DeMille explains why he considers Merriam the superior candidate.

The fate of one of the State's largest industries—motion pictures—hangs in the balance at the coming gubernatorial election, Cecil B. DeMille, pioneer in films and one of its outstanding producers said yesterday. He announced his support of Frank C. Merriam, Republican nominee for office.

Southern California is faced with the loss of his industry and its huge pay rolls if the electorate fails to rally to the support of Merriam and retain him in office for the forthcoming term, DeMille declared.

Industry in Danger

"Few people in Southern California realize," he said, "that they are in danger of having this industry move out of the State; that hundreds of thousands of persons, directly and indirectly employed in pictures and those engaged in trading with them face the prospect of being thrown out of work.

"In supporting Frank C. Merriam for the office of Governor of California. I do so with the knowledge of his proven ability as an able economist and leader who is aware of this situation and able to save the

THE 1934 CALIFORNIA GUBERNATORIAL ELECTION | 11

State this wholesale wave of unemployment and the consequent loss of millions of dollars.

Look for Excuse

"Increased taxation of the motion-picture industry is just what the eastern financiers are looking for as an excuse to move the industry to New York.

"Political enthusiasms are insignificant when one is confronted with as grave a situation as this. After watching this industry grow from its infancy to the point where it is the source of income for hundreds of thousands of persons in Southern California who benefit by the millions of dollars the industry places in circulation here. I would naturally have no other alternative than to vote into office the one man, Frank C. Merriam, who can and will save this industry for us."

1.2 RICHARD SHERIDAN AMES, "THE SCREEN ENTERS POLITICS: WILL HOLLYWOOD PRODUCE MORE PROPAGANDA?" [EXCERPT]

After it was revealed that the Hollywood moguls had produced fake newsreels about the 1934 California gubernatorial candidate Upton Sinclair, *Harper's* magazine published an article by Richard Sheridan Ames in which he denounced the moguls' actions and warned Americans about the influence of Hollywood in politics.

The movies have tasted blood. It was, in this instance, the blood of Upton Sinclair. But it was political blood, tasting strongly of victory, and sweet indeed to that Goliath of the arts, hitherto so vulnerable to the slingshots of reformers and detractors, including that very Sinclair whose book about William Fox held no blandishments for Hollywood.

Mr. Sinclair's threat to California meant ruin to the movie magnates, so they believed. Before they took serious thought some of them had appeared ridiculous in press dispatches. They promised the hasty exodus of themselves and their glittering chattels if the Democratic candidate should be elected, and were straightway beguiled by seductive offers from Arizona and Florida. New York City had been fooled so often before that it didn't bother to be coquettish. And sensible Californians couldn't quite see one hundred million dollars' worth of equipment emigrating overnight nor imagine the film industry in exile, getting along without the physical geography of the Golden State. It is a fact, not known to everyone, that there exist in California fair substitutes for most of the world's scenery, from Algerian sand dunes to Bavarian forests and Polynesian isles. The Sacramento river, for example, has been "ghosting" for the Mississippi for years. Studio location experts have maps of the State which tell them just where to go to film a Sudanese landscape or the French Riviera.

No one had ever taken the movies very seriously, so the studio manifestoes died with the editions in which they were printed. Had the political battle been fought along the usual lines no reinforcements would have been sought in Hollywood. But by mid-October conservatives of both parties realized that Sinclair could not be stopped by ordinary methods. Having agreed upon a campaign of fear and personal vituperation, backed by superabundant cash, the coalition strategists implored Hollywood's aid in an intense last-minute program of visual education.

So the screen entered politics. Surprised patrons of neighborhood movie houses were suddenly treated to pictures of an indigent army disembarking from box cars on Los Angeles sidings. These repulsive looking bums appeared to have swarmed in from all corners of the United States, determined to enjoy the easy pickings of the promised Sinclair regime. Their appearance was enough to terrify any citizen who already had a job and a roof over his head. This interpretation of current events was strangely moving, although those with critical eyes wondered why the vagrants were wearing make-up; and some with good memories at once recognized excerpts from the Warner Brothers' previous film fiction "Wild Boys of the Road." The Sinclair cohorts exposed this fraud and the movies were forced to abandon the use of stock shots thereafter. But they had plenty of cameras, and imagination.

Never really favoring the methods of Russian film realism, Hollywood nevertheless exceeded the best efforts of Mr. Sinclair's own Eisenstein. Gorki's "Lower Depths" were mild compared to the camera's gleanings in the camps of Sinclair followers. With an art seldom equalled in million-dollar productions, Hollywood, mordantly selective, photographed the down-and-outs, the wanderers, and the jail birds. It satirized, distorted, and at times nearly burlesqued—to its own detriment. But on the whole it manufactured some very telling celluloid in record time, and not since "The Kaiser, the Beast of Berlin" during war days had it so hypnotized the mob mind.

A large number of forces combined to defeat Sinclair, but the margin of victory was scarcely sufficient to merit loud hosannas from those who fear the organization of the EPIC movement and the Never-Say-Die attitude of its leader. The movies may have been instrumental in defeating the Social-Democrats. They think so. But the campaign went to the head of an industry which always has been easy to frighten and never quite sure of itself. For years the movies have been accused of pandering to the lowest tastes. They were regarded as mere entertainment factories and, in spite of their enormous potential power, they were given no adult privileges, no mature responsibilities in the national economy. A giant, kept too long in swaddling clothes, the motion picture has just discovered its own power. It was the Sinclair campaign which was responsible for this discovery, and neither the results nor the future prospects are pleasant.

. . .

Before election the Screen Writers Guild went on record "to criticize indignantly the fascism of the bosses in demanding contributions to their campaigns, asking for instances of employees discharged for refusing, with the intention of bringing suit for criminal conspiracy, a Federal offense, against offending studios." Did disinterestedness cause the studios to import C. C. Pettijohn, general counsel of the Hays organization in New York, to handle the campaign against Sinclair? What prompted Rob Wagner in his *Script*, California's liberal weekly, read by all film workers, to write: "In this recent campaign the studios broke precedent and under the bludgeoning leadership of Louis B. Mayer lined up brutally—fake interviews for instance—against the other fellows." The militant editor wrote merely what everybody in the industry already knew—that the producer's anti-Sinclair films were deliberately dishonest. When Sinclair converts were shown on the screen, actual members of the EPIC organization weren't used. The film men picked the most appalling figures they could find, put words into their mouths, and thus identified them with Sinclair's movement.

Nor is the first skirmish to be all. When the legislature convenes in January it will contain a belligerent Sinclair minority, eager for revenge against the industry which administered a knock-out blow to its leader. Already plans are laid for an investigation of the movies, salaries, and taxes, conditions under which women labor, instances of despotism. Movie money helped to elect Governor Merriam, and the Hollywood magnates expect him to veto any measure which would mean increased taxes or State regulation of their product. But they fear the publicity which would result from such an investigation. Sinclair's is a master mind for ferreting out combustible facts—the Fox book proved how well he knew the movies. Hollywood prefers to let the public and federal government forget about lots of things.

It would not relish, for example, a detailed inquiry into the manner in which taxes are paid on film negatives. To avoid California taxation unfinished negatives are shipped to New York at just the proper time. When these valuable properties have been proved non-existent in Hollywood vaults, they are whisked out of Manhattan so that they may escape a tax penalty there. Their taxable status is never quite certain on either coast. The cans of celluloid have been known to travel to Arizona, just over the California border, their departure being timed as exactly as the arrival of the avenging hero in a film melodrama.

Having begun its fight with Sinclair, Hollywood has discovered that, like Indian warfare, it may be never ending. At any moment Sinclair may let out a war whoop and Hollywood will have to man its fortifications. The worst of it is that it costs Sinclair nothing except the exercise of his typewriter. It may cost Hollywood plenty, as the last campaign showed. And, more seriously, this sort of running fight may extend to other States and eventually arouse Washington.

As Will Hays once said: "Everyone has two businesses, his own and the movies." If the California legislature moves for State censorship, other States may try it. If California investigates the movies, New York and the federal government may seek a few facts too.

. . .

What if Hollywood decides to convert the nation to any of its principles? It has the money, the studios, and the talent. It controls the major theaters and can command the best advertising media. Hollywood pays the stars whose glamour hypnotizes spectators. It knows all the tricks with which to beguile and amuse them. It knows how to arouse mass emotion. The game of outwitting the censors for many years has taught the producers innumerable strategies. They know how to make almost any situation palatable to the person of average intelligence. Is there anything then to prevent the motion picture industry from flooding the United States with adroit propaganda of its own choosing so long as it contains nothing seditious or of an immoral character? Could it not attack any left-wing organization or liberal minority with the same methods it used against Upton Sinclair? Could it not pervert truth, play tricks with superimposed voices, backgrounds, and canny substitutions? What it has done once it can do again if occasion arises, and there is no constitutional provision or Federal commission to interfere. Only the law courts, ordinarily slow and tedious, could offer opportunity for opposition with injunctions or libel suits, and the cinema retains some of the best lawyers in the world.

. . .

Hollywood does not like the New Deal any better than most corporate business likes it, although it prefers pleasant relations with Washington. But its screen fare has not exhibited a zeal for the Democratic war against depression comparable to the patriotic fury with which it responded in the war for democracy. Its heart isn't in the struggle for national rehabilitation, though it is glad for the extra quarters the emergency relief bureaus put in the otherwise empty pockets of some ten million unemployed movie patrons. But where is the epic of the New Deal equal to the "Birth of a Nation"? What picture has been produced or announced dealing with reforestation, reclamation, the drought, the Brain Trust, national housing, the flagellation of Wall Street, or the new Washington? The movies are respectfully attentive to the Chief Executive and his key men in the newsreels, and that's all. No film halo has ever adorned the Roosevelt experiment.

Until 1936 the films can pepper Sinclair with shrapnel and put out a few feeler films to test the temper of the times. These pictures will doubtless be tinted faintly pro-Fascist, as the others have been. There will be some more red baiting and no traffic with socialism in any of its forms— at least on the part of the major studios. Since the Republican opposition appears too weak to warrant movie backing any longer, the cinema will try to keep on good terms with the Administration, which was sufficiently agreeable to make the industry's own Joseph P. Kennedy chairman of the commission set up by Congress to police Wall Street. Such favors make for a polite interchange of courtesies.

. . .

The screen alone of all the mediums of propaganda permits the accused no reply. Radio time can be bought and newsprint is fairly accessible to all. But while our democracy still prides itself on the constitutional guarantee of the right of free speech, no group or faction can talk back to the motion picture. Its owners and distributors have a virtual monopoly and their control brooks no interference other than the disposition of the public to remain outside of cinema theaters.

Will the nation be warned by California's recent experience? Will its legislators end their vacillation and proceed to the long promised Congressional investigation of cinema tactics, and not be sidetracked from important issues by talk about morals? No more serious affront to the thoughtful citizen's sense of justice has ever been offered than by the screen's first venture into partisan politics. Government regulation might lead eventually to federal propaganda and the obvious danger of Washington politics. But it would determine responsibility; and a complete and unbiased investigation of the screen would place the important facts squarely before the American people.

CHAPTER 2

Mr. Hollywood Goes to Washington: 1952 Presidential Election

2.1 GEORGE MURPHY WITH VICTOR LASKY, *SAY . . . DIDN'T YOU USED TO BE GEORGE MURPHY?* [EXCERPT]

A popular dancer and actor who performed in a number of films in the 1930s and 1940s, George Murphy became increasingly involved in politics in the late 1940s and 1950s. After successfully staging the Republican Party's first Lincoln Day box supper in 1948, Murphy became the self-described "Ziegfeld of the Republican party" and produced several party conventions and inaugural celebrations over the next decade. In this excerpt from his autobiography, *Say . . . Didn't You Used to Be George Murphy?*, he describes his efforts to make the productions more entertaining and, thus, more popular. Murphy would go on to chair the California Republican State Central Committee and to win election to the United States Senate, where he served until 1971.

Not long after the disastrous 1948 Presidential election, Louis Mayer asked me to drop by his office. He had received a call from Eric Johnston, head of the Motion Picture Association in Washington, asking whether I would be available to stage the Republican party's first Lincoln Day box supper in the nation's capital.

The price of admission was to be one dollar and the idea was to change the image of the party from a rich man's organization to one that more ordinary people could identify with.

At first, I must confess, I was not too anxious to fly East. I had only recently come through a tough campaign and was frankly eager to get back to making films and seeing a little more of my family. Besides I was still active in a multitude of other activities including the Screen Actors Guild, which has always been important in my life.

But Mayer would brook no objections. "George," he said in his quiet, authoritative way, "I think you'd better go and see what you can do."

Once again I was forced to tell Julie I would be going away—this time, however, for just a few days. By this time Julie had become used to my sudden departures, and I must say she was a good sport about my extra-curricular activities. Occasionally she would joke, "If you don't get away from some of these committees, I'll divorce you." But there was one thing she never objected to, and that was my work for the Republican party.

I arrived in Washington on a Thursday. The box supper was scheduled for the following Monday at the Uline Arena. They had sold only two hundred tickets at this point. We had half an hour of radio time and my job was to arrange the broadcast as well as a program at the Arena for the rest of the evening.

The first meeting was held at the apartment of Senator Owen Brewster of Maine at the Mayflower Hotel. There wasn't much time and I hadn't flown all those miles to argue with anyone. I got right down to brass tacks.

Usually a political broadcast in those days involved a long-winded orator who would frequently force the listener to change stations. I proposed that we use nine Republican Senators and nine Congressmen, each of whom would talk for only one minute or less on some pertinent subject.

"It just can't be done," I was told.

Senator Taft was one of the disbelievers. "How can I say anything worthwhile in one minute?" he asked.

"Senator," I said, "all you have to say is something like this: 'I've been accused of having written a slave labor law. All I can tell you is that after one year of this so-called slave labor law there are more people at work under higher salaries and better working conditions than ever in the history of our country.'"

Though Taft and his Congressional colleagues were doubtful, they were game enough to try out what this crazy actor from Hollywood was proposing.

I had a little more difficulty selling the idea of hiring Fred Waring to provide the music for the rest of the program. The Republican leaders thought the fee—I think it was about seventy-five hundred dollars—was too steep. Actually Waring was charging the rock-bottom minimum for his huge contingent of musicians and singers.

"Why Waring?" I was asked.

"Simply because we don't have time to put a program of entertainment together and Fred can do ten minutes, a half hour or two hours, if necessary. I have no idea what is going to happen Monday night and we need Waring for insurance."

Still kicking like steers, the leadership reluctantly agreed that I could hire Waring. Fortunately, he was available.

Meanwhile the Washington press corps had learned that this Hollywood character was in town and all sorts of stories about what I was doing began to circulate around the rumor-ridden town. I made a big mystery of what I was about and that only helped the publicity.

The Republican leaders had hoped for about three thousand people at the Uline Arena that Monday night. Instead, eleven thousand showed up. We ran out of box suppers, but no one seemed to mind. The half-hour broadcast went off better than any of its participants expected, even though—because the cheering and applause took so much time—poor Joe Martin couldn't make the final summation.

The show did a great deal to lift the spirits of the Republican leadership and rank-and-file at a time when, following the 1948 defeat, it looked as if our party was finished for a long time to come. It was so successful that from then on I became, in effect, the Ziegfeld of the Republican party.

. . .

There were many occasions in the ensuing years when I was tempted to try television acting. I had had some experience in radio. Among other things, I had been the master of ceremonies of the Motion Picture Relief Fund radio show which raised enough money to build our Actors' Home in the Valley.

Once I got a very excited call from Lew Wasserman, who was then the number one man at Music Corporation of America (M.C.A.), asking if I would read a script. I said I would be glad to do so. Before you could say Harvey Snodgrass three times, the script was delivered to my door. After reading it through, I phoned Lew and said, "Yes, I think I would be very interested in this particular series."

"That's just great," Wasserman said. "I'll get on it right away."

That was the last I heard from him. Two days later I went over to the M.C.A. office and asked what had happened. They said they weren't sure. I suggested that they call New York, which they did. On the other end of the phone was a vice-president of one of the top networks, who said politely, "Murphy is not acceptable to our network because of his political activity."

Later I was barred from working on two other TV shows because of the objections of this particular gentleman. The fact that I was being "blacklisted" because of my political beliefs did upset me for a time, but there was little I could do about it. I was always amused by the caterwauling of my liberal friends whenever they discovered that some radical or other could not get a job in Hollywood. Very few of them ever had any compassion for those on the other side of the political fence who faced the same problem.

At any rate, I'm sorry that the network gentleman kept me out of television, because had I done the three series I would have been a very rich man today and wouldn't have to worry so much about paying the bills. On the other hand, had I not been "blacklisted," I might have ended up in television and not in the United States Senate. And I'd rather be where I am.

Just before I decided to run for the Senate, one of my favorite writers at Universal called me about a television series in which he thought I would fit very well. I went over to the studio and had lunch with him. After we discussed the series, I asked him which network he had in mind and he told me.

"Sorry," I said, "it's no good. I'm barred from that network."

"George," he replied, "I just don't believe it."

I assured him it was no figment of my imagination. He asked me whether I would mind if he checked out my story.

"Of course not," I said, "Go ahead."

My writer friend called me back three days later. "I'm stunned, but you're right," he said. "That guy in New York said he won't have anything to do with you."

Apparently the antagonism this network executive felt towards me because of my politics had lasted all those years.

I had one other chance to appear on television. I was offered the part of the doctor in the television version of *Peyton Place*, which turned out to be a mighty profitable series for Twentieth Century-Fox. I decided to turn down the offer because I had heard it was a pretty dirty book and, at that point in my life, I thought I'd rather not get involved in projects of that nature.

On another occasion, too, I guess I was a "square." I had been asked to play two weeks in Las Vegas for more money than I had ever been paid in my life. But I decided that wasn't right either. I explained that I didn't think I should be shilling for a gambling joint and I thanked them very much. The only time I ever appeared in Las Vegas was to make a speech at the Knife and Fork Club, which has nothing to do with the gambling fraternity. Maybe it was just as well.

Even though I stopped making films, I remained with M-G-M, working full time as the studio's "official ambassador," representing the studio at exhibitor's conventions and speaking before groups such as the PTA. Because of my close associations with labor, I was also appointed liaison between Metro and the unions. Since I was now representing management, I was forced to resign my membership in the Screen Actors Guild. But I have always maintained strong ties with the S.A.G. and its leaders. And I still proudly carry my membership card in the Guild.

After what amounted to a power struggle with Dore Schary, my dear friend and mentor Louis B. Mayer resigned as head of the studio in 1951. Mayer's departure was a blow to me, and I made no secret of my feelings. Nevertheless, despite our differing political philosophies, Schary and I got along very well. Schary, of course, was as well-known in Democratic councils as I was on the other side.

He was quoted as saying of me: "I've known George since I wrote a *Broadway Melody* script for him back in 1939. In that time he has brought more dignity than any other one person to our business. He's never been afraid to say exactly where he stands. When he was once warned that all actors get criticized for taking a political position, he just said, 'I happen to be a citizen before I am an actor.' There haven't been enough guys like that in Hollywood. He would be a first-class man for anybody's side."

But I was on the Republican side and I devoted what time I could to that cause. In 1952 I had helped to stage-manage the Republican convention held in the International Amphitheater in Chicago. It was one of the most exciting conventions I have ever attended, featuring as it did an epic struggle for the Presidential nomination between the two giants of the Republican party—Dwight David Eisenhower and Robert Alphonso Taft.

As a member of the California delegation, I was pledged to vote for Earl Warren at the convention. But I never considered the Governor as a serious contender, even though he did himself.

The night before I left for Chicago, Louis Mayer asked me over to his house. He was an ardent Taft supporter and he began to preach the virtues of the man from Ohio.

"I agree with you one hundred percent about Taft," I told Mayer. "He would make a great President. My only question is whether he can win. The Republican party needs a winner. That's why I'm for Eisenhower."

. . .

On my first day of the 1952 convention in Chicago, I reported to Mrs. F. Peavey Heffelfinger, a national committeewoman from Minnesota who was chairman of the Entertainment and Decorations Committee.

A charming lady, when she saw me she gave me a big hug and a kiss and said, "I'm so glad you're here." And that was the last time I saw her.

From then on I was on my own, and it wasn't easy. One of the first problems to arise was the tickets. It seemed that despite all the months of planning that went into the convention, someone had forgotten to have the tickets printed in a union plant. They arrived at our headquarters in the Stevens Hotel (now the Conrad Hilton) by the many thousands without the union "bug." This was tantamount to political suicide among union voters so we had them hurriedly redone in several union plants.

Then there was the problem of getting entertainers. Very little had been done before I arrived on the scene, and the matter was dumped in my lap. There was no program, no budget, and very little hope, but somehow I managed to get some excellent talents to appear at the convention.

The nicest tribute I received for my efforts came from the aforementioned Mrs. Heffelfinger. Talking to Dorothy Brandon of the *New York Herald-Tribune*, the lady from Minnesota described me as "that wonderful man who calms turbulent theatrical temperaments and gets our shows on the platform through sheer muscular endeavor. . . . George Murphy is the littlest man at the convention—he is humble, helpful and hefty. Why, he isn't above hauling chairs, checking on choir aggregations and finding a secluded resting place for our great soloists before the opening ceremonies. He's the man who thinks and does everything."

The truth is that I couldn't have done anything without the help of a lot of other "little" people who were always there when I needed them. When things were really rough they would restore your faith in humanity. They were there to work for a cause they believed in and not for any personal gain.

Sure, there were plenty of aggravations. I remember one man who was in charge of distributing the tickets. This poor fellow later had a heart attack and I've always thought it was because of the emotional strain he endured at the convention. I learned quickly that if you let things prey on your mind there is no place you can lose your cool more quickly than at a political convention.

A thousand and one things can go wrong and you've got to try to stay on top of them. For example, before the convention began, I paid a visit to the Amphitheater to test the sound equipment. The chief electrician, a bit annoyed, told me not to worry, that everything would be fine. I wasn't satisfied and I insisted on a test.

It turned out that my fears were justified. The speakers were so placed that the delegates in the first fifteen rows—the most important people at the convention—would not have been able to hear any of the proceedings. On my instructions, the electricians worked all night placing speakers under the stage.

Would you believe that eight years later at the Republican convention in that very same hall we had the same problem? "Now fellows," I told the electricians who had welcomed me warmly, "don't you remember what happened eight years ago?" Glumly they proceeded to work all night again.

. . .

I first got to meet General Eisenhower several weeks after the convention at an election rally at the Pan-Pacific Auditorium in Los Angeles. I was in charge of the rally.

Mamie Eisenhower introduced me to her distinguished husband. "Oh, there's Murphy," she said on spotting me. "My mother says you're the finest fellow for getting a lady down the stairs that she ever met."

Mrs. Eisenhower was referring to the time I accompanied her mother, Mrs. Doud, down a steep staircase in order to get her out of the convention hall without being trampled by the crowds.

The Pan-Pacific rally went off like clockwork. Actually there were two rallies. Inside the auditorium some seven thousand partisans were gathered to cheer Ike to the rafters. Outside, and for this innovation I took full credit, I arranged for the General to address some fifteen thousand people gathered in a parking lot. Eisenhower ad-libbed his outdoor speech and I think it came off much better than the prepared speech he delivered inside.

Eisenhower was that kind of man. When he ad-libbed, he spoke from the heart and wasn't mouthing words prepared by speech-writers. True, he occasionally got his syntax mixed up, but the people couldn't have cared less. They loved him. They trusted him and believed in him—and they elected him.

Eisenhower was so pleased with his Pan-Pacific appearances that he made inquiries as to who had made the arrangements. He was told it was George Murphy. The next day I received a call from one of his aides who said the General wanted me to join his campaign tour.

"As much as I'd like to," I said, "I'm afraid that I can't. I'm still under contract to M-G-M."

At seven o'clock the next morning, I got a call at home from the big boss in New York, Nicholas Schenck.

"George," said Schenck, "I want you to do something for me. Pack your bag and come to New York immediately. Report to the Commodore Hotel. You are assigned to General Eisenhower for the duration of the campaign. Help in any way you can."

Shortly after I arrived at the Commodore, where the Republican campaign headquarters was located, I was taken in to see Eisenhower who quickly got to the point.

"I want you to arrange all my rallies," he said.

"Anything you say, sir," I said, "but only on one condition."

"What's that?"

"Please don't make any official announcement. In every town there are at least two or three groups already at odds with each other about how to run a meeting. Just let me go into a city quietly and have a free hand. If I get into any trouble and need you, I will call you to bail me out."

"Agreed," the General said, shaking my hand.

And that was the way I worked throughout the campaign, preceding Eisenhower wherever he went, arranging rally after rally, seldom seeing the candidate or even talking to him, but somehow getting the job done. All I can say is that the General was happy with the results. Being a military man, he most of all valued good timing, and that was what he usually got.

The final rally of the campaign was to be held in Boston Garden. This was the big one since it also involved a national hour-long television program which was to feature the Eisenhowers and the Nixons. I went to Boston several days before the rally.

. . .

There were a lot of problems connected with putting on that rally at the Boston Garden. About three bickering groups, each with its own idea of how to run things, finally got together at my urging. My big problem was a Wild West rodeo show that was to close the previous night. There were two feet of dirt on the Garden floor, dozens of horses and cattle, and last but not least, Leo Carillo.

"Can you cut your performance short tonight?" I asked Leo. Leo was obliging. Though a good Democrat, he generally supported Republicans, particularly if he thought they were going to win. He had always been a great fan of Earl Warren's.

At about one a.m. the next morning the bulldozers were busy and we began moving in our own paraphernalia. One basic problem was the pungent aroma left by the animals. We brought in some huge fans to blow the stuff out. By the time the rally started the Garden smelled a little more like a political arena.

But my troubles weren't over. By six o'clock the Garden was nearly packed. I had hired half-a-dozen vaudeville acts to keep the crowd amused, but the electrician wasn't there to turn on the microphones. Someone had told him to come in at seven-thirty. When he did finally arrive, he couldn't get the mikes to work properly.

Meantime the large group of entertainers, headed by Fred Waring, was stranded in New York. We had chartered an airplane to bring the group to Boston. The plane was scheduled to leave LaGuardia Airport at four-thirty p.m., but it was still on the ground an hour later because of pouring rain and poor visibility in Boston. Finally the plane took off and the microphones at the Garden began to function properly, and my vaudeville acts kept the crowd happy until the big show arrived.

My final problem was with Senator Henry Cabot Lodge.

"Cabot," I said, "the General will be upstairs in the Garden Club. When he leaves there, I will give you a hand signal and you just say, 'And now, ladies and gentlemen, it is my privilege to present the next President of the United States, General Dwight David Eisenhower.' "

"My dear Murph," Lodge said. "If you don't mind, I would like to read a short introduction which I have written. It's kind of precious to me—"

"Now, Senator," I said, "I've been doing these rallies for a long time—"

"Well, Murph, I do feel I have to insist on reading the statement."

Shrugging my shoulders, I said, "Okay, you do it your way, but don't say I didn't warn you."

The original plan was to have an hour and a half of political speeches before the Presidential candidate arrived. I said it was too much and succeeded in cutting the verbiage down to two twenty-minute segments. The rest was entertainment. The huge crowd packing the auditorium was waiting to explode.

General and Mrs. Eisenhower and their party had hardly left the Garden Club upstairs when the crowd knew they were coming. How they sensed it I'll never know. The crowd started to roar. The noise was deafening.

And there was poor Cabot Lodge at the microphone trying to read from a paper in front of him. The crowd just didn't want to listen. Finally I went over to the Senator and said, "Cabot, I don't think you have to say anything. They know the General is in the hall."

"I guess you're right," Cabot said with a happy, good-natured smile.

It was truly an exciting night, and it was over before I realized that I had completely forgotten to eat for forty-eight hours.

All the months of campaigning ended at the stroke of midnight. I had planned to take the first plane back to New York, but General Eisenhower asked me to join the rest of the staff on the campaign train. We left Boston about one o'clock.

Instead of going immediately to their bedrooms, as they had during all those hectic weeks of travel, the General and Mrs. Eisenhower came to the conference car where all the staff and the entertainers had gathered.

"I understand," the General said, "that before I arrive at a meeting you people provide great entertainment and whip up enthusiasm. Could you show me what you do?"

So we restaged what we had done at the Boston Garden several hours before. Bob Montgomery made a short speech, and Fred Waring and his orchestra, as well as several singers, provided the entertainment. I told a couple of "Eisenhower stories"—ones I had used in the camp shows— and the General responded with a few stories of his own. This went on for at least three hours and the General seemed to have the time of his life. Dawn was breaking when we arrived in New York. Before that day ended, Dwight David Eisenhower was elected President of the United States.

The Republicans, having been out of power for twenty years, prepared to go all-out on a big bang-up Inauguration celebration. I was promptly named director of entertainment, and once again my headaches began. I flew to Washington and found myself quartered in a couple of bare, beaverboard rooms in a crackerbox eyesore on Pennsylvania Avenue left over from World War II.

"Murphy's madhouse" was the way my good friend Bill Henry of the *Los Angeles Times* described my place of work. Bill came over to interview me just as I was nearing the end of my inaugural chores. With just hours left to go, crisis after crisis developed. And I was in the center of the storm, hoping that my sanity would hold out until it was all over.

Bill Henry wrote: "George Murphy, fortunately, has long years of physical accomplishments to his credit and with the good athlete's ability to relax, he seems to be holding up remarkably well despite the harassments of the job and the lack of anything resembling real rest. George has been through this sort of thing in fair weather and foul and he manages, somehow, to preserve a sense of balance."

The demand for tickets was so great that I found myself masterminding three inaugural balls with six dance bands. The President-elect promised to attend [two], and kept his promise.

For one of the balls we came up with the idea of having a "grand march" or "grand promenade" lead by some two hundred of the top socialites in Washington. Leroy Prinz was assigned to getting the thing into shape. It wasn't easy. At one point Leroy asked Mrs. Marjorie Post, in his most polite way, to move on cue to the music. He explained to her that in the old days, when he was directing chorus girls for Ziegfeld, he had issued such orders a little differently.

"How did you do it in those days?" Mrs. Post asked.

"I would have yelled, 'Get your rear end over there in a hurry and get moving to the music,' " Prinz said.

Mrs. Post, fascinated by this bit of show business lore, laughed uproariously. "That's the funniest thing I ever heard," she said.

One result of that episode was that Leroy got a column in the society section of the *Washington Post* which he's never forgotten.

In addition I had to plan the Inaugural Festival at the Uline Arena. I had almost no problems with the fine entertainers I invited. They were willing to do their best for this historic occasion. My problems were with the managers and press agents. For example, some chap from New York was terribly upset because he didn't think his ballet dancers were getting a good enough spot. He was so mad that he said he'd only bring half as many dancers and they would dance only half as long. I said to myself

Former President Dwight D. Eisenhower and actor-turned-politician George Murphy at a luncheon in honor of George Murphy on July 15, 1964, during Murphy's campaign for the United States Senate. Murphy had worked on both of Eisenhower's presidential campaigns in the 1950s and became a successful politician in his own right, serving in the Senate until 1971. Dwight D. Eisenhower Presidential Library.

that was just dandy, since it made it all the easier to cope with an already overlong list of entertainers.

As it was the Festival ran for four hours, twice as long as I had planned. But the audience seemed happy. Among the stellar personalities making appearances were Yehudi Menuhin, Ethel Merman, Edgar Bergen, Marge and Gower Champion, Dorothy Shay, Sid Caesar, the De Marcos, Jarmila Novotna, Fred Waring, Abbott and Costello, William Gaxton, Irene Dunne and, again and again, the production team of Leroy Prinz and George Murphy.

. . .

After the Inauguration I returned home to resume my work at Metro as well as my extracurricular activities which by now included membership on the Republican state central committee. In October 1953, Governor Warren was named Chief Justice of the Supreme Court, and Lieutenant Governor Goodwin Knight became Governor. A. Ronald Button, the Republican State Chairman, was made a national committeeman. One day I received a telephone call from "Goody" Knight. The new Governor tersely told me that, after meeting with both Vice-president Nixon and Senator Knowland, he had picked me as the new State Chairman.

When I hesitated, being somewhat overwhelmed, Knight said bluntly, "George, you've got to take it. You're the only guy in the state that nobody's mad at!"

2.2   LETTER FROM DORE SCHARY TO ADLAI STEVENSON

Isidore "Dore" Schary worked as a director, writer, and producer in Hollywood, starting in the 1930s. He was known for his partiality to "message" movies and for his involvement in the Democratic Party. By 1955, Schary was serving as president of MGM studios and working extensively with the two-time Democratic presidential candidate Adlai Stevenson. Schary hosted fundraisers, produced film reels, and, as this letter illustrates, gave Stevenson advice on how to improve his appearance on television.

Dear Adlai:

Have just finished reading Michael Straight's report in New Republic regarding the dinner in Chicago. Mr. Straight gives you the nod over the other contenders, but I felt that the story had a strained quality.

I heard your speech and saw you on TV, and told Harry Ashmore something of what I felt. I thought you looked fine. Don't let the TV lads talk you into pancake makeup—the slight shine on your brow looked good and real. Someone, however, should check on the height of the mike—in Chicago they covered part of your face, and that doesn't look good, even on Robert Taylor. The words you said were rich and an abundant harvest—perhaps too abundant—because you were forced to hurry your delivery and as a result some of the sock points were too rapidly winged away into the ether. Please, Guv, a little slower on the pace. Allow the audience to absorb as you go along. Speed is fine for Walter Winchell because no one much cares what he talks about.

The chatter around—and I mean around—on studio sets—and a gas station—the train conductor on The Lark—a cab driver in San Francisco—and a waitress (not very pretty) in the Circus Cafe in Long Beach—is still upbeat about Stevenson, but with a recurrent question: "Is Truman for him?" The fact that this remains a question on so many minds—Stevenson minds—is significant. A couple of nights ago here in Los Angeles Truman spoke to some 800 non-partisans (though heavily Democratic). The affair was for the Truman Library. It was hosted by Ed Pauley, who conducted the proceedings a little foggily through the effects of numerous and ample jolts of "Kaintuck" bourbon. It was rather elegant and gay, though it kept getting a little fuzzy along with Pauley's diction.

Harry S. Truman's reception was terrific. He is well-liked and respected and his warm reputation is growing along with the affection people feel for him as a man who quit as a winner and as a tough and fearless leader. This you must know—but I cannot report it to you strongly enough.

Among the rank and files he is still a block-buster, and his support is not only a necessity, it is, as the live hounds say, "the most." Of course the hard rock Repubs don't like him, but those kind of fellows don't like you, either. I feel that the people who will vote for you will not walk out if Truman begins sounding the tocsin for you.

Of course you have heard the latest—that since Eisenhower's coronary most top people are hoping they get one, because apparently it's an indication that you're in good health. It begins to look that if a man gets a good report on a cardiograph he's in terrible shape.

I thought you'd like to have this interim report—more later.

Meanwhile, as always, my very fondest.

DS:lb

Hon. Adlai E. Stevenson
231 South LaSalle Street
Chicago 4, Illinois

CHAPTER 3

Network: 1960 Presidential Election

3.1 VICKI DAITCH, ORAL HISTORY INTERVIEW WITH DON HEWITT [EXCERPT]

Don Hewitt started his journalism career in 1942 and would go on to direct the documentary news program *See It Now*, as well as the 1960 presidential debates between John F. Kennedy and Richard Nixon, before creating *60 Minutes*, the CBS news magazine in 1968. In this excerpt from his oral history with the John F. Kennedy Presidential Library, Hewitt discusses the Kennedy/Nixon "debates," the impact of television on politics, and Kennedy's relationship with the singer and actor Frank Sinatra, a partnership which ultimately connected the President to the Mob.

Hewitt: The first time I ever met Jack Kennedy it was, I think, two weeks before the first Nixon [Richard M. Nixon]-Kennedy debate, which actually was never a debate. That was a misnomer. It was a confrontation and a joint news conference, but nobody ever debated. How that word came to be, I don't know. We met in a hangar at Midway Airport. He was campaigning in the Midwest. He diverted his plane to Midway, which is a small airport, not O'Hare, downtown Chicago.

We met in a hangar. My recollection is I think that Ted Sorensen [Theodore C. Sorensen] was with him, but I don't recall that that much. It's a lot of years ago. And he was curious, you know, where do I stand? Do I stand? Do I sit? How much time do I have to answer? Can he interrupt? Can I interrupt? He wanted to know everything. Nixon I never saw until he arrived that night in the studio. Kennedy knew how important this television appearance would be. Nixon kissed it off as just another campaign appearance.

He arrived in the studio that night. He looked like death warmed over. He'd had a staphylococcus infection. He banged his knee on the car door getting out. He walked in, he looked pretty bad. I was standing there talking to him, and all of a sudden I noticed out of the corner of my eye Jack Kennedy sort of arrived. And it was awesome. Here was this guy running for president of the United States who looked like a matinee idol. Well tailored, well tanned, in command of himself, command of the language. I guess I'd never seen a matinee idol president before. As we stood there, and I kept telling what each one was going to do, I felt like a referee at a fight, like I was giving them a last-minute "Give me a good clean fight!" etc., etc.

Daitch: Right.

Hewitt: And then I said to both of them, "Would you like some makeup?" I had with me a lady named Frannie Arvold [Frances Arvold], who was the best makeup person I knew, and I brought her to Chicago. I said, "Would you like some makeup?" Kennedy, who didn't need any, said, "No, thank you, not really." Nixon, who needed makeup, also said no, I'm convinced, because he didn't want history to record that that night he was made up and Kennedy wasn't. So they took him back in a room, in an office. And the guys that are with him, his handlers, made him up. . . .

. . .

That night was a great night for Jack Kennedy, and the worst night that ever happened in American politics. That's the night the politicians looked at us and said, "That's the only way to campaign." And television looked at them and said, "They're a bottomless pit of advertising dollars." From that day on nobody has ever run for office in the United States without amassing a war chest to buy television time, and it all winged off that night.

It cost Franklin Roosevelt [Franklin D. Roosevelt] $2.2 million to get elected president. In today's money that's 26, 27, 28 million dollars. Hillary Clinton [Hillary Rodham Clinton] and Rick Lazio [Enrico A. Lazio] spent twice that on television commercials for one Senate seat. That night the democratic process became hostage to money. I don't think before that night anybody had ever heard the term fund-raiser. Every time a president leaves the Oval Office, it's for a fund-raiser. The

Hewitt: fund-raiser is to get money for television time. The only way to
(cont.)   get money for television time is to do favors for people who give
        you money.

        . . .

        I also left there thinking, we just elected a president, when the
debate was over. Because he [Kennedy] was better tailored, better looking, more articulate. I said, "That's not how you want to elect a president, by his performance in a debate." Now, I think we got the right man but for the wrong reason. I'm not sure that's how you should pick your president. That's how you pick Miss America, who is the more attractive? That's not the way to pick a president, who's the more attractive of the two people? But it happened in that case. We got the more attractive guy, and he happened to be the better guy, and he made a pretty damned good president.

        Now, about the makeup. It wasn't 'til almost 40 years later that I learned from Ted Sorensen that they also made up Kennedy that night. I never knew that.

Daitch: Really!

Hewitt: He said we put some powder on him. I said, "Well, whatever you did, you did it better than the Nixon people did." That's the first time I ever knew about it. Because I'd been going around for years telling this story of the no makeup, and it wasn't true.

        . . .

        Oh, yes. Are you kidding? Judith Exner [Judith Campbell Exner]. . . . Now, Tina Sinatra told me, and then she said it on our air, that Joe Kennedy [Joseph P. Kennedy, Sr.] called her father, and said, "We need help in West Virginia. We've got to get the labor vote because it's going to Hubert Humphrey [Hubert H. Humphrey]." And Frank Sinatra [Francis A. Sinatra] went to Sam Giancana [Samuel M. Giancana] and The Mob and got the votes that won West Virginia. I think also Illinois, but I know West Virginia.

Daitch: Through the Mine Workers' Union?

Hewitt: I don't know, but some union in West Virginia, which was Kennedy's first big triumph when he beat Hubert Humphrey. Several years later, when Bobby started going after The Mob, Sam Giancana called Sinatra and said, "We made that sonofabitch president. What is he doing to us? Sinatra, according to Tina, said to The Mob, "Your fight's with me, not them. If you're unhappy, I'm the guy that was the go-between. What do you want?"

Sinatra played 13 dates with the Rat Pack with Sammy Davis [Sammy Davis, Jr.] and that whole crowd, Dean Martin, at a club called the Villa Venice in Chicago for nothing, 13 dates, to pay back The Mob for their being had by Bobby. This is Tina Sinatra telling me this. Then Sinatra went before the Gaming Commission in Nevada to get a license to operate a gambling casino at Cal-Neva Lodge, and he was asked about these 13 dates he played for The Mob in Chicago.

Daitch: So people knew about that.

Hewitt: And he said it never happened. Tina said to me, "He lied. He told me he lied." So there was. . . . That's the whole Judith Exner, Sam Giancana, Frank Sinatra. It was a side of Jack Kennedy that was indiscreet. I mean as far as. . . . It's like Bill Clinton [William J. Clinton]. I think it was more cerebral than sexual. I mean he didn't know that a young kid was going to brag about having it off with the president. Jack Kennedy didn't realize. . . . Well, most of the women who had things with Jack Kennedy were very secret about it. Judith Exner wasn't. It's almost irresistible to say you're having an affair with the president.

So it was reckless. You don't do that. It's like with Bill Clinton, it was reckless. I've always figured that Hillary went on about that the Right Wing was using this to get him. I said, "You know, if you consider yourself a firewall between Sane America and the crazy Right Wing, you'd better take better care of that firewall." You can't do that. You can't have a thing with an intern in the Oval Office. You can't invite the top mobster in America's girlfriend to spend the night with you in the White House.

So, you know, he was very human, but it wasn't very smart. And it's hubris. It's no one tells the Kennedys what they can do and can't do. Not good.

Daitch: No. And maybe not just the Kennedys. I mean if there's something about that position or power, because a huge percentage of our presidents have had. . . .

Hewitt: Yes, sure. But the girlfriend of a top gangster in America, especially when that guy had helped him win, bad stuff.

. . .

I've got to tell you: I look back on debates, what they call them.

Hewitt:
(cont.)
The first one was about Nixon's makeup. One of them was about Ronald Reagan [Ronald W. Reagan] saying to Jimmy Carter [James E. Carter], "There you go again." One of them was about Michael Dukakis [Michael S. Dukakis] being asked what he would do if his wife got raped. One of them was about Jerry Ford's [Gerald R. Ford] gaff about Poland not being behind the Iron Curtain. And Al Gore [Albert A. Gore, Jr.] and Bush [George W. Bush] was about absolutely nothing, and nobody can remember one thing either one of them ever said.

So the debates are. . . . I'll go back to what they produced. They produced this awful marriage of television and politics which is about money. And when a guy like Mitch McConnell [Addison Mitchell McConnell, Jr.] says, "You cannot deny anyone the right to buy as much television time as he wants

President John F. Kennedy and the singer and actor Frank Sinatra at Kennedy's inaugural ceremony in 1961. Sinatra had been a vocal supporter of Kennedy, but the entertainer's connections to organized crime led the President to cut ties with him. Sinatra would go on to support the Republican Party in subsequent years. Motion Picture and Television Archive.

because that's a violation of the First Amendment," The Founding Fathers would turn over in their graves if they heard that. What First Amendment and television time? They didn't know what television was.

Daitch: Right.

Hewitt: You've got to realize that they lived in a time when you communicated through pamphlets. That's how Tom Paine [Thomas Paine] communicated with the world, pamphleteers. See, I believe, this is a little off track, but I believe that my people, journalists, have an exaggerated sense of their own importance, have an exaggerated sense of what the First Amendment gives us permission to do.

Those guys never heard about hidden cameras and debates that reached the world and satellites that send word around the world. They didn't know anything about that. So we have interpreted the First Amendment to give us rights that I don't think those guys ever even contemplated. That's a little off the beaten path of what debates do. But I really think that debate comes from a terrible chapter in American history.

Daitch: It wouldn't have had to, right? Because wasn't the intent of the debates to offer free time? It was at the expense of the networks.

Hewitt: Nobody bought time before that. Nobody ever heard. . . . Now all of a sudden these guys are saying, "Jesus! We can buy time on every local station in America. They'll sell us the time to do what we did there." They knew that night that the only way you can get elected president of the United States was to be an appealing television performer. Therefore, they would buy the time to appear on stage as a television pol [politician].

Before that the only thing that ever happened was Dwight Eisenhower had hired Robert Montgomery, the actor, to help him, and the Young & Rubicam, the advertising agency, to do some television commercials. Up to that point, nobody ever even heard of it. No, it was an awful day.

CHAPTER 4

All the President's Men: 1964 Presidential Election

4.1 RONALD REAGAN, "A TIME FOR CHOOSING" [EXCERPT]

Ronald Reagan had enjoyed a successful career in Hollywood with such hit movies as *Knute Rockne, All American*, and *Bedtime for Bonzo* and served as the president of the Screen Actors Guild from 1947 until 1952 and again in 1959. Although he had once identified as a New Deal Democrat, Reagan began endorsing Republican candidates in the 1950s, formally switched parties in 1962, and began stumping for Republican presidential candidate Barry Goldwater in 1964. Reagan's speech for Goldwater, excerpted below, was the first for which a Hollywood actor received national airtime, and it was an unqualified hit, bringing in over eight million dollars to Goldwater's campaign and earning its nickname "The Speech."

Thank you. Thank you very much. Thank you and good evening. The sponsor has been identified, but unlike most television programs, the performer hasn't been provided with a script. As a matter of fact, I have been permitted to choose my own words and discuss my own ideas regarding the choice that we face in the next few weeks.

I have spent most of my life as a Democrat. I recently have seen fit to follow another course. I believe that the issues confronting us cross party lines. Now, one side in this campaign has been telling us that the issues of this election are the maintenance of peace and prosperity. The line has been used, "We've never had it so good."

But I have an uncomfortable feeling that this prosperity isn't something on which we can base our hopes for the future. No nation in history has ever survived a tax burden that reached a third of its national income. Today, 37 cents out of every dollar earned in this country is the tax collector's share, and yet our government continues to spend 17 million dollars a day more than the government takes in. We haven't balanced our budget 28 out of the last 34 years. We've raised our debt limit three times in the last twelve months, and now our national debt is one and a half times bigger than all the combined debts of all the nations of the world. We have 15 billion dollars in gold in our treasury; we don't own an ounce. Foreign dollar claims are 27.3 billion dollars. And we've just had announced that the dollar of 1939 will now purchase 45 cents in its total value.

As for the peace that we would preserve, I wonder who among us would like to approach the wife or mother whose husband or son has died in South Vietnam and ask them if they think this is a peace that should be maintained indefinitely. Do they mean peace, or do they mean we just want to be left in peace? There can be no real peace while one American is dying some place in the world for the rest of us. We're at war with the most dangerous enemy that has ever faced mankind in his long climb from the swamp to the stars, and it's been said if we lose that war, and in so doing lose this way of freedom of ours, history will record with the greatest astonishment that those who had the most to lose did the least to prevent its happening. Well I think it's time we ask ourselves if we still know the freedoms that were intended for us by the Founding Fathers.

Not too long ago, two friends of mine were talking to a Cuban refugee, a businessman who had escaped from Castro, and in the midst of his story one of my friends turned to the other and said, "We don't know how lucky we are." And the Cuban stopped and said, "How lucky you are? I had someplace to escape to." And in that sentence he told us the entire story. If we lose freedom here, there's no place to escape to. This is the last stand on earth.

. . .

This is the issue of this election: Whether we believe in our capacity for self-government or whether we abandon the American revolution and confess that a little intellectual elite in a far-distant capitol can plan our lives for us better than we can plan them ourselves.

. . .

Well, I, for one, resent it when a representative of the people refers to you and me, the free men and women of this country, as "the masses." This is a term we haven't applied to ourselves in America. But beyond that, "the full power of centralized government"—this was the very thing the Founding Fathers sought to minimize. They knew that governments don't control things. A government can't control the economy without controlling people. And they know when a government sets out to do that, it must use force and coercion to achieve its purpose. They also knew, those Founding Fathers, that outside of its legitimate functions, government does nothing as well or as economically as the private sector of the economy.

. . .

Now—so now we declare "war on poverty," or "You, too, can be a Bobby Baker." Now do they honestly expect us to believe that if we add 1 billion dollars to the 45 billion we're spending, one more program to the 30-odd we have—and remember, this new program doesn't replace any, it just duplicates existing programs—do they believe that poverty is suddenly going to disappear by magic? Well, in all fairness I should explain there is one part of the new program that isn't duplicated. This is the youth feature. We're now going to solve the dropout problem, juvenile delinquency, by reinstituting something like the old CCC camps [Civilian Conservation Corps], and we're going to put our young people in these camps. But again we do some arithmetic, and we find that we're going to spend each year just on room and board for each young person we help 4,700 dollars a year. We can send them to Harvard for 2,700! Course, don't get me wrong. I'm not suggesting Harvard is the answer to juvenile delinquency.

But seriously, what are we doing to those we seek to help? Not too long ago, a judge called me here in Los Angeles. He told me of a young woman who'd come before him for a divorce. She had six children, was pregnant with her seventh. Under his questioning, she revealed her husband was a laborer earning 250 dollars a month. She wanted a divorce to get an 80 dollar raise. She's eligible for 330 dollars a month in the Aid to Dependent Children Program. She got the idea from two women in her neighborhood who'd already done that very thing.

Yet anytime you and I question the schemes of the do-gooders, we're denounced as being against their humanitarian goals. They say we're always "against" things—we're never "for" anything.

Well, the trouble with our liberal friends is not that they're ignorant; it's just that they know so much that isn't so.

. . .

No government ever voluntarily reduces itself in size. So governments' programs, once launched, never disappear.

Actually, a government bureau is the nearest thing to eternal life we'll ever see on this earth.

Federal employees—federal employees number two and a half million; and federal, state, and local, one out of six of the nation's work force employed by government. These proliferating bureaus with their thousands of regulations have cost us many of our constitutional safeguards. How many of us realize that today federal agents can invade a man's property without a warrant? They can impose a fine without a formal hearing, let alone a trial by jury? And they can seize and sell his property at auction to enforce the payment of that fine. In Chico County, Arkansas, James Wier over-planted his rice allotment. The government obtained a 17,000 dollar judgment. And a U.S. marshal sold his 960-acre farm at auction. The government said it was necessary as a warning to others to make the system work.

. . .

Now it doesn't require expropriation or confiscation of private property or business to impose socialism on a people. What does it mean whether you hold the deed to the—or the title to your business or property if the government holds the power of life and death over that business or property? And such machinery already exists. The government can find some charge to bring against any concern it chooses to prosecute. Every businessman has his own tale of harassment. Somewhere a perversion has taken place. Our natural, unalienable rights are now considered to be a dispensation of government, and freedom has never been so fragile, so close to slipping from our grasp as it is at this moment.

Our Democratic opponents seem unwilling to debate these issues. They want to make you and I believe that this is a contest between two men—that we're to choose just between two personalities.

Well what of this man that they would destroy—and in destroying, they would destroy that which he represents, the ideas that you and I hold dear? Is he the brash and shallow and trigger-happy man they say he is? Well I've been privileged to know him "when." I knew him long before he ever dreamed of trying for high office, and I can tell you personally I've never known a man in my life I believed so incapable of doing a dishonest or dishonorable thing.

This is a man who, in his own business before he entered politics, instituted a profit-sharing plan before unions had ever thought of it. He put in health and medical insurance for all his employees. He took 50 percent of the profits before taxes and set up a retirement program, a pension plan for all his employees. He sent monthly checks for life to an employee who was ill and couldn't work. He provides nursing care for the children of mothers who work in the stores. When Mexico was ravaged by the floods in the Rio Grande, he climbed in his airplane and flew medicine and supplies down there.

. . .

Those who would trade our freedom for the soup kitchen of the welfare state have told us they have a utopian solution of peace without victory.

They call their policy "accommodation." And they say if we'll only avoid any direct confrontation with the enemy, he'll forget his evil ways and learn to love us. All who oppose them are indicted as warmongers. They say we offer simple answers to complex problems. Well, perhaps there is a simple answer—not an easy answer—but simple: If you and I have the courage to tell our elected officials that we want our national policy based on what we know in our hearts is morally right.

. . .

Admittedly, there's a risk in any course we follow other than this, but every lesson of history tells us that the greater risk lies in appeasement, and this is the specter our well-meaning liberal friends refuse to face—that their policy of accommodation is appeasement, and it gives no choice between peace and war, only between fight or surrender. If we continue to accommodate, continue to back and retreat, eventually we have to face the final demand—the ultimatum. And what then—when Nikita Khrushchev has told his people he knows what our answer will be? He has told them that we're retreating under the pressure of the Cold War, and someday when the time comes to deliver the final ultimatum, our surrender will be voluntary, because by that time we will have been weakened from within spiritually, morally, and economically. He believes this because from our side he's heard voices pleading for "peace at any price" or "better Red than dead," or as one commentator put it, he'd rather "live on his knees than die on his feet." And therein lies the road to war, because those voices don't speak for the rest of us.

You and I know and do not believe that life is so dear and peace so sweet as to be purchased at the price of chains and slavery. If nothing in life is worth dying for, when did this begin—just in the face of this enemy? Or should Moses have told the children of Israel to live in slavery under the pharaohs? Should Christ have refused the cross? Should the patriots at Concord Bridge have thrown down their guns and refused to fire the shot heard 'round the world? The martyrs of history were not fools, and our honored dead who gave their lives to stop the advance of the Nazis didn't die in vain. Where, then, is the road to peace? Well it's a simple answer after all.

You and I have the courage to say to our enemies, "There is a price we will not pay." "There is a point beyond which they must not advance." And this—this is the meaning in the phrase of Barry Goldwater's "peace through strength." Winston Churchill said, "The destiny of man is not measured by material computations. When great forces are on the move in the world, we learn we're spirits—not animals." And he said, "There's something going on in time and space, and beyond time and space, which, whether we like it or not, spells duty."

You and I have a rendezvous with destiny.

4.2   MEMO FROM BESS ABELL TO LYNDON JOHNSON

An outpouring of celebrity support during Lyndon Johnson's 1964 presidential campaign led his staff to brainstorm about new ways celebrities could help the administration. In this memo by Bess Abell, social secretary to Mrs. Johnson, Abell describes her ideas to recruit celebrities to bring positive attention to LBJ's legislative proposals and programs.

March 3, 1965
Memo to: The President
From: Bess Abell
Re: Recruiting entertainers on a volunteer basis to participate in the President's program of economic opportunity, manpower retraining, plans for progress, etc.

The entertainers who criss-crossed the country last Summer and Fall on behalf of your campaign and those of other Democratic candidates were working not for money, not for publicity, but because they believed in a cause.

They still do. They believe in your program, in your hopes for the Great Society, and are eager to participate.

The following memorandum has evolved pretty much from discussion we've had over the weekend with an attractive young folk singing group—the Brothers Four. These young men have a great social conscience. They frequently appear at large charity benefits where they find themselves singing for the privileged who pay $5 or $10 for a ticket, when they would rather give a concert in a tiny mining town in Appalachia or a slum area in Chicago—telling young people the importance of staying in school or helping to gather a crowd for an administration spokesman in much the same way they did during the campaign.

They strongly believe—and, from the limited contact I have had with those in the entertainment fields, I agree—their feelings are typical, i.e., that show people want to and can contribute a great deal by performing in their own fields of specialization.

What Could Be Done

Their hope is to perform voluntarily all of the work and coordination necessary to ensure that talent is available for any of the Administration's [unintelligible]—where the use of such talent seems appropriate.

- Perform in community relations programs, manpower retraining camps and high schools in distressed areas both to help reduce drop-outs and to recruit for other Federal programs.
- Assist recruiting efforts for Federal Service (Peace Corps, National Service Corps, etc.)
- Provide assistance wherever the Administration considers it appropriate.
- Not least, their efforts could contribute a great deal in demonstrating to the disadvantaged that they are not forgotten by the Administration and by the rest of the Nation.

How It Would Be Done

The organization could consist of a small executive group, appointed by the President, referred to perhaps as a "steering committee," who would in turn recruit talent from the rest of the entertainment industry. The make-up of such a committee should be representative of the entertainment industry as a whole, including:

- A movie executive, a recording company executive
- A screen and/or stage actor or actress, a great producer, someone from the Metropolitan Opera
- And from the worlds of popular and folk music. There are others, of course.

No Funds Required

They would volunteer to provide all the funds necessary to provide whatever coordination is necessary between the group and the Administration and they would not require any Federal funds in any part of the execution of their programs. All the coordination necessary could be accomplished by one employee in a small office in Washington.

I foresee this as being handled in a similar way to the "recruiting" of talent for the campaign, i.e., schedules of willing entertainers were obtained and matched with requests for appearances. Once the programs got underway it became quite contagious and pretty much took care of itself.

Of course, you or someone on your staff would be able to exercise policy control over publicity and appropriateness of entertainers and entertainment.

Not only would this show a vast segment of a major American industry supporting the President in his efforts to provide economic opportunity and equal rights, but their assistance can in ever so many case be beneficial in furthering the programs.

Recommendation

I believe there is a yearning among young artists to do this—and to work with you.

May I please place this before a meeting of your Assistants—such as: Jack Valenti, Horace Busby and Eric Goldman—next week? I truly believe this is in your interest.

_____X_____yes _____ no _____ talk to me

Bess Abell

Press agent Jack Valenti and President Lyndon B. Johnson in 1964. The first "special assistant" to Johnson's White House, Valenti was also an influential link between Hollywood and the President. In 1966, Valenti resigned his White House commission to become president of the Motion Picture Association of America and in 1968 created the MPAA film rating system. Motion Picture and Television Archive.

CHAPTER 5

Do It for the Gipper:
1966 California Gubernatorial Election

5.1 STEPHEN STERN, ORAL HISTORY INTERVIEW WITH STANLEY PLOG, "MORE THAN JUST AN ACTOR: THE EARLY CAMPAIGNS OF RONALD REAGAN" [EXCERPT]

Stanley Plog, a professor of psychology at the University of California at Los Angeles, worked with Ronald Reagan on his California gubernatorial campaign in 1966. In this excerpted oral history with the UCLA Special Collections Library, Plog discusses how Reagan's opponent, Edmund "Pat" Brown, tried to use Reagan's background as an actor against him and how that strategy backfired.

Stern: And how did you become involved with the Reagan project to begin with?

Plog: I started a Republican club on campus because I am a Republican and ran into such terrible resistance, simply because everything was so liberal on the campuses. I got a lot of static from people; and the people who were Republicans, even those who were tenured professors, just amazed me. They were afraid to identify themselves. I was not tenured, and I didn't care who knew [I was a Republican]. And I finally said, "Oh, to hell with it. We need some academic involvement in the Republican party; I will look for some good brains outside of academia. One of the people I came in contact with was a fellow named Bob Krueger, who headed up a company called Planning Research Corporation. Bob joined some of our meetings. He also had trouble finding academic Republicans. He had contact somehow to the Reagan campaign, and they were looking for the kind of help that I could give. Bob gave my name to them and we got together. What really kicked that off was that Reagan in January of 1966, I guess it was, when he made his announcement—for the 1966 campaign it

Plog:
(cont.) was, I guess—and said, "Would you believe that 15.1 percent of the population of California is on welfare?" Well, the fact is, it was 5.1 at that time, not 15.1. So the guys who really got Reagan going, like Holmes Tuttle and Henry Salvatori, said no more of this. "If he's going after it he's going to have a professional campaign. We're going to get some good research background for him. Go out and find it." They didn't want any more goofs like that. They contacted me and we put together a program for them that included several elements. Our primary task was not surveying—we did some of that, too. Rather it was putting together all the data, the background information, position papers, and issue papers for Reagan about California.

. . .

Stern: And what were your findings at that meeting about how he takes in information, and what the nature of your preparation would have to be?

Plog: Two things. Number one, I have worked in a variety of political campaigns, and Reagan, unquestionably, has the most integrated political philosophy that I've seen in anyone. There's no question of that although he's a pragmatist, as you've seen in his actions. What he believes has a logical framework and a consistency to it that most candidates don't have. Most candidates have leanings one direction or the other, liberal or conservative. But, if you ever take the various things that they have voted for and line them up, there are terrible, terrible inconsistencies. If you take Reagan's position on most things, you'll find a great amount of consistency, because he has fundamental beliefs. These are based on many Revolutionary times and early constitutional writers, about the nature and concept of democracy. Everything, for him, flows from the constitution and he considers it important. It made it easier to write for him.

The second thing is that he needed a cross-referencing and indexing system which allowed us to provide information on cards. We used five-by-eight cards which we put in black notebooks (three-ring binder notebooks). He was able to pull out cards to work on a speech and insert them back in the notebook afterwards. We developed a cross-referenced index system that allowed him to work quickly and efficiently. So he ended up at the end with, I think, with thirteen of these black research books, which actually became an issue in the campaign. Pat Brown brought it up.

. . .

Stern: Did you then have to present to him even what the basic issues were, that you found of interest to the voting public at the time?

Plog: Definitely. The primary thing was to educate him on the politics and issues of California because, all along, that guy has been focused on national politics. He has always wanted to be president, not governor.

Stern: Did you sense that from the very beginning?

Plog: He knew zero about California when we came in. I mean zero. The first time we heard him, he was still giving "The Speech," as it was called, which is a speech that he gave in support of Barry Goldwater to convince people to vote for Goldwater. That was during the campaign itself. That was the speech we heard at—I don't know where it was—the Beverly Hilton where we heard him for the first time.

. . .

It was a beautiful, fun campaign because, once that happened [the walkout incident], there were two strategies that the Brown campaign employed; they employed them consistently. And they were terrible strategies. One is, "He's only an actor." And [Edmund G. (Pat)] Brown made that terrible mistake of saying in an ad that "He's only an actor and, remember, an actor killed Lincoln." The other side of it was, playing up that he's an emotional, unstable kind of guy. And every campaign he [Reagan] has been in, people have brought that up. They've tried to use that against him, and that is so easy to handle. Both of those things are so easy to handle. Reagan has a sense of righteousness about things, and that translates into a belief that there is an American sense of justice about things. If things are wrong, you should get angry about it, because that is very Western, very American, and very right to do. The voters will always understand that, he believed. What he didn't quite catch is that the voters would understand that if it were presented straightforwardly in full context. But the press did not present it that way. It's a beautiful issue to write up and play out of proportion. We had to convince him—and we kept working on it for some time—"Whatever happens, regardless of what happens, remember, this is a chess game. And if your opponent is making these kinds of moves, remember, we've got him trapped. You absolutely are not going to be checkmated. Here's how it's going to happen, and they're going to try this all the time." The more we could intellectualize with him, so that he

Plog:
(cont.) could see it was a strategy on their part and that we had counter moves planned, the more he could handle it. Now the issue becomes intellectualized; it's not an emotional thing. When something unplanned happened, he was less emotionally involved. We had to work on that quite a bit for a while, because he wanted to get angry in return—when a sense of fair play or justice was called for. It was a long campaign, and the opposition, Pat Brown's campaign, tried to set up all kinds of situations for him to get angry about—they planted questions and did a number of things to embarrass him. But he never did get angry in public again. He always kept his cool in all kinds of situations in which they tried to trap him. Obviously, the opposite happened. The voting public began to say, "Hey, this guy's pretty cool, isn't he, man?" That's the image he has right now, because a variety of other circumstances have happened, you know, the shooting and other situations. But that was a very simple, straightforward campaign (the gubernatorial race) in terms of what was going on. The other side was dumb; they really were.

. . .

Yes, some of that, but he is also quick on the draw himself. He did a beautiful thing, for example, at my alma mater, Occidental College. He went out for a speech one night, and they had some students of the sixties type—you know, long hair and sandals, and looking kind of scraggly—parading around with signs and everything, "Down with Reagan, Down with Nancy," et cetera, and "Who Wants Boraxo in Sacramento." And they got up in the balcony of the auditorium we were in and paraded around a while, and he just waited till they kind of stopped and settled down a bit. Most of the signs had something to do with Boraxo, which was the sponsor of "Death Valley Days." He looked at the group of demonstrators and quietly said, "That may be only soap to you, but it was bread and butter to me." That just wowed the audience, and that group could not do anything any more—they couldn't demonstrate, they couldn't parade, they couldn't do anything, because they'd been chopped, just beautifully, with a little quick retort. Now everyone settled down to listen to his speech.

Stern: While we're on the general discussion of Reagan's image-creating, did you have any input into the use of the terms Creative Society or Citizen Politician that he was known for?

Plog: Citizen Politician came from the Spencer-Roberts group; the Creative Society came from us.

Stern: Did you feel that those terms were apt or useful for the campaign?

Plog: Yes, because from the Spencer-Roberts side, they needed some way of taking him out of just being an actor, which was the charge and, more importantly, not having been in politics. You had to have the idea conveyed that it was not necessary to be in politics previously to be in politics now. And that was an effective answer to that charge. The Creative Society and the reason for that was that the sixties, if you remember, was a heavy time of labels coming out of government. You had to be *for* things, and everything we worked on for him was focused on developing a positive program, with conservative underpinnings. You can't just stand up on the political platform and say that you will do things for people without putting some kind of an umbrella term together, a handle that you can grab onto and say, "That's what he's doing." That's the reason for the Creative Society.

. . .

Stern: Do you have any insight as to why the press was so antagonistic towards Reagan?

Plog: It's not with the man. It's with the fact that the press is liberal anyway, and this guy to them was a throwback, he's an anachronism to what is going on today.

Stern: Did his acting career have anything to do with their attitude towards him?

Plog: That was a way of characterizing him, but if he happened to be a very thoughtful, energetic, good-looking, exceptional public speaker—which Reagan is—who spoke liberal things, they'd love him. I'm oversimplifying everything, liberal and conservative, but those are shorthand ways of at least saying basically what you're talking about.

5.2 RONALD REAGAN INAUGURAL ADDRESS, JANUARY 5, 1967 [EXCERPT]

When Ronald Reagan won the governorship of California, he launched a political career that would culminate in the presidency of the United States. Reagan's inaugural address as governor illustrates his political ascendancy and signals the rise of conservatism in American politics.

Governor Ronald Reagan, with Nancy Reagan, speaking at the Governor's Inaugural Ball in Sacramento, California, on January 5, 1967. The first prominent actor to successfully run for office, Reagan's victory inspired other entertainers to launch their own candidacies, including George Murphy, Sonny Bono, and Arnold Schwarzenegger. Ronald Reagan Presidential Library.

Lieutenant Governor Finch, fellow Constitutional Officers, Justice McComb, Honorable Members of the Senate, Speaker Unruh, and Members of the Assembly, Distinguished Guests:

To a number of us, this is a first and hence a solemn and momentous occasion, and yet, on the broad page of state and national history, what is taking place here is almost commonplace routine. We are participating in the orderly transfer of administrative authority by the direction of the people. And this is the simple magic which makes a commonplace routine a near miracle to many of the world's inhabitants: the continuing fact that the people, by democratic process, can delegate this power, yet retain custody of it.

Perhaps you and I have lived with this miracle too long to be properly appreciative. Freedom is a fragile thing and is never more than one generation away from extinction. It is not ours by inheritance; it must be fought for and defended constantly by each generation, for it comes only once to a people. Those who have known freedom and then lost it have never known it again.

Knowing this, it is hard to explain those who even today would question the people's capacity for self rule. Will they answer this: If no one among us is capable of governing himself, then who among us has the capacity to govern someone else? Using the temporary authority granted by the people, an increasing number lately have sought to control the means of production as if this could be done without eventually controlling those who produce. Always this is explained as necessary to the people's welfare. But, "The deterioration of every government begins with the decay of the principle upon which it was founded." This is true today as it was when it was written in 1748.

Government is the people's business, and every man, woman and child becomes a shareholder with the first penny of tax paid. With all the profound wording of the Constitution, probably the most meaningful words are the first three, "We, the People." Those of us here today who have been elected to constitutional office of legislative position are in that three word phrase. We are of the people, chosen by them to see that no permanent structure of government ever encroaches on freedom or assumes a power beyond that freely granted by the people. We stand between the taxpayer and the taxspender.

It is inconceivable to me that anyone could accept this delegated authority without asking God's help. I pray that we who legislate and administer will be granted wisdom and strength beyond our own limited power; that with divine guidance we can avoid easy expedients as we work to build a state where liberty under law and justice can triumph, where compassion can govern and and wherein the people can participate and prosper because of their government and not in spite of it.

The path we will chart is not an easy one. It demands much of those chosen to govern, but also from those who did the choosing. And let there be no mistake about this; We have come to a crossroad—a time of decision—and the path we follow turns away from any idea that government and those who serve it are omnipotent. It is a path impossible to follow unless we have faith in the collective wisdom and genius of the people. Along this path government will lead but not rule, listen but not lecture. It is the path of a Creative Society.

A number of problems were discussed during the campaign and I see no reason to change the subject now. Campaign oratory on the issues of crime, pollution of air and water, conservation, welfare and expanded educational facilities does not mean that the issues will go away because the campaign has ended. Problems remain to be solved and they challenge all of us. Government will lead, of course, but the answer must come from all of you.

We will make specific proposals and we will solicit other ideas. In the area of crime, where we have double our proportionate share, we will propose legislation to give back to local communities the right to pass and enforce ordinances which will enable the police to more adequately protect these communities. Legislation already drafted will be submitted, calling upon the Legislature clearly to state in the future whether newly adopted laws are intended to preempt the right of local governments to legislate in the same field. Hopefully, this will free judges from having to guess the intent of those who passed the legislation in the first place.

At the same time, I pledge my support and fullest effort to a plan which will remove from politics, once and for all, the appointment of judges . . . not that I believe I'll be overburdened with making judicial appointments in the immediate future.

Just as we assume a responsibility to guard our young people up to a certain age from the possible harmful effects of alcohol and tobacco, so do I believe we have a right and a responsibility to protect them from the even more harmful effects of smut and pornography. We can and must frame legislation that will accomplish this without endangering freedom of speech and the press.

When fiscally feasible, we hope to create a California crime technological foundation utilizing both public and private resources in a major effort to employ the most scientific techniques to control crime. At such a time, we should explore the idea of a state police academy to assure that police from even the smallest communities can have the most advanced training. We lead the nation in many things; we are going to stop leading in crime. Californians should be able to walk our streets safely day or night. The law abiding are entitled to at least as much protection as the lawbreakers.

While on the subject of crime . . . those with a grievance can seek redress in the courts or Legislature, but not in the streets. Lawlessness by the mob, as with the individual, will not be tolerated. We will act firmly and quickly to put down riot or insurrection wherever and whenever the situation requires.

Welfare is another of our major problems. We are a humane and generous people and we accept without reservation our obligation to help the aged, disabled and those unfortunates who, through no fault of their own, must depend on their fellow man. But we are not going to perpetuate poverty by substituting a permanent dole for a paycheck. There is no humanity or charity in destroying self-reliance, dignity and self-respect . . . the very substance of moral fiber.

We seek reforms that will, wherever possible, change relief check to paycheck. Spencer Williams, Administrator of Health and Welfare, is assessing the amount of work that could be done in public installations by welfare recipients. This not being done in any punitive sense, but as a beginning step in rehabilitation to give the individual the self-respect that goes with performing a useful service.

But this is not the ultimate answer. Only private industry in the last analysis can provide jobs with a future. Lieutenant Governor Robert Finch will be liaison between government and the private sector in an all-out program of job training and education leading to real employment.

A truly great citizen of our state and a fine American, Mr. H. C. McClellan, has agreed to institute a statewide program patterned after the one he directed so successfully in the "curfew area" of Los Angeles. There, in the year and a half since the tragic riots, fully half of the unemployed have been channeled into productive jobs in the private industry, and more than 2600 businesses are involved. Mr. McClellan will be serving without pay and the entire statewide program will be privately financed. While it will be directed at all who lack opportunity, it offers hope especially to those minorities who have a disproportionate share of poverty and unemployment.

In the whole area of welfare, everything will be done to reduce administrative overhead, cut red tape and return control as much as possible to the county level. And the goal will be investment in, and salvage of, human beings.

. . .

Just as a man is entitled to a voice in government, so he should certainly have that right in the very personal matter of earning a living. I have always supported the principle of the union shop even though that includes a certain amount of compulsion with regard to union membership. For that reason it seems to me that government must accept a responsibility for safeguarding each union member's democratic rights within his union. For that reason we will submit legislative proposals to guarantee each union member a secret ballot in his union on policy matters and the use of union dues.

. . .

If we accept the present budget as absolutely necessary and add on projected increases plus funding for property tax relief (which I believe is absolutely essential and for which we are preparing a detailed and comprehensive program), our deficit in the coming year would reach three-quarters of a billion dollars.

But Californians are already burdened with combined state and local taxes $113 per capita higher than the national average. Our property tax contributes to a slump in the real estate and building trades industries and makes it well nigh impossible for many citizens to continue owning their own homes.

For many years now, you and I have been shushed like children and told there are no simple answers to the complex problems which are beyond our comprehension.

Well, the truth is, there are simple answers—there just are not easy ones. The time has come for us to decide whether collectively we can afford everything and anything we think of simply because we think of it. The time has come to run a check to see if all the services government provides were in answer to demands or were just goodies dreamed up for our supposed betterment. The time has come to match outgo to income, instead of always doing it the other way around.

The cost of California's government is too high; it adversely affects our business climate. We have a phenomenal growth with hundreds of thousands of people joining us each year. Of course the overall cost of government must go up to provide necessary services for these newcomers, but growth should mean increased prosperity and thus a lightening of the load each individual must bear. If this isn't true, then you and I should be planning how we can put a fence along the Colorado River and seal our borders.

Well, we aren't going to do that. We are going to squeeze and cut and trim until we reduce the cost of government. It won't be easy, nor will it be pleasant, and it will involve every department of government, starting

Bodybuilder and actor Arnold Schwarzenegger and President Ronald Reagan at the Republican National Convention in Dallas, Texas on August 23, 1984. Schwarzenegger increasingly became involved in Republican politics in the 1980s and 1990s. He became California's thirty-eighth governor in 2003 during a special recall election and was reelected in 2006 for a second term. Ronald Reagan Presidential Library.

with the Governor's office. I have already informed the Legislature of the reorganization we hope to effect with their help in the executive branch and I have asked for their cooperation and support.

The new Director of Finance is in complete agreement that we turn to additional sources of revenue only if it becomes clear that economies alone cannot balance the budget.

Disraeli said: "Man is not a creature of circumstances. Circumstances are the creatures of men." You and I will shape our circumstances to fit needs.

Let me reaffirm a promise made during the months of campaigning. I believe in your right to know all the facts concerning the people's business. Independent firms are making an audit of state finances. When it is completed, you will have audit. You will have all the information you need to make the decisions which must be made. This is not just a problem for the administration; it is a problem for all of us to solve together. I know that you can face any prospect and do anything that has to be done as long as you know the truth of what you are up against.

We will put our fiscal house in order. And as we do, we will build those things we need to make our state a better place in which to live and we will enjoy them more, knowing we can afford them and they are paid for.

. . .

If this is a dream, it is a good dream, worthy of our generation and worth passing on to the next.

Let this day mark the beginning.

PART II

Public Policy

In the polarized political environment, actors joined in public debates over gun control, the nuclear arms race, HIV–AIDS disease research, and environmental policies. While Hollywood stood mostly on the Left, a few dissident voices were heard. Most notable in this respect was Charlton Heston.

Like Ronald Reagan before him, Heston served as president of the Screen Actors Guild and like Reagan he started out a liberal Democrat, but it was a "change of heart" in the Democratic Party that prompted his conservatism. In 1956, Heston campaigned for Democratic presidential candidates Adlai Stevenson in 1956 and John F. Kennedy in 1960. In the early 1960s, Heston emerged as one of Hollywood's most outspoken civil rights activists, making national news in 1961 when he joined a picket line in Oklahoma City protesting segregated restaurants in that city. In 1963, he helped organize a small, but visible, Hollywood contingent for the March on Washington, walking side-by-side with Martin Luther King, Jr.

In 1964, Heston publicly endorsed Lyndon Baines Johnson in his race for the presidency against conservative Republican Barry Goldwater, who campaigned on the slogan, "In Your Heart You Know He Is Right." Later in his autobiography, Heston claimed that during the campaign he saw a Goldwater billboard in 1964 while driving to work on a Los Angeles freeway and realized that Goldwater *was* right. Heston's political transformation, however, was not evident at first. When Senator Robert F. Kennedy was assassinated during the Democratic primary race in 1968, Heston joined fellow actors Gregory Peck, Kirk Douglas, and James Stewart in supporting President Johnson's Gun Control Act of 1968. In the 1972 presidential race, Heston publicly supported Republican Richard Nixon, but it was not until Ronald Reagan ran for president in 1980 that Heston stood firmly in the Republican camp. During these years, Heston contributed to the conservative magazine *National Review*, and worked for conservative causes. During the Reagan years, Heston spoke and debated publicly on behalf of a strong national defense policy. Using his fame to support the right to bear arms, Heston also became a spokesman for the National Rifle Association (NRA). "You can have this gun, when you pry it out of my cold, dead hands," he repeatedly warned—famous words in defense of gun ownership testified to this deeply rooted rugged individualism.

Heston emerged as Hollywood's most prominent conservative in these years, but there were others who continued to use media and celebrity to promote their political views. Screenwriter and director John Milius expressed his support for the right to bear arms, his belief in law and order, and his commitment to a strong national defense in his movies *Magnum Force* (1973) and the classic *Red Dawn* (1993). Actor Tom Selleck also became active in the National Rifle Association, drawing criticism from liberal Hollywood, most visibly Rosie O'Donnell, when he appeared on her afternoon television program in May 1999.

If Hollywood divided over the right to bear arms, more vociferous debate occurred over nuclear weapons, especially when a massive arms buildup was launched by the Reagan administration in the 1980s. Although fiercely anti-Communist, Reagan's ideology was tempered by a deep fear of nuclear war. Reagan, however, believed that the Soviet Union should not be allowed to gain advantage in the arms race and that any arms reduction with that country needed to be mutual and verifiable.

Reagan's arms buildup intensified fears that the world was headed toward a nuclear holocaust. One of the most watched television events of the decade was *The Day After,* a melodramatic movie that appeared on ABC television in November, 1983. This Sunday night movie drew an audience of 100 million, including President Ronald Reagan himself.

Bearing the brunt of a massive peace movement in the United States and Europe, as well as a barrage of criticism from the mainstream media and complaints within his own administration, Reagan showed exceptional tenacity in pursuing this hard-line strategy. The administration spent a total of $2.7 trillion for defense in the next eight years. Under Reagan, conventional military strength was increased and strategic capability enlarged through new Trident missile submarines and more inter-continental ballistic missiles (ICBMs) added to the nuclear arsenal.

In order to counter the Soviet placement of SS-20 missiles in Europe in 1977, Reagan called for installing new intermediate-range ballistic missiles. At the same time, Reagan proposed to the Soviet Union what was called the "zero option"—a proposal that offered not to deploy any American missiles in Europe in exchange for the dismantling of all intermediate-range ballistic missiles by the Soviet Union. As a result of Reagan's proposal, negotiations on intermediate-range missiles were opened in Geneva by the Americans and the Soviets.

While these negotiations were being conducted, peace demonstrations were held throughout Europe and the United States calling for a "nuclear freeze"—a complete halt of the production of new weapons on both sides. The mass movement that attracted demonstrators in the United States and Europe condemned the Soviet and American arms race, but it directed most of its activity against the Reagan administration and the United States. For example, in the fall of 1982, an estimated 750,000 marchers turned out in New York's Central Park to hear Hollywood celebrities—Ed Asner, Martin Sheen, Harry Belafonte, as well as rock singers, Bruce Sprinsteen, Jackson Brown, and Bonnie Raitt—condemn the Reagan administration. Conservatives such as Charlton Heston defended Reagan's nuclear policy. It is improbable that the "nuclear freeze" movement supported by some in Hollywood, or Heston's defense of the administration's policy influenced American or Soviet policy, but ultimately the Soviets agreed to a treaty based on Reagan's zero option.

During the 1980s, the HIV–AIDS disease drew public attention as it reached epidemic proportions, primarily among gay men and drug users, and spread to the blood supply for transfusions. As the disease spread, homosexuals and other concerned citizens called for federal intervention for research, treatment, and care for those infected with the disease.

When actor Rock Hudson announced he had contracted HIV–AIDS, national attention focused on the disease. The revelation that the masculine and virile Hudson was gay may have led some Americans to reconsider their perception of gay men. Activists claimed that more research was needed and accused the Reagan administration of not committing federal research money to what had become a national pandemic.

The Reagan administration treated the HIV–AIDS issue as a public health issue and there is no archival evidence that the White House sought to exploit the epidemic in pursuit of an anti-gay agenda aimed at appeasing the religious Right. Nonetheless, this controversy spilled over into Hollywood politics as actors such as Elizabeth Taylor, a close friend of Rock Hudson's, pressed for more federal funding. In 1987, Reagan called for a one-billion-dollar spending program for AIDS prevention and research. In attendance at the speech, Taylor believed that Hudson's death had served to awaken the American public to HIV–AIDS.

While AIDS activism attracted many in Hollywood, so did environmentalism. The environmental issue, however, tended to cut across political lines. For example, Republican Heston remained an environmental activist and starred in the movie *Soylent Green* (1973) because of his fear of global over-population.

In the 1990s, many in Hollywood expressed concern about the environment. Environmental activist organizations such as the Environmental Media Association purposefully recruited young celebrities to sell their message. Former Vice President Al Gore, a long-time environmentalist, also called on Hollywood to sell his message when he made the documentary, *An Inconvenient Truth*, for which he won an Academy Award. No other issue provoked the ire of conservative commentators as much as the environmental activism on the so-called "Left Coast."

CHAPTER 6

Go Ahead, Make My Day: Gun Control

6.1 MEMOS FROM LIZ CARPENTER AND JOE CALIFANO TO LYNDON JOHNSON

Celebrities first entered the gun control debate in 1968 when President Johnson proposed restrictions on the sales of rifles and long guns. As these White House memos from presidential aides Elizabeth Carpenter and Joseph Califano illustrate, Hugh O'Brian, known for playing the lawman Wyatt Earp in a television series, spontaneously formed a group of "cowboy" actors, including Gregory Peck and Charlton Heston, in support of this legislation. The Johnson administration then "guided" O'Brian's efforts by providing him with research and soundbites.

Memorandum
The White House
Washington
8:45 a.m.—Tuesday June 11, 1968
To: The President
From: Liz

Hugh O'Brien (sic.) called last night to say that he would like to head a committee—perhaps with Gregory Peck—to push the President's bill for more gun control.

O'Brien (sic.) said he believes it will be helpful because he has played the part of Wyatt Earp and has been a Marine, and is identified with guns. "I am a sportsman and I would be glad to register my guns," he said.

He feels that Gregory Peck feels the same way.

O'Brien (sic.) said they would be glad to take out ads, go on national TV shows, try to enlist the theatre owners of America, and he is anxious to set it up and make it very much in support of the President's proposal.

This might be a way to dramatize this issue, get a more effective lobby going, and make it your cause in the most dramatic way. He was inspired by the speech you made to your commission's opening effort which he said was carried widely on TV out there.

Someone should give him some direction.

*   *   *

Memorandum
The White House
Washington
June 20, 1968 Thursday, 8:00 p.m.
For: The President
From: Joe Califano

I thought you might be interested in the attached statement which Hugh O'Brien (sic.) read on the Joey Bishop Show last Tuesday. This was a statement subscribed to by Kirk Douglas, James Stewart, Gregory Peck and Charleton (sic.) Heston and has been widely circulated throughout the country.

The statement was prepared by Levinson and Middleton and was "slipped" to Hugh O'Brien (sic.) through Jack Valenti.

6.2   BEAU BRIDGES AND CHARLTON HESTON, "GUNS: OPEN SEASON OR CEASE-FIRE?"

Charlton Heston eventually believed his support of President Johnson's gun control proposals a mistake and began a long relationship with the National Rifle Association in the 1970s. He successfully raised money, lobbied, and generated publicity for the organization, and his identification with the NRA led him to debate Beau Bridges, who played the presidential aide James Brady in an HBO film about the assassination attempt on Ronald Reagan that left Brady paralyzed, in *Elle* magazine in 1993. Heston went on to serve as the president of the NRA from 1998 until 2003.

Take Two: One Topic, Two Voices. Is the Right to Bear Arms Shooting Holes in the Fabric of our Society?

Beau Bridges won an Emmy for his portrayal of James Brady in an HBO film about the presidential assassination attempt that left Brady paralyzed.

It was a bright, peaceful Sunday morning, 20 years ago. I was sitting in a small fast-food restaurant on Ventura Boulevard in the San Fernando Valley, enjoying a cup of coffee and the newspaper. A flash of color caught my eye, as a tall young man wearing a red bandanna around his neck entered and wove his way through the customers.

Suddenly, the red bandanna was covering the young man's face, and he was pressing a handgun into the temple of the cashier, demanding money. He waved the gun toward the patrons and ordered us all to lie facedown on the floor. Frozen with fear, I couldn't move. His shaking hand then jammed the barrel of his pistol between my eyes and he repeated his request. At that moment, he was the most important person in my life. A noise in the kitchen spun him around and he went back to investigate. I sprinted out of the restaurant and called the police. The gunman returned to the customer section and fired his weapon, wounding a woman in the leg. The police arrested the man before anyone else was seriously injured.

This was the incident that first brought my attention to the urgent need for responsible gun-safety legislation. No one should ever have to experience the gut-wrenching fear that comes when you are staring down the barrel of a gun held by a person who is out of control. And I was one of the lucky ones; he didn't pull the trigger.

I have fond memories of occasional hunting trips in my early teens with my grandfather and father. My grandfather was a lifelong hunter. He respected the power of guns and he wanted me to do the same. Gun safety was important to him. When I was 18 and in Coast Guard boot camp, I learned to fire an M-1 rifle. Our tough company commander extolled the importance of gun safety to his new recruits.

I believe that our constitutional right to bear arms should be protected. However, we need to understand the responsibility involved in exercising this right—especially in today's world of automatic rifles and powerful handguns. In the 18th century, when our forefathers created our Constitution, the existing weapons were mere slingshots compared to the sophisticated weaponry of today. These days, it is easier to purchase a gun in half the states than it is to get a driver's license. This is not right. Handguns in the hands of minors, criminals, drunks, drug users, and the mentally incompetent take the lives of more than 20,000 Americans every year, in homicides, accidents, and suicides.

On March 30, 1981, John Hinkley pulled a $29 revolver from his pocket and shot President Reagan and three of the president's aides. The most critically wounded was his press secretary, James Brady. Mr. Brady survived, and with the loving support of his wife, Sarah, and son, Scott, he was able to return to an active, vital life. However, he lives his life in a wheelchair, with a piece of bullet forever lodged in his brain.

Sarah and James Brady continue to lead a major effort to establish "the Brady bill," which ensures a five-working-day waiting period before a person can purchase a gun. This legislation alone would not end gun violence in America, but at least it would be a start. It would provide a cooling-off period for anyone contemplating a harmful act with a firearm. It would give law-enforcement agencies the chance to eliminate irresponsible gun purchases, through background checks. It would also help stem the flow of illegal handguns to the black market by preventing the cash-and-carry, over-the-counter sale of these weapons to criminals—with virtually no questions asked. More than 90 percent of guns used in crime in New York City come from outside the state, most from states like Georgia, Virginia, and Ohio, which lack strong handgun laws. A national, uniform law is vital.

America's law-enforcement community is also united in its support of a ban on semiautomatic assault weapons—guns designed for combat use, now used to mow down humans, quickly and efficiently. "The availability of firearms is tied to the growing drug trade, and today's criminal is armed to kill. His weapons of choice range from the A R-15 military assault rifle to the 9-mm. semiautomatic pistol." This quote is from Phillip C. McGuire, associate director of law enforcement with the Bureau of Alcohol, Tobacco, and Firearms, August 2, 1988.

Recent Gallup polls found that 91 percent of Americans support a waiting period and background check for handgun purchasers and that 72 percent of all Americans, including 68 percent of gun owners, favored a ban on the sale and production of military-style assault weapons. President Clinton and four living ex-presidents support a waiting period. Despite the polls, Congress has refused to act. Standing in the way is the largest single-issue lobby in the nation—the National Rifle Association. The NRA, with its nearly 3 million members, not only blocks new laws but also works to repeal existing laws. The NRA has fought to allow the sale of plastic, undetectable handguns, cop-killer bullets, and machine guns. With an annual budget of $70 million, the NRA has the money, the numbers, and the clout to influence and intimidate Congress.

While our nation's political leaders continue their long-winded debates over the issue of gun safety, our children continue to die by gunfire at the rate of 12 a day. We must take responsibility for our right to bear arms and pass a gun-safety law now, designed to protect us all.

Charlton Heston—a distinguished actor, writer, and director—is a politically and socially active citizen on a variety of public issues.

There are few issues on which so many intelligent people have spent so much rhetoric pursuing so little reason as gun control. Within recent memory both *The New York Times* and *Time* magazine published challenges to the private ownership of firearms. That these august publications, staunch defenders of American liberties, should openly support the abrogation of the Second Amendment of the Bill of Rights seems aberrant.

There's been a great deal of public hoo-ha lately about media bias. Given the demographics and cultural background of most of the press corps, this may be both undeniable and unavoidable. Still, we should require more objective reporting on the gun issue. It's been consistently, and grievously, flawed. From the beginning, gun-control advocates and their media supporters have proposed first one sort of firearm, then another, in a sort of flavor-of-the-month approach. After the Kennedy assassination, they demanded bans on importing the Italian 6.5-mm. Carcano that Oswald used to kill the president. Then small-caliber handguns became the devil gun of choice. If only the cheap, concealable Saturday night special were kept out of the hands of impressionable lowlifes, their irresistible urge to kill each other would somehow disappear. Later, as airplane hijackings proliferated, the plastic gun was targeted: "It can pass undetected through airport security." This fad evaporated when it became clear that there's no such thing as a plastic gun. Currently, the gun-ban effort is focused on "military semiautomatics," sometimes described as "assault-type weapons." Antigun enthusiasts (though probably few of them can even correctly define such weapons) insist they're the "weapon of choice of Colombian drug dealers, thus they should be banned." For the record, in this country, less than one percent of all murders involve a semiautomatic assault weapon.

However wrongly expressed, the concern of gun-control enthusiasts is real. "More than 30,000 people a year are killed by guns!" they proclaim. "The slaughter must cease." They ignore, or do not know, that 55 percent are suicides, and about 8 percent are justifiable homicides by law-enforcement officers or citizens acting in self-defense.

The antigun groups have hold of the wrong end of the stick. First, let's consider: how many guns are there in the U.S.? Estimates vary, but there are surely some 200 million firearms in private hands. As a boy, I was raised in a tiny hamlet in upstate Michigan. There were about 100 people living there, owning at least 250 firearms, most of them used for hunting for the table, the rest for sport and collecting. None were really regarded then as defensive weapons; there was almost no crime in the county.

The gun controllers insist the answer to gun crime is to remove firearms from the American landscape, stubbornly denying the obvious: it (a) is impossible and (b) does nothing to deal with criminal violence. Over two decades, a web of legislation in various cities and states restricting firearms has in no instance reduced their use in crime. The irrefutable adage applies: Guns don't kill people. People kill people.

The draconian, though unstated, goal of gun-control groups is legislation prohibiting the purchase, use, or even ownership of all firearms. They have virtually achieved this in New York and Washington, D.C. The two cities, one our largest, the other the nation's capital, now compete for this title; Murder Capital of America. New York, with just three percent of our population, accounts for more than an eighth of all handgun-related unjustifiable homicides in the country. Bernhard Goetz, denied a carry permit by the City of New York after being injured by muggers, used a gun in self-defense against a gang of thugs. He was jailed for unlawful possession, while the thugs went free, one of whom was later arrested for rape and robbery.

Some localities have legislated waiting periods, which theoretically allow police to check gun purchasers for criminal records. Criminals, of course, don't buy guns—they steal them. That is, after all, what they do for a living. The irrationality of this approach was demonstrated in Los Angeles last April, during the riots. California has a waiting period. When the rioters overwhelmed the LAPD's response capacity, householders found they were unable to purchase firearms to defend their homes, while roaming criminal bands broke into gun shops and stole what they wanted. It's a lesson Angelenos won't forget. Almost a third of all states now permit handguns to be carried by the law-abiding. The thoughtful won't be surprised to learn that every one of those states now enjoys a lowered crime rate.

Let's turn now to the Bill of Rights, the cornerstone of our liberty, envied around the world as the bulwark of individual freedoms against the intrusion of the government. Its Second Amendment states: ". . . the right of the people to keep and bear arms, shall not be infringed."

"They meant a militia," anxious critics cry. No, they did not. The Founding Fathers, among them some of the best minds in our history, meant exactly what they said. Adams, Madison, Jefferson, Paine—all wrote separately and specifically, defining the right of all Americans to use arms. "The right of the people" is a phrase found only three times in the Bill of Rights. As in the Second, so in the First Amendment: it defines every individual citizen's right—to speak out, or to bear a gun. The British derided us then as "a rabble in arms." We're still armed, and still free, thanks to those dead white men who made our revolution, and codified our freedoms. God bless them—every one.

6.3   TRANSCRIPT FROM THE ROSIE O'DONNELL SHOW, ON WHICH TOM SELLECK WAS A GUEST, MAY 19, 1999

An even more famous, but less civil, celebrity gun debate took place between television talk show host and gun control supporter, Rosie O'Donnell, and actor and National Rifle Association spokesperson, Tom Selleck, on an episode of her show in 1999. As this transcript illustrates, Selleck threatened to walk off the set for what he believed to be hostile questioning from O'Donnell. Gun control seemed to inspire more passionate and divisive debate amongst celebrities than almost any other issue, although O'Donnell became less vocal on the subject when it was revealed that her bodyguards carried concealed weapons.

Rosie: We're here with Tom Selleck who's member of the NRA. Three months ago you joined the NRA.

Tom: I did. I actually joined to do an ad. Because, I've done a lot of consensus work for like the last 7 to 8 years and what disturbs me and I think disturbs a lot of Americans is the whole idea of politics now-a-days which seems to be, 'if you disagree with me, you must be evil' as opposed to 'if you disagree with me, you must be stupid'. That's very American.

You know, the demonizing of a group like the NRA is very disturbing. And that coupled with the idea that the government is getting into the idea of suing. We did it for noble reasons with tobacco. I think it was a mistake. Then they moved to gun

Tom: (cont.) makers, now they're suing television shows. Oliver Stone there's a suit on his movie.

I think the First Amendment, the Second Amendment, and all of the Bill of Rights are extremely important. And somebody needs to stand up at times where . . . maybe some of our politicians are demagogue-ing issues. Reasonable people should disagree in this country; we should celebrate that, not consider it a threat.

Rosie: Right, but I think that the reason that people are so extreme against the NRA is because the NRA has such a militant strength, especially a power in Washington to veto or to stronghold any sensible gun law. They have been against every sensible gun law, until yesterday, including trigger locks, so that children, which there are 500 a year that die, don't get killed.

Tom: I'm not a spokesman for the NRA. In fact, all I can tell you is, I was a member when I was kid. I was a junior NRA member. I learned firearm safety. And from what I can see in the last three months, they don't do a lot of the stuff that you assume that they do.

Rosie: I don't assume.

Tom: They are for trigger locks. The NRA is for a lot of things as long as they're voluntary.

Rosie: They're against the registering of guns. We have to register cars. Why shouldn't we register guns so that when a crime is committed we can trace who has owned it?

Tom: You know, I understand how you feel. This is a really contentious issue. Probably as contentious, and potentially as troubling as the abortion issue in this country. All I can tell you is, rushes to pass legislation at a time of national crisis or mourning. I don't really think are proper. And more importantly, nothing in any of this legislation would have done anything to prevent that awful tragedy in Littleton.

What I see in the work I've done with kids is, is troubling direction in our culture. And where I see consensus, which is I think we ought to concentrate on in our culture is . . . look . . . nobody argues anymore whether they're Conservatives or Liberal whether our society is going in the wrong direction. They may argue trying to quantify how far it's gone wrong or why it's gone that far wrong, whether it's guns, or television, or the Internet, or whatever. But there's consensus saying that something's happened. Guns were much more accessible 40 years ago.

A kid could walk into a pawn shop or a hardware store and buy a high capacity magazine weapon that could kill a lot of people and they didn't do it.

The question we should be asking is . . . look . . . suicide is a tragedy. And it's a horrible thing. But 30 or 40 years ago, particularly men, and even young men, when they were suicidal, they went, and unfortunately, blew their brains out. In today's world, someone who is suicidal sits home, nurses their grievance, develops a rage, and is just a suicidal but they take 20 people with them. There's something changed in our culture. That's not a simple . . .

Rosie: But you can't say that guns don't bear a responsibility. If the makers of the TEC-9 assault rifle . . . Why wouldn't the NRA be against assault rifles? This is a gun that can shoot five bullets in a second. This is the gun that those boys brought into the school. Why the NRA wouldn't say as a matter of compromise, 'we agree, assault weapons are not good'?

Tom: I'm not . . . I can't speak for the NRA.

Rosie: But you're their spokesperson Tom, so you have to be responsible for what they say.

Tom: But I'm not a spokesperson. I'm not a spokesperson for the NRA.

Rosie: But if you put your name out and say, 'I, Tom Selleck . . .

Tom: Don't put words in my mouth. I'm not a spokesperson. Remember how calm you said you'd be? Now you're questioning my humanity.

Rosie: No, not your humanity. I think you're a very humane man. I'm saying that if you . . .

Tom: Let's just say that I disagree with you but I think you're being stupid.

Rosie: But you can't say that I will not take responsibility for anything the NRA represents if you're saying that you're going to do an ad for the NRA.

Tom: Really?

Rosie: You can't say that. Do you think you can?

Tom: Look . . . you're carefully skirting the issue. It's an act of moral vanity, Rosie, to assume that someone who disagrees with your political agenda to solve our problems, cares any less or is any less shocked . . .

Rosie: I never said you cared less.

Tom: Well, let me finish . . .

Rosie: Tom, I don't think you cared less. Nor do I think the men in the NRA cared less.

Tom: The women too.

Rosie: And the women. I simply said, why can there not be a compromise on the issue . . .

Tom: There IS a compromise! There's a compromise in enforcing laws. There's a compromise with not allowing kids with guns in school. The problem is, and what you don't seem to realize . . . you seem to have some sort of . . . look, we all hang out with people we agree with. And you have a one very one-sided view of the fact of what you don't understand . . .

Rosie: As does the NRA and the people you hang out with at the NRA have a one-sided view as well.

Tom: I don't hang out with people of the NRA . . .

Rosie: OK, well, you're saying that I hang out with people with my views. I'm just saying . . .

Tom: I said people tend to . . .

Rosie: We all tend to. The NRA does and the un-NRA does.

Tom: You know, this is a nice one-sided conversation but you keep interrupting me. Remember how civil you said we were going to be?

Rosie: I let you talk for four minutes without saying one thing! I did. I didn't say one thing! I simply asked a question on what their philosophies are. And you don't want to . . .

Tom: I told you . . . look, when do you want to get to television and violence . . .

Rosie: I agree! I agree.

Tom: . . . and game shows . . .

Rosie: Game shows?

Tom: . . . and how do you reconcile . . .

Rosie: You mean video games? I agree!

Tom: Please let me finish! Let me say just one thing. What you're really talking about . . . at least what I'm talking about . . . is are we a responsible enough society, in terms of television, in terms of guns, in terms of everything else, to be this free? That should frame the debate. My answer unfortunately, in this culture, is 'probably not'. But I'm going to go down with the Civil Liberties ship, and all the Bill of Rights, and apply them equally. That's the way I feel. You can ask me specific questions about anything, but it's simply stupid political rhetoric.

Rosie: Well, it's not stupid political rhetoric. We also have freedom of speech, but you're not allowed to scream 'fire' in a crowded movie theater because it threatens the safety of other people.

Tom: I understand.

Rosie: Assault weapons threaten the safety of other people. There's no reason, in my opinion, to have them. You want to have a hunting rifle? Great! You want to have a handgun?

Tom: Do you really think the Second Amendment to the Constitution is to guarantee hunting and target shooting? Do you really think that's what the Founding Fathers meant?

Rosie: I think the Second Amendment is in the Constitution so that we can have muskets when the British people come over in 1800. I don't think it's in the Constitution to have assault weapons in the year 2000. But I'm wrong? I guess . . .

Tom: *(nods his head)*

Rosie: You know, this is the problem. Here's what happens. The people with opposing views, there is no compromise because, you feel attacked, I feel attacked. You feel less understood . . .

Tom: I haven't attacked you. I've disagreed with you.

Rosie: And I've disagreed with you as well. But mine comes in the form of attacking because . . .

Tom: I haven't mentioned assault weapons once. I haven't mentioned a lot of things once. The nature of this debate . . . I didn't come on your show to have a debate. I came on your show to plug a movie. That's what's I'm doing here.

Rosie: And that's what we did.

Tom: If you think it's proper to have a debate about the NRA, I'm trying to be fair with you.

Rosie: As I am trying to . . .

Tom: But this is absurd. You're calling me a spokesman for the NRA.

Rosie: Tom, if you are a celebrity and you're doing an ad that says, 'I am the NRA', then what should have been . . .

Tom: Have you read the ads?

Rosie: I have read the ads.

Tom: Good.

Rosie: Did *you* read the ads?

Tom: I said them. I read them when I say them.

Rosie: Well, I do too. Well, this is not supposed to be a personal . . .

Tom: Well it's certainly very entertaining, look at the audience, they're just laughing and having a great old time.

Rosie: Well it's a serious subject. I don't think it's a lot to laugh about.

Tom: Well, that's fine.

Rosie: All right, well, this has not gone the way I had hoped it had gone. But, I would like to thank you for appearing anyway, knowing that we have differing views. I was happy that you decided to come on the show. And if you feel insulted by my questions, I apologize, because it was not a personal attack. I was meant to bring up the subject as it is in the consciousness of so many today. That was my intent. And if it was wrong, I apologize to you, on a personal level.

Tom: It's your show and you can talk about it after I leave too.

Rosie: Well, I thought I would give you an opportunity to discuss your side of it. Which is what I hope that I did. And if I was wrong I'm sorry. *(Tom looks away from Rosie)* Well, obviously, it didn't do much good.

Comedian Rosie O'Donnell, former White House Press Secretary James Brady, and New York Rep. Carolyn McCarthy (D-NY) at the Handgun Control dinner in New York, May 1, 2000. The lives of both Brady and McCarthy were affected by gun violence. O'Donnell was honored at the dinner for her commitment to hand gun control. She had supported gun control policies on her daytime talk show and had even argued with guest Tom Selleck for his support of the National Rifle Association during one episode. AP Photo/Ron Frehm.

6.4 "I'M THE NRA" ADVERTISEMENT WITH TOM SELLECK

In order to combat its image as an extremist organization, the National Rifle Association started a new advertising campaign called "I'm the NRA" in the 1980s. Although first undertaken to showcase a cross-section of everyday gun owners, the NRA began recruiting celebrities, such as the actor Charlton Heston, the singer Charlie Daniels, and the basketball player Karl Malone as well. As this advertisement with the actor Tom Selleck illustrates, the campaign often emphasized traditional values, hunter safety, and wildlife conservation, and the NRA recruited celebrities known for identifying with those qualities.

I know people have strong feelings about guns. Some like all guns always. Some like some guns sometimes. Some like no guns ever. Reasonable people are free to differ.

But we cannot differ on the freedom. The magnificent minds who created our country — like Mason, Jefferson, Adams and Paine — knew the individual right to choose to own firearms is essential to a free people.

We don't have to agree on every thing, just that one thing. That's how and why NRA works. **I'm The NRA.**

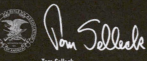

Tom Selleck
Actor, Father, Hunter, Recreational Shooter

Did You Know... "During debate over the U.S. Constitution, our Founding Fathers often wrote about firearm freedom as an individual right — but never as a 'collective' or 'state's' right. 'No free man shall ever be debarred the use of arms,' wrote Thomas Jefferson, who considered the Second Amendment a guarantee of an individual freedom just like the rest of the Bill of Rights."

Wayne LaPierre, NRA Executive Vice President

CHAPTER 7

To Freeze or Not to Freeze: Nuclear Buildup

7.1 TRANSCRIPT FROM NUCLEAR FREEZE DEBATE BETWEEN CHARLTON HESTON AND PAUL NEWMAN ON ABC'S *THE LAST WORD*, OCTOBER 30, 1982

The actors Charlton Heston's and Paul Newman's involvement in the nuclear freeze initiative campaign in California (which included appearing in commercials, interviews, and rallies) led them to debate on ABC's news program *The Last Word* in 1982. The host felt obligated to explain why two actors would be debating a subject out of their realm of expertise, but, as this transcript illustrates, the call-in guests seemed to take them seriously and the two men did a reputable job, although Newman received flack for being ill-informed on Soviet treaty violations.

Ted Koppel: Last night on *The Last Word*, much of the broadcast was devoted to the nuclear freeze issue. Well, tonight Greg Jackson is back to pick up on that theme. Greg.

Greg Jackson: Ted, for sure I hadn't planned on being in Los Angeles, but I guess you move where the viewers tell you. Let me begin at the beginning. More than 184,000 people called us last night to register their opinion on the question: Are you in favor or are you opposed to a bilateral U.S./Soviet freeze on nuclear weapons? Here are the results. Voting yes, 78,356 people. Voting no, 105,703. The no vote winning by some 27,000 calls. Now, of course, our survey was not statistically scientific. And later we'll give you the outcome of a more formal poll on the same question which had opposite results, and we'll try to explain why. Also last night if you were watching us, you know our switchboard was swamped with calls for

Greg Jackson:
(cont.)

Paul Newman and Charlton Heston. Mr. Newman arguing for the nuclear freeze, Mr. Heston against it. Tonight out in Los Angeles, we're with these two famous and serious men, and they will go at it face to face in a debate, and you again can take part by calling in with your questions . . .

. . . Last night on *The Last Word*, Phil Donahue's guest was Paul Newman discussing with some passion his feelings in favor of the nuclear freeze movement. We also talked with Charlton Heston who's against the nuclear freeze. In the course of the evening, it came out that Mr. Newman had refused to debate Mr. Heston face to face and by night's end he called and said he changed his mind, and we are here now to give them a chance to make their cases live from Los Angeles. Before I start, a last and I guess frank word or question we all are asking: what are these performers doing becoming public spokesmen on extremely complex issues that don't have anything to do with their art or expertise? Now both Mr. Newman and Mr. Heston acknowledge they are not military scientists. But experts we've checked with say that they are obviously intelligent and responsible in their arguments, and I think anyone who watched the program last night will agree. Serious men committed and truly talented at communicating so that we can understand both sides of the nuclear freeze question. And that's true whether you agree with them or not. Both men have agreed that Mr. Newman will begin. Mr. Newman, your position on the nuclear freeze?

Paul Newman:

Thank you. I'm here tonight as a concerned American citizen and as a former United States delegate to the United Nations special session on disarmament. I am concerned because today the United States and the Soviet Union possess the equivalent of one million Hiroshima bombs, an amount equal to four tons for every man, woman and child on this planet. And I am concerned because America's nuclear weapons policy is moving away from deterrence, which has kept the peace for thirty-seven years, and is moving toward the incredible proposition that we can fight and win a nuclear war. That's why I support a verifiable freeze on the production, testing, and the deployment of nuclear arms by both sides. A nuclear weapons freeze is the best and it is the quickest way for the people to gain control of this mindless, technological explosion that threatens the life on this planet. And the freeze is not based on trusting the Russians. If it were, I certainly wouldn't be for it, because every separate element of the freeze depends on strict verification. And that's why the former director of the CIA, William Colby, supports the freeze, came to California to speak for the freeze and endorse it, and testified before Congress that the freeze can be verified. The freeze is bi-lateral and the various referendums across the country call on both the United States and the Soviet Union to sit down and to negotiate an immediate halt to the nuclear arms race. If the Soviets don't agree, the deal is off, but it would be criminal not to make the effort because time is starting to run out. Today the United States and the Soviet Union have about 50,000 nuclear devices. We have about 30,000. The Soviets have 20,000. And if you look at those awesome numbers, this endless bickering about which side is ahead is almost grotesque. The fact is that we have enough nuclear weapons to deter the Soviets and the Soviets have enough to deter us. Just take a brief look at the history of the arms race, and it discloses the following: we developed the atom bomb, the Soviets followed; we developed the hydrogen bomb, the Soviets soon followed; we developed multiple warheads, more accurate warheads, solid propellants, the Soviets soon followed. And this administration came into office and initiated a further weapons buildup, and right on schedule—two days ago!—we heard Soviet President Breshnev say that he would not allow the Soviets to fall behind. So off we go again, playing this nuclear game of leap-frog. The nuclear freeze offers the only logical alternative to a race in which there are no winners. On Tuesday,

Paul Newman: **(cont.)**	citizens here in California and in many other states and counties and cities across the United States will have the opportunity to vote for a nuclear arms freeze. This vote is not a vote on an arms agreement. It is a message that Americans, as Americans we have not abdicated from our democratic right to advise the president on matters of great import. As President Eisenhower said, "The people want peace. In fact, the people want peace so bad that governments just better get out of their way and let them have it."
Greg Jackson:	Thank you Mr. Newman. Mr. Heston?
Charlton Heston:	As Paul says, next week Americans in a number of states are going to vote on a nuclear freeze initiative. A lot of voters feel, as Paul does, that the nuclear freeze would somehow bring us the peace, the world, we all seek. As Paul and I have followed each other around the state the past couple of weeks, I've heard people talk about the passion Paul brings to his conviction. I'm very glad he's agreed to come and debate this with me here tonight, but I hope passion won't have any part in what we say. This is too important for that. I heard an actor, not Paul, supporting the freeze by saying, "No, I haven't read anything about it. I don't need to, this is a gut issue." Yeah, indeed it is, but you can't think with your guts. You can think of the search for peace as a moral obligation, incumbent on every human being. A great philosopher, Hegel I think it was, talked about that. The most important of all moral obligations, he said, is to think clearly. I hope very much Paul and I can think clearly here tonight and I beg all of you to think clearly in the polling booth next Tuesday. OK, let me be brief and clear. A nuclear freeze will not serve the cause of peace because it is unnegotiable, unequal, and unverifiable. It would divert the energies of the American negotiations now in progress in Geneva where we're trying not just to freeze nuclear arms but to reduce them. A nuclear freeze initiative, if it's passed, would send a false message to the Soviet Union, which is ignorant of the open function of the democratic process in a free society, a false message

of weakness of will and commitment on the part of the American people. A nuclear freeze would not lock the armed forces of the United States and our allies, which have been successful as Paul says for thirty-seven years in deterring the Soviet Union from launching World War III. It would lock us into a position of strategic inferiority, which would in fact increase the danger of the war we all fear. A hundred year ago, no it was more than that, a great man Stonewall Jackson said, "Do not take counsel of your fears." Now, he didn't mean don't know your fears, just don't be guided by them. I think that's good advice. We live, God knows we always have, in an infinitely dangerous world. Well, none of us get out of it alive, but while we're here, please let's put the infinite treasure of the peace of the world in the hands of those we trust, not those we fear.

Greg Jackson: Thank you. Opening statements from Mr. Newman and Mr. Heston. As we get into this, I can see now that one term that constantly comes up, "unilateral," which obviously means only one side halts nuclear development, hoping the other side will, I presume, and "bilateral," which means the only way the deal goes through is if both sides agree to it. You can call with your questions for Paul Newman or Charlton Heston right after this . . .

. . . We're talking with Paul Newman, who is for the nuclear freeze, and Charlton Heston, who's against it, and we'll be taking your phone calls on whether the United States and the Soviet Union should freeze the production of nuclear weapons. Incidentally, as many of you know, that question will be on Tuesday's ballot in nine states plus the District of Columbia. For your information the states are Arizona, California, Oregon, Michigan, Rhode Island, Montana, North Dakota, Massachusetts, and New Jersey. Wisconsin has already voted in favor of a freeze. Gentlemen, what does this mean, this referendum? Both of you, I mean, in fact, we all know, however the vote comes out next Tuesday, it doesn't

Greg Jackson: have any binding effect on the President. Why all of
(cont.) your energy? Either one of you first.
Charlton Heston: Paul.
Paul Newman: Well, I think it's really very, very important to understand that the people really of this country control
what goes on in Washington. I think it's very, very
. . . you know, Eisenhower warned us in his Farewell
Address to be careful that national policy was not
determined by the technologically elite. And word
comes down from the White House that we
citizens really don't have enough information to
make intelligent decisions about an issue like this.
Well the fact of the matter is that the whole
premise and cornerstone of a democracy is that the
people send the messages back to Congress and to
people in Washington about what our feelings are
and it's then up to Washington to respond to the
people.

Greg Jackson: Well, let me ask that then. The vote so far, in these
other referendum have been in favor of nuclear
freeze.

Charlton Heston: I think that's because perhaps those who favor a
freeze are perhaps unaware that the current negotiations in Geneva are not for a freeze but for a reduction in nuclear arms, which obviously would reduce
the danger of war. To send this message to the Soviet
Union, as I said in my opening statement, would be
a false message. They don't understand the democratic process. Democracy is rare in the world. We're
very fortunate to be able to have this kind of an
exchange.

Greg Jackson: May we go to our first phone caller. Yes, you're on
the air.

Caller: . . . My question is to Mr. Newman. Do you think
Russia would take a nuclear freeze on our part to be
a show of weakness as a world power?

Paul Newman: There's no way that the Soviet Union can take the
insistence that we have a nuclear freeze, a bilateral
freeze, as a show of weakness on our part. We both
have occasions when there are things that accrue to
both sides to mutual benefit. If you're talking about

annihilation, then that is what the benefit is to both sides. Just because you're calling for a freeze of nuclear weapons is not necessarily an admission of weakness.

Greg Jackson [to Charlton Heston]: I know that's a major point of yours. Just briefly, that question was to Mr. Newman, but I know you don't agree.

Charlton Heston: Wouldn't it be lovely if the Soviet citizens could vote on reduction of nuclear arms, Paul. Of course, the Soviet citizens are not able to take part in the political process.

Paul Newman: It's very simple. We have three nuclear treaties with the Soviet Union. It didn't make any difference who initiated these treaties. In our situation, the government initiated the treaties and the government of the Soviets. The important part is that we have the treaties, that they have been lived up to, and it does not seem necessarily relevant who initiates them. The point is to have the treaty.

Charlton Heston: With respect, Paul, the question was about a freeze, not the treaties. The treaties, of course, have been frequently violated, which I know you don't agree with, but that's another question. There was an interesting item in the UP wire today. "San Jose, California. The head of a Soviet delegation in California to promote a freeze of nuclear weapons denies the visit as an attempt to manipulate the American peace movement. He also denies the visit is directly tied to the current campaign for a nuclear freeze initiative on the California ballot. He maintains it's merely a coincidence that the group happens to be in the state just before the election in which voters will decide on a nuclear freeze."

Greg Jackson: Mr. Heston, I think your disbelief is obvious. Pause just a moment. We'll be back right after this. . . .

. . . We are discussing the nuclear freeze with Paul Newman, Charlton Heston. I'd like to go to the phones. Somebody out there, a question for either.

Caller: . . . I'd like to ask Charlton Heston if he knows who's ahead in the nuclear arms race.

Charlton Heston: All of the information I have received from the Defense Department over the last two days indicates that there is a serious strategic shortfall, particularly, and I think that this is a point that hasn't been made yet, Paul, and it's one of the things that disturbs me most about the nuclear freeze initiative as it's voiced in California. It states that there will be a freeze on the testing, production, and deployment, not only of nuclear missiles, but of carrier systems. According to the SALT I negotiations, carrier systems is defined as aircraft. The strategic air command consists entirely of B-52 bombers, none of which was built later than 1962, all of which are sub-sonic aircraft, now entirely obsolete for their original missions.

Greg Jackson: Mr. Newman?

Paul Newman: Well, it really is very interesting that the two chairmans [sic] of the Joint Chiefs of Staff both said in testimony in front of the United States Senate that they would not be willing to trade our military capability for the capability of the Russians. [talking over Heston] And so far as the Air Corps is concerned, Lou Allen, a retired head of the Air Corps, has already said that he would not be willing to trade the Air Force capability with the capability of the Russians. And it's also not true, Charlton. We have seventy F-11s that are supersonic. The Russians have about 160 long-range bombers and 100 of those are propeller-driven, so I wouldn't worry very much about calling our B-52s antiquated. They have been redesigned. We've been spending billions and billions of dollars . . .

Charlton Heston: Paul, those aircraft are older than the men that are flying them.

Paul Newman: That's just like saying that a Cadillac Seville from fifteen years ago is the same as a Cadillac Seville from today. The B-52 no longer has anything to do with . . . except the name.

Charlton Heston: Not according to the Air Force.

Paul Newman: Well, according to Lou Allen, and he's the retired head of the Air Force, and I will take his word for it.

Greg Jackson:	OK, again this isn't trying to get proof. It's your two positions. I'd like to go to another phone call.
	. . .
Caller:	. . . I'd like to ask Mr. Heston, just how many nuclear bombs will it take to blow up Russia? How many do we need?
Charlton Heston:	Fewer than we have now, ma'am, fewer than we have now. That's why I approve of the government's efforts to negotiate a reduction in nuclear forces.
Greg Jackson:	I'm sorry, you said we don't have enough bombs?
Charlton Heston:	No, she said "how many do we need?"
Greg Jackson:	Yes?
Charlton Heston:	I said *fewer* than we have.
Greg Jackson:	Cut it in half, what would you say?
Charlton Heston:	Yes, in the intermediate range missiles, the administration proposal is to reduce them to zero. The Russians have so far . . . we have zero, as it happens. We also have a commitment to NATO, to install the Pershing missiles next year, a commitment which the Europeans took seriously enough that a German Socialist government fell two weeks ago to be replaced by a government that . . . [interrupted by PN]
Paul Newman:	You also talk about an imbalance in intermediate range missiles. We also have twenty submarines that we maintain off the coast of Russia . . .
Charlton Heston:	That's true.
Paul Newman:	. . . and they have, we have, 3,000 [CH interrupts]
Charlton Heston:	The Europeans want those Pershings.
Paul Newman:	We have 3,000 warheads that are sitting off the coast on submarines that are on station 365 days a week, so that's just another one of, uh, you know funneling improper facts in, because that would give us . . .
Charlton Heston:	You feel those missiles shouldn't be there?
Paul Newman:	Of course they should be there, but when you talk of the tremendous disadvantage that we have, and we have 3,000 warheads sitting off the coast of Russia all the time, it seems to me we've got a tremendous advantage. If we freeze that advantage now, that would be to our advantage.
Greg Jackson:	OK, gentlemen, no more questions. I'm not taking any more phone calls. This is it. You got the last word, the both of you. Mr. Heston?

Charlton Heston: I feel that the commitment of the government to reducing nuclear arms is significant. Those are the people elected and appointed to preserve the security of the United States. I accept their commitment. I am a little bemused by the feeling that somehow this is not to be trusted. As for the Russian position, I think Breshnev made a statement yesterday, he made another statement in 1973 I think is significant, he said "trust his comrades, for by 1985 we will have achieved our objectives, a shift in the balance of forces, that will enable us to exert our will."

Paul Newman: On one of the programs, Charlton, you said that the SALT Treaty had been violated forty times. If that is true, why hasn't the President terminated the treaties that we have with the Soviet Union, and why, if there have been so many violations of SALT II, is he at this very moment trying to have two teams negotiating in Geneva on arms reduction talks. Now as I said before, the only problem with the arms reduction talks, is if it takes ten years, you're talking about putting another 11,000 warheads on these very, very destabilizing weapons—the Trident II, the Pershing II, and the MX—and cutting down all that reaction time, and finally, meaning that the planet, life on this planet, may very well be determined by computers and unfortunately, the Russian computers are not as accurate as ours. The danger is twice as great.

Charlton Heston: Paul, the Soviet record on treaty compliance is familiar to the world. We've got to do the best we can. I know we're winding up here, [PN interrupts]

Paul Newman: I'm talking about the three *nuclear* treaties. I'm not talking about going back to 1921.

Charlton Heston: Well, I have a list of violations here . . .

Paul Newman: I'm not talking about going back to 1921.

Charlton Heston: Tell you what. Let's make it more simply, Paul, if this were the summer of 1939, instead of the fall of 1982, would you vote for nuclear freeze with Adolph Hitler?

Paul Newman: I'm trying to say that our . . . the Russian compliance, we have machinery in Geneva to monitor the Russian compliance of the nuclear treaties that we have with them. There have been six instances where the Soviets have accused us of noncompliance, and eight instances where we have accused the Soviets of non-compliance. In all of those cases, those fourteen cases, the conclusions have come to mutual agreement . . .

Charlton Heston: Here's a list of fifty-one, Paul.

Paul Newman: What?

Charlton Heston: Here's a list of fifty-one violations.

Paul Newman: Who is [sic] those composed by, Mickey Mouse?

Charlton Heston: No. Here's a list of the sources.

Paul Newman: Why, why would the President not terminate the agreements that we have, if there were all those violations that you're talking about?

Charlton Heston: I suppose that's one of the reasons the Senate refused to ratify SALT II.

Paul Newman: Oh.

Charlton Heston: Isn't that what you mentioned?

Paul Newman: No, no we refused to ratify SALT II because of Frank Church's remarks about troops in Cuba, not because of any cases of violations.

Charlton Heston: You really think that?

Paul Newman: Well, of course.

Charlton Heston: I disagree with you.

Paul Newman: It's been published many, many times, in many newspapers.

Greg Jackson: Gentlemen, thank you both. You're obviously very committed.

Charlton Heston: Thank you for loaning us your audience. I appreciate the chance.

[host makes concluding remarks, including . . .]

Greg Jackson: . . . I don't know if you changed anyone's minds, but I'm absolutely positive there's no one out there that doesn't think you're committed, serious, and you've done your homework.

Charlton Heston: Well, I still wish we could have done this debate in Moscow, but I'm glad we got a chance to do it [smiling].

Greg Jackson: OK.

CHAPTER 8

Pillow Talk: AIDS Research

8.1 ARMY ARCHERD, "TWENTY YEARS WITH AIDS AND H'W'D"

AIDS was first recognized in 1981, but numerous misperceptions arose over how the disease spread. In his popular column in the Hollywood trade paper *Variety*, Army Archerd discusses how the news that Rock Hudson, one of the most popular movie stars of his time, was suffering from AIDS mobilized Hollywood's biggest stars, including Elizabeth Taylor, to raise public awareness about the disease.

Good Morning

I was the most hated man—in some circles—in Hollywood on Tuesday, July 23 1985. It was the day I wrote, with heavy heart, the most difficult and most astounding column of my career. It started with, "The whispering campaign on Rock Hudson can—and should stop. He has flown to Paris for further help. The Institute Pasteur has been very active in research on Acquired Immune Deficiency Syndrome." I went on to write, "Doctors warn that the dread disease (AIDS) is going to reach catastrophic proportions in all communities if a cure is not soon found." Unfortunately, that prediction proved true. This month marks the 20th anniversary of the disease, which was first observed in June 1981. In 1985, AIDS was unknown to almost everyone; for much of the world, Hudson was the first person they knew to contract the whispered-about disease. For the first time, they had a face to put with the disease. My 1985 column resulted in international response, questions—and immediate denials from Hudson's camp. When his press agent declined to confirm it, even the then-editor of this paper, Thomas M. Pryor, wanted me to "correct" my story. I told him my facts were accurate: I had known about Hudson's illness and had a copy (under lock and key) of the diagnosis in which Hudson's doctor had given him confirmation six months earlier. Yet even after that diagnosis, Hudson continued lifestyle that no AIDS patient (or partner) today would condone. When Hudson collapsed at the Pasteur Institute, I reported he was then transferred to the American Hospital in Paris after the White House (Ronald Reagan) had gotten a request from longtime supporter Hudson. But the White House noted they would offer assistance "to any American citizen." The American hospital in Paris denied that he had inoperable cancer. After my column ran, Hudson's press agent Dale Olson would issue a statement "to clear up confusion and speculation about the medical condition" of Hudson. The confusion was caused by Hudson's camp. And while Hudson knew he had AIDS, Olson says "He never admitted it to me" ... On July 31, Hudson, now confirmed as suffering from AIDS, was admitted to UCLA Medical Center at 3 a.m., having arrived from Paris in a chartered Air France 747.

Hollywood Was Stunned

As was I, when I first learned of Hudson's illness and his ensuing deterioration, which became evident to all when he "winged to Carmel (July 16) to help longtime friend Doris Day launch her new pet TV series," as I wrote at the time. "His illness was no secret to close Hollywood friends but its true nature was divulged to very, very few." When my story appeared, some of those friends and former associates berated me for the story. "How could you do that to Rock," wrote one of his former press agents. When Elizabeth Taylor was giving a press party for friend Carole Bayer Sager at Tiffany's, the publicist told me, "If I invite you, Elizabeth will *not* show up." Taylor soon thereafter became one of the staunchest supporters, fundraisers and contributors to AmFar ... Four years later, Hudson was again in the news: In 1989, Marc Christian, a former lover of his, went to court vs. the Hudson estate saying the actor had kept his illness a secret from Christian, saying it was he, not Hudson, who went public with Hudson's illness. But the New York Times, on Feb. 15, 1989, reminded Christian, "It was not he who first went public with confirmation of Rock Hudson's fatal attraction. That was done by a longtime *Variety* columnist, Army Archerd, who printed the information a few months before Hudson's death. Mr. Archerd was both applauded and scorned at the time by a town and an industry with a schizophrenic attitude toward homosexuality, privately accepting as they had been of Hudson's double life, but publicly squeamishly fearful of just what

Middle America might think." When I wrote the story, I told the L.A. Times I wanted to help the AIDS education campaign and at the same time respect Hudson's dignity, and "I wanted to print it (the story) as painlessly yet as effectively as possible so that the message would come across." I also knew that by acknowledgment by celebrity, some of the most worthwhile causes have achieved recognition and assistance. For instance the health problems of First Ladies Betty Ford and Nancy Reagan, and men's prostate problem making news thanks to President Reagan's advice for early examinations. AIDS didn't get the White House's attention until friend Hudson's affliction. Two years later, the FDA's drug-approval program's weakness was highlighted.

In Its Current Cover Story

"AIDS at 20—A Special Report," Newsweek quotes Elizabeth Taylor as saying that friends started calling her with, "Don't go near this one (an AIDS fund-raiser). It's not a sympathetic charity." However, Taylor is quoted as saying, "Then a couple of months before the (AIDS benefit) dinner it came out (*guess where!—ed.*) that Rock had AIDS. All of a sudden the city did a total spin, It was like, 'Oh, one of us got it, it's not just bums in the gutter'." But as the New York Times pointed out (in 1989) "Without Army Archerd's column there is a very real chance that the world might have suspected but never known what killed Rock Hudson." Hudson died Oct. 2, 1985, of complications from AIDS. His secret may have been his vanity—but it was not in vain.

8.2 RONALD REAGAN, "REMARKS AT THE AMERICAN FOUNDATION FOR AIDS RESEARCH AWARDS DINNER," MAY 31, 1987

As public awareness about AIDS grew, critics accused the Reagan administration of reacting too slowly to take federal action against it. Even though some of Ronald Reagan's supporters on the Religious Right proclaimed that AIDS was God's punishment against homosexuals for their "immoral" lifestyle, Hollywood luminaries like Elizabeth Taylor and Rock Hudson urged Reagan to take a leading role in the fight against the disease. In this 1987 speech, at which Taylor was present, Reagan calls for a one-billion-dollar spending program on AIDS prevention and research and also calls for treating AIDS victims with "compassion" and "kindness."

The President, Dr. Silverman, Elizabeth, Don Ross, award winners, ladies and gentlemen, I hope Elizabeth won't mind, but some years ago when I was doing a television show, "General Electric Theater," part of my work required visiting the General Electric plants, 139 of them, and meeting all the employees.

And knowing better than to have a canned speech for them, I would go and suggest that they might ask questions. And every place I went, the first question was "Is Elizabeth Taylor really that pretty?" [Laughter] And being the soul of honesty, I would say, "You bet." [Applause]

But you know, fundraisers always remind me of one of my favorite but most well-worn stories. I've been telling it for years, so if you've heard it, please indulge me. A man had just been elected chairman of his community's annual charity drive. And he went over all the records, and he noticed something about one individual in town, a very wealthy man. And so, he paid a call on him, introduced himself as to what he was doing, and he said, "Our records show that you have never contributed anything to our charity." And the man said, "Well, do your records show that I also have a brother who, as the result of a disabling accident, is permanently disabled and cannot provide for himself? Do your records show that I have an invalid mother and a widowed sister with several small children and no father to support them?" And the chairman, a little abashed and embarrassed, said, "Well, no, our records don't show that." The man said, "Well, I don't give anything to them. Why should I give something to you?" [Laughter]

Well, I do want to thank each of you for giving to the fight against AIDS. And I want to thank the American Foundation for AIDS Research and our award recipients for their contributions, as well. I'm especially pleased a member of the administration is one of tonight's recipients. Dr. [C. Everett] Koop is what every Surgeon General should be. He's an honest man, a good doctor, and an advocate for the public health. I also want to thank other doctors and researchers who aren't here tonight. Those individuals showed genuine courage in the early days of the disease when we didn't know how AIDS was spreading its death. They took personal risks for medical knowledge and for their patients' well-being, and that deserves our gratitude and recognition.

I want to talk tonight about the disease that has brought us all together. It has been talked about, and I'm going to continue. The poet W.H. Auden said that true men of action in our times are not the politicians and statesmen but the scientists. I believe that's especially true when it comes to the AIDS epidemic. Those of us in government can educate our citizens about the dangers. We can encourage safe behavior. We can test to determine how widespread the virus is. We can do any number of things. But only medical science can ever truly defeat AIDS. We've made remarkable progress, as you've heard, already. To think we didn't even know we had a disease until June of 1981, when five cases appeared in California. The AIDS virus itself was discovered in 1984. The blood test became available in 1985. A treatment drug, AZT, has been brought to market in record time, and others are coming. Work on a vaccine is now underway in many laboratories, as you've been told.

In addition to all the private and corporate research underway here at home and around the world, this fiscal year the Federal Government plans to spend $317 million on AIDS research and $766 million overall. Next year we intend to spend 30 percent more on research: $413 million out of $1 billion overall. Spending on AIDS has been one of the fastest growing parts of the budget, and, ladies and gentlemen, it deserves to be. We're also tearing down the regulatory barriers so as to move AIDS from the pharmaceutical laboratory to the marketplace as quickly as possible. It makes no sense, and in fact it's cruel, to keep the hope of new drugs from dying patients. And I don't blame those who are out marching and protesting to get AIDS drugs released before the I's were—or the T's were crossed and the I's were dotted. I sympathize with them, and we'll supply help and hope as quickly as we can.

Science is clearly capable of breathtaking advances, but it's not capable of miracles. Because of AIDS' long incubation period, it'll take years to know if a vaccine works. These tests require time, and this is a problem money cannot overcome. We will not have a vaccine on the market until the mid- to late 1990's, at best. Since we don't have a cure for the disease and we don't have a vaccine against it, the question is how do we deal with it in the meantime? How do we protect the citizens of this nation, and where do we start? For one thing, it's absolutely essential that the American people understand the nature and the extent of the AIDS problem. And it's important that Federal and State Governments do the same.

I recently announced my intention to create a national commission on AIDS because of the consequences of this disease on our society. We need some comprehensive answers. What can we do to defend Americans not infected with the virus? How can we best care for those who are ill and dying? How do we deal with a disease that may swamp our health care system? The commission will help crystallize America's best ideas on how to deal with the AIDS crisis. We know some things already: the cold statistics. But I'm not going to read you gruesome facts on how many thousands have died or most certainly will die. I'm not going to break down the numbers and categories of those we've lost, because I don't want Americans to think AIDS simply affects only certain groups. AIDS affects all of us.

What our citizens must know is this: America faces a disease that is fatal and spreading. And this calls for urgency, not panic. It calls for compassion, not blame. And it calls for understanding, not ignorance. It's also important that America not reject those who have the disease, but care for them with dignity and kindness. Final judgment is up to God; our part is to ease the suffering and to find a cure. This is a battle against disease, not against our fellow Americans. We mustn't allow those with the AIDS virus to suffer discrimination. I agree with Secretary of Education Bennett: We must firmly oppose discrimination against those who have AIDS. We must prevent the persecution, through ignorance or malice, of our fellow citizens.

As dangerous and deadly as AIDS is, many of the fears surrounding it are unfounded. These fears are based on ignorance. I was told of a newspaper photo of a baby in a hospital crib with a sign that said, "AIDS—Do Not Touch." Fortunately, that photo was taken several years ago, and we now know there's no basis for this kind of fear. But similar incidents are still happening elsewhere in this country. I read of one man with AIDS who returned to work to find anonymous notes on his desk with such messages as, "Don't use our water fountain." I was told of a situation in Florida where 3 young brothers—ages 10, 9, and 7—were all hemophiliacs carrying the AIDS virus. The pastor asked the entire family not to come back to their church. Ladies and gentlemen, this is old-fashioned fear, and it has no place in the "home of the brave."

The Public Health Service has stated that there's no medical reason for barring a person with the virus from any routine school or work activity. There's no reason for those who carry the AIDS virus to wear a scarlet A. AIDS is not a casually contagious disease. We're still learning about how AIDS is transmitted, but experts tell us you don't get it from telephones or swimming pools or drinking fountains. You don't get it from shaking hands or sitting on a bus or anywhere else, for that matter. And most important, you don't get AIDS by donating blood. Education is critical to clearing up the fears. Education is also crucial to stopping the transmission of the disease. Since we don't yet have a cure or a vaccine, the only thing that can halt the spread of AIDS right now is a change in the behavior of those Americans who are at risk.

As I've said before, the Federal role is to provide scientific, factual information. Corporations can help get the information out, so can community and religious groups, and of course so can the schools, with guidance from the parents and with the commitment, I hope, that AIDS education or any aspect of sex education will not be value-neutral. A dean of St. Paul's Cathedral in London once said: "The aim of education is the knowledge not of facts, but of values." Well, that's not too far off. Education is knowing how to adapt, to grow, to understand ourselves and the world around us. And values are how we guide ourselves through the decisions of life. How we behave sexually is one of those decisions. As Surgeon General Koop has pointed out, if children are taught their own worth, we can expect them to treat themselves and others with greater respect. And wherever you have self-respect and mutual respect, you don't have drug abuse and sexual promiscuity, which of course are the two major causes of AIDS. Nancy, too, has found from her work that self-esteem is the best defense against drug abuse.

Now, we know there will be those who will go right ahead. So, yes, after there is a moral base, then you can discuss preventives and other scientific measures. And there's another aspect of teaching values that needs to be mentioned here. As individuals, we have a moral obligation not to endanger others, and that can mean endangering others with a gun, with a car, or with a virus. If a person has reason to believe that he or she may be a carrier, that person has a moral duty to be tested for AIDS; human decency requires it. And the reason is very simple: Innocent people are being infected by this virus, and some of them are going to acquire AIDS and die.

Let me tell you a story about innocent, unknowing people. A doctor in a rural county in Kentucky treated a woman who caught the AIDS virus from her husband, who was an IV-drug user. They later got divorced, neither knowing that they were infected. They remarried other people, and now one of them has already transmitted the disease to her new husband. Just as most individuals don't know they carry the virus, no one knows to what extent the virus has infected our entire society. AIDS is surreptitiously spreading throughout our population, and yet we have no accurate measure of its scope. It's time we knew exactly what we were facing, and that's why I support some routine testing.

I've asked the Department of Health and Human Services to determine as soon as possible the extent to which the AIDS virus has penetrated our society and to predict its future dimensions. I've also asked HHS to add the AIDS virus to the list of contagious diseases for which immigrants and aliens seeking permanent residence in the United States can be denied entry.

[Audience members: "Boo-oo-o!"]

They are presently denied entry for other contagious diseases. I've asked the Department of Justice to plan for testing all Federal prisoners, as looking into ways to protect uninfected inmates and their families. In addition, I've asked for a review of other Federal responsibilities, such as veterans hospitals, to see if testing might be appropriate in those areas. This is in addition to the testing already underway in our military and foreign service.

[Audience members: "No! No!"]

Now let me turn to what the States can do. Some are already at work. While recognizing the individual's choice, I encourage States to offer routine testing for those who seek marriage licenses and for those who visit sexually transmitted disease or drug abuse clinics. And I encourage States to require routine testing in State and local prisons. Not only will testing

The actor Rock Hudson, with Nancy and Ronald Reagan, at a White House dinner for President De La Madrid of Mexico on May 15, 1984. Three weeks later, Hudson was diagnosed with AIDS and in July 1985, he issued a press release stating he was dying of the disease. He passed away October 2, 1985. Hudson was one of the first major Hollywood celebrities to die of an AIDS related illness. His death gave AIDS a face and mobilized Hollywood stars to press for federal funding for prevention and treatment of the disease. Ronald Reagan Presidential Library.

give us more information on which to make decisions, but in the case of marriage licenses, it might prevent at least some babies from being born with AIDS. And anyone who knows how viciously AIDS attacks the body cannot object to this humane consideration. I should think that everyone getting married would want to be tested.

You know, it's been said that when the night is darkest, we see the stars. And there have been some shining moments throughout this horrible AIDS epidemic. I'm talking about all those volunteers across the country who've ministered to the sick and the helpless. For example, last year about 450 volunteers from the Shanti Project provided 130,000 hours of emotional and practical support for 87 percent of San Francisco's AIDS patients. That kind of compassion has been duplicated all over the country, and it symbolizes the best tradition of caring. And I encourage Americans to follow that example and volunteer to help their fellow citizens who have AIDS.

In closing, let me read to you something I saw in the paper that also embodies the American spirit. It's something that a young man with AIDS recently said. He said: "While I do accept death, I think the fight for life is important, and I'm going to fight the disease with every breath I have." Ladies and gentlemen, so must we. Thank you.

Note: The President spoke at 8:16 p.m. at the Potomac Restaurant. In his opening remarks, he referred to Dr. Mervyn Silverman, president of the American Foundation for AIDS Research; Elizabeth Taylor; and Donald Ross, chairman of the board of New York Life Insurance Co.

CHAPTER 9

Soylent Green Is People: The Environment

9.1 NORMAN LEAR, "FROM THE DESK OF NORMAN LEAR"

The Environmental Media Association was founded in 1989 to mobilize the entertainment industry in educating people about environmental issues. In addition to creating "celebrity-driven eco-focused events," the EMA works with writers, directors, and producers to incorporate environmental issues into their plotlines and stories. This memo from the television writer and producer Norman Lear, who created such popular series as *All in the Family, The Jeffersons, One Day at a Time*, and *Good Times*, explains the strategy of the EMA's efforts regarding environmental messages in television sitcoms and dramas.

The logline for the episode is quintessential Happy Days: "Richie goes to a local college and Fonzie takes him to the library to meet some girls." For a sitcom in the 70s, this is standard stuff, but what happens after this episode airs on September 27, 1977 is far from standard. Millions of kids watching the show see the Fonz take out a library card—his first, mind you, which is a big deal by Happy Days standards. Younger viewers are duly impressed. In the days that follow, according to the series creator, Garry Marshall, requests for library cards zoom by more than 500% nationwide.

Dissolve to eleven years later. Dr. Jay Winsten, director of The Harvard Alcohol Project, comes to Hollywood with a new idea: the "designated driver." Winsten meets with writers and producers of The Cosby Show, Cheers, LA Law and dozens of other prime time series. He asks them to incorporate story beats that will introduce this new concept to the drinking public. The TV community responds, and starting in November 1988, over 160 prime time episodes include subplots, scenes, or dialogue telling viewers it's okay to party as long as someone stays sober for the drive home. One year later, a Gallup poll finds 67% of adults surveyed recognize the term "designated driver." In 1991, Winsten's new idea is a listing in Webster's College Dictionary.

The following year, the Environmental Media Association applies Winsten's technique for a campaign on recycling. EMA asks TV shows to depict recycling on camera to convey that this can be a simple, routine behavior in any American household. Home Improvement, Baywatch, Hearts Afire, Lois & Clark, and several other series follow through, and even increase efforts to recycle on their own sets. Coupled with national public service campaigns on TV, radio, and in print, this effort contributes to unprecedented growth in recycling nationwide. Old news? The notion that prime time series can deliver important messages and have a positive impact on society may be a familiar one. You've probably heard other examples from All in the Family, Murphy Brown, Ellen—you name it.

There's even a measure of cynicism on the subject, especially when a logline includes those five dreaded words "a very special episode of . . ." But that's not what we're talking about. EMA has been working with prime time TV series since 1989. We provide accurate information when stories deal with environmental issues, and we encourage writers to address this subject whenever possible—but never at the expense of story, character, or the entertainment value of the episode. Our annual Environmental Media Awards recognize programs that convey environmental messages in the most entertaining and creative ways, because we understand a critical fact: if the audience isn't entertained, they won't stay around for any message. In recent years, series such as The Simpsons, Home Improvement, and The X-Files have won multiple EMA awards, proving over and over that the environment can play in prime time.

So, we have a fairly simple "ask": as you break your stories this season, please consider the environmental issues described below. Of all the issues out there, we believe these are ten of the most important, and we've capsulized them here for your consideration. [Editors' note: we have included one issue.]

If you'd like to know more, we'd be happy to provide additional information or connect you with experts who can. If any of these issues can be addressed in dialogue or subplots, through characters or even props, it will help U.S. expand environmental awareness among literally millions of viewers. As awareness is the step immediately before activism, it's a crucial step, and you are uniquely positioned to help people take it. We hope you will.

Actress Cameron Diaz and former Vice President Al Gore at the "Save Our Selves" Global Climate Crisis Campaign Concert announcement held at the California Science Center on February 15, 2007, in Los Angeles, California. Diaz was one of several young celebrities to tout environmental causes, and Gore used film to sell his message about global climate change when he made the documentary *An Inconvenient Truth* (2006). AP Photo/Benkey.

Population

According to a growing number of environmentalists, this is the crux of all our environmental problems: too many people chasing too few resources. In developing nations such as Haiti and Rwanda, we have already witnessed the ecological disasters wrought when a rapidly growing populace literally overwhelms its natural resources. If the world's population doubles in the next century as predicted, we could all share their fate. In the U.S., we have high rates of teenage pregnancy, congestion in classrooms, and increasingly charged battles over immigration law—all symptoms of the same problem.

To help slow the rate of population growth, government agencies and environmental groups are promoting easier access to family planning; educational programs on fertility options, adoption, and contraception; and more programs that provide workplace opportunities for women, giving them alternatives where none existed before. The ultimate goal: to reduce the pressure on the planet to meet the needs of its inhabitants. The world's population increases by 3 people each second, equal to about 220,000 per day, nearly 81 million per year. In an hour in 1998, there are an average of 15,177 births and 6,196 natural deaths, resulting in a net population growth of 8,980. The population has grown more since 1950 than it did during the previous four million years. As (could be) seen on TV . . . a family elects to adopt rather than have another child; a poster for "Zero Population Growth" appears in a teenager's bedroom; a couple decides to stop after having two children and debate vasectomy vs. tubal ligation.

9.2   ANN COULTER, "LET THEM EAT TOFU!"

As concerns about global warming grew at the turn of the twenty-first century, a number of celebrities, like Cameron Diaz and Leonardo DiCaprio, became increasingly identified with the environmental movement. Conservative commentators often questioned the validity of global warming and complained about the "hypocrisy" of wealthy, jet-setting celebrities who touted "green" causes while living lavish lifestyles. This editorial by conservative columnist Ann Coulter illustrates the frustration of many on the Right with the environmental activism of the "Left Coast."

Even right-wingers who know that "global warming" is a crock do not seem to grasp what the tree-huggers are demanding. Liberals want mass starvation and human devastation.

Forget the lunacy of people claiming to tell us the precise temperature of planet Earth in 1918 based on tree rings. Or the fact that in the '70s liberals were issuing similarly dire warnings about "global cooling."

Simply consider what noted climatologists Al Gore and Melissa Etheridge are demanding that we do to combat their nutty conjectures about "global warming." They want us to starve the productive sector of fossil fuel and allow the world's factories to grind to a halt. This means an end to material growth and a cataclysmic reduction in wealth.

There are more reputable scientists defending astrology than defending "global warming," but liberals simply announce that the debate has been resolved in their favor and demand that we shut down all production.

They think they can live in a world of only Malibu and East Hampton—with no Trentons or Detroits. It does not occur to them that someone has to manufacture the tiles and steel and glass and solar panels that go into those "eco-friendly" mansions, and someone has to truck it all to their beachfront properties, and someone else has to transport all the workers there to build it. (And then someone has to drive the fleets of trucks delivering the pachysandra and bottled water every day.)

Liberals are already comfortably ensconced in their beachfront estates, which they expect to be unaffected by their negative growth prescriptions for the rest of us.

There was more energy consumed in the manufacture, construction and maintenance of Leonardo DiCaprio's Malibu home than is needed to light the entire city of Albuquerque, where there are surely several men who can actually act. But he has solar panels to warm his house six degrees on chilly Malibu nights.

Liberals haven't the foggiest idea how the industrial world works. They act as if America could reduce its vast energy consumption by using fluorescent bulbs and driving hybrid cars rather than SUVs. They have no idea how light miraculously appears when they flick a switch or what allows them to go to the bathroom indoors in winter—luxuries Americans are not likely to abandon because Leo DiCaprio had solar panels trucked into his Malibu estate.

Our lives depend on fossil fuel. Steel plants, chemical plants, rubber plants, pharmaceutical plants, glass plants, paper plants—those run on energy. There are no Mother Earth nursery designs in stylish organic cotton without gas-belching factories, ships and trucks, and temperature-controlled, well-lighted stores. Windmills can't even produce enough energy to manufacture a windmill.

Because of the industrialization of agriculture—using massive amounts of fossil fuel—only 2 percent of Americans work in farming. And yet they produce enough food to feed all 300 million Americans, with plenty left over for export. When are liberals going to break the news to their friends in Darfur that they all have to starve to death to save the planet?

"Global warming" is the left's pagan rage against mankind. If we can't produce industrial waste, then we can't produce. Some of us—not the ones with mansions in Malibu and Nashville is my guess—are going to have to die. To say we need to reduce our energy consumption is like saying we need to reduce our oxygen consumption.

Liberals have always had a thing about eliminating humans. Stalin wanted to eliminate the kulaks and Ukranians, vegetarian atheist Adolf Hitler wanted to eliminate the Jews, Planned Parenthood founder Margaret Sanger wanted to eliminate poor blacks, DDT opponent Rachel Carson wanted to eliminate Africans (introduction to her book "Silent

Spring" written by ... Al Gore!), and population-control guru Paul Ehrlich wants to eliminate all humans.

But global warming is the most insane, psychotic idea liberals have ever concocted to kill off "useless eaters." If we have to live in a pure "natural" environment like the Indians, then our entire transcontinental nation can only support about 1 million human beings. Sorry, fellas—299 million of you are going to have to go.

Proving that the "global warming" campaign is nothing but hatred of humanity, these are the exact same people who destroyed the nuclear power industry in this country 30 years ago.

If we accept for purposes of argument their claim that the only way the human race can survive is with clean energy that doesn't emit carbon dioxide, environmentalists waited until they had safely destroyed the nuclear power industry to tell us that. This proves they never intended for us to survive.

"Global warming" is the liberal's stalking horse for their ultimate fantasy: The whole U.S. will look like Amagansett, with no one living in it except their even-tempered maids (for "diversity"), themselves and their coterie (all, presumably, living in solar-heated mansions, except the maids who will do without electricity altogether). The entire fuel-guzzling, tacky, beer-drinking, NASCAR-watching middle class with their over-large families will simply have to die.

It seems not to have occurred to the jet set that when California is as poor as Mexico, they might have trouble finding a maid. Without trucking, packaging, manufacturing, shipping and refrigeration in their Bel-Air fantasy world, they'll be chasing the rear-end of an animal every time their stomachs growl and killing small animals for pelts to keep their genitals warm.

IN VIETNAM
THE WIND
DOESN'T BLOW
IT SUCKS
BORN
TO
KiLL
Stanley Kubrick's
FULL
METAL
JACKET
WARNER BROS PRESENTS STANLEY KUBRICK'S FULL METAL JACKET
STARRING
MATTHEW MODINE ADAM BALDWIN VINCENT D'ONOFRIO LEE ERMEY DORIAN HAREWOOD ARLISS HOWARD
KEVYN MAJOR HOWARD ED O'ROSS SCREENPLAY BY STANLEY KUBRICK MICHAEL HERR GUSTAV HASFORD
BASED ON THE NOVEL THE SHORT-TIMERS BY GUSTAV HASFORD CO PRODUCER PHILIP HOBBS EXECUTIVE PRODUCER JAN HARLAN PRODUCED AND DIRECTED BY STANLEY KUBRICK
WARNER BROS

PART III

War and Patriotism

World War II unified Hollywood as the industry rallied to fight Fascism.

Actors, directors, producers, and technicians joined the armed services; those who did not join led recruitment and bond drives and entertained troops on the war front. Movies were made aimed at building troop and the entire nation's morale. Political and employer–employee differences were set aside—at least for the time being.

War unified Hollywood, but this was the last war—other than perhaps the Korean War (1950–3)—that received the unqualified support of people in the film industry. Divisions over the Vietnam War, the Gulf War, and the Iraq War deeply divided the American people and Hollywood inevitably reflected these differences.

Political differences in Hollywood became evident even as World War II drew to a close. The issue of Communists in the film industry, especially in unions including the technicians' unions and the talent guilds—the screen actors, directors, and writers guilds—led to heated factionalism in the 1930s. During World War II, Communist factions in these unions increased their influence, setting the stage for a counter-attack by anti-Communists in Hollywood.

In 1944 Hollywood anti-Communists banded together for the first time in a political organization, the Motion Picture Alliance for the Preservation of American Ideals, with the avowed purpose to fight Communists within the industry. The group was formed by a small group of actors, screenwriters, and directors. The war was drawing to a close and many conservatives expected the Soviet Union to emerge as a world power bent on global domination. Although small, the organization attracted immediate media attention when Gary Cooper, studio head Walt Disney, and John Wayne's sidekick Ward Bond enlisted in the cause. Over the next few years others came to support the Alliance: actors Clark Gable, Gary Cooper, and Spencer Tracy, to name a few. Dancer Ginger Rogers and her mother Lela Rogers (a former U.S. marine and screenwriter) joined the Alliance. The fiercely anti-Communist novelist and screenwriter Ayn Rand was an early member. Her anti-Communism was easily matched by influential Hollywood columnist Hedda Hopper, who secretly cooperated with the FBI in reporting suspected Communists.

The Alliance had a single goal: The weeding out of Communists from the film industry. Convinced that Communists were in control of the Screenwriters Guild and the technical guilds in the Conference of Studio Unions, the leaders of the Alliance called on studio heads to address the Communist problem. Members of the Alliance maintained that the Communists wanted to gain control of Hollywood through the unions in order to propagandize America and the world through movies. Alliance members held that Hollywood films scripted by Communists were full of sly innuendo about corrupt politicians and greedy businessmen in materialistic America. Political commentary, they asserted, was being placed subtly into scripts to erode traditional American values.

The Alliance urged Congress to investigate Communist influence in Hollywood. In 1947, the House Un-American Activities Committee (HUAC), chaired by J. Parnell Thomas (R-New Jersey) answered the call to investigate Communist influence in the film industry. HUAC issued subpoenas to forty-three studio executives, labor leaders, and filmmakers, evenly divided between so-called friendly and unfriendly witnesses.

This counter-attack on Communists within the film industry was set within a context of labor conflict with the studios and union rivalry between the Conference of Studio Unions (CSU), headed by the combative Herb Sorrell, and the larger International Alliance of Theatrical and Stage Employees (IATSE), led by Roy Brewer. In 1945, the CSU went on strike winning a huge pay increase for its 7,000 members in pre-production crafts including carpenters, set designers, painters, and others. This made CSU members among the nation's highest-paid salary workers in the United States. As leader of the rival to the CSU, Roy Brewer of the IATSE attacked the CSU as Communist-controlled and intransigent in its negotiations. In September 1946, the CSU went out on strike over a flap with the IATSE over the construction of sets. The strike lasted thirteen months, ending only in late October 1947 when Sorrell's own painters union voted to cross the picket lines. This occurred only days before HUAC opened its hearings.

The first week of the hearings brought "friendly" witnesses, those sympathetic to the hearings, including film stars Ronald Reagan, Gary Cooper, and Robert Taylor, screenwriter and novelist Ayn Rand, and leading Hollywood producers, directors, and studio executives.

As the week drew to a close, the media was in a complete frenzy as ten former and active Communists were called to the stand to testify. Of these ten "unfriendly witnesses"—John Howard Lawson, Dalton Trumbo, Albert Maltz, Alvah Bessie, Samuel Ornitz, Herbert Biberman, Ring Lardner, Jr., Adrian Scott, Edward Dmytryk, and Lester Cole—eight were screenwriters. Dmytryk was a director and Scott a producer. These witnesses became known as the Hollywood Ten.

Liberals in Hollywood organized the Committee for the First Amendment in support of the unfriendly witnesses accused of Communist involvement. Spearheading the committee were directors John Huster, William Wyler, and Billy Wilder, joined by actors Humphrey Bogart, Katharine Hepburn, Groucho Marx, Danny Kaye, and Lauren Bacall.

Until the ten unfriendly witnesses took the stand, the national media had been critical of HUAC's investigation into alleged Communist influence in the film industry. Lead editorials in the *New York Times* and the *Washington Post* blasted the proceedings. News articles of the hearings focused on the appearance of preening celebrity witnesses and foolish statements made by the "friendlies" (e.g. when Walt Disney mistakenly called the League of Women Voters a Communist front), and the inability of the hearings to prove that explicit Communist propaganda had been inserted into Hollywood films. In the media's eye, the first round had gone against the committee and its friendly witnesses.

The ten unfriendly witnesses who took the stand in the second week undertook a strategy of refusing to answer questions and attacking the hearings as unconstitutional and as the first step toward fascism in America. This strategy presented the Hollywood Left at its worst—arrogant, intolerant, and out of touch with mainstream America. After witnessing the performance of the "unfriendlies" at the hearings, many liberal supporters including Humphrey Bogart and his wife Lauren Bacall retreated to Hollywood and quickly distanced themselves from the entire business. Director Billy Wilder captured liberal sentiment in his reputed quip: "Of the unfriendly ten, only two had any talent; the other eight were just unfriendly."

In late November 1947, Congress voted overwhelmingly to cite the ten unfriendly witnesses with contempt. The same day, fifty top industry executives met behind closed doors for a two-day session at New York's Waldorf Astoria Hotel. Fearing a public backlash, the studio executives acted quickly. Following the Waldorf Astoria meeting, the studio heads announced that they had agreed to an industry policy of not employing known Communists. In announcing this new policy, the studios acknowledged the dangers of hurting innocent people and the risk of creating an atmosphere of fear: "Creative work at its best cannot be carried on in an atmosphere of fear." To prevent this from happening, the association pledged itself to "eliminate any subversive, to protect the innocent, and to safeguard free speech and a free screen wherever threatened." The statement declared that none of the ten would be employed in Hollywood until he was acquitted and purged himself of contempt. Following this announcement, Communist factions were defeated in elections in the Screenwriters Guild. Members of the Screen Actors Guild voted to require loyalty oaths of its members, although a similar proposal was defeated in the Screen Directors Guild in 1950.

The Hollywood Red Scare had begun. It lasted until the late 1950s when the blacklist began to break down, as blacklisted screenwriters such as Dalton Trumbo and Albert Maltz were surreptitiously hired by studio and independent film producers. The end of the blacklist came in early 1960 when director Otto Preminger publicly announced that Dalton Trumbo was the screenwriter for the about to be released film, *Exodus*. Six months later producer-actor Kirk Douglas announced that Universal Pictures would give Trumbo screen credit for scripting the block-buster film *Spartacus*. Since being blacklisted Trumbo had scripted seventeen films under various names. Even as the blacklist ended, its effects in Hollywood left deep political wounds in the industry.

While Republicans remained a distinct force in Hollywood politics—most visibly represented by actors Ronald Reagan, John Wayne, George Murphy, director John Ford, and producer Cecil B. DeMille, among many others—the Democratic Party drew the most support within Hollywood. Liberalism remained the prevailing sentiment in Hollywood until the mid-1960s. The escalation of United States involvement in Vietnam split the Democratic Party nationally and divided Hollywood.

Nevertheless, the 1960s were difficult years for the Republican Party and conservatism. In Hollywood the older studio system had completely collapsed, replaced by independent filmmakers who projected new values on the American screen. An ageing Hollywood Right became increasingly agitated as counter-cultural values entered mainstream America. Division over the war in Vietnam ignited passions on both sides.

The Hollywood Right turned to the movies and the media to promote support for the Vietnam War. John Wayne threw his support behind the Vietnam War with full enthusiasm. He spoke at patriotic rallies and devoted time and money to conservative causes. His most notable pro-war statement was made in his movie *The Green Berets*, which opened in the summer of 1968, after the Tet offensive in Vietnam and the assassinations of Martin Luther King, Jr. and Bobby Kennedy. The movie, starring the ageing Wayne as a combat officer, is about a liberal journalist (played by David Janssen) who awakens to the reality that if Vietnam fell, Southeast Asia would fall to Communism. Although the film drew anti-war protests across the country, *The Green Berets* was a box office smash. It was one of the top ten grossing films in 1968, with domestic sales approaching $20 million. It tapped into the smoldering resentment of many white working-class people. It was the only pro-war film to come out during the Vietnam period.

By the time of the film's release, however, majority opinion in the United States had begun to swing against the war and a number of celebrities had become involved in anti-Vietnam War protest. The most high-profile and controversial activist was actress Jane Fonda. Fonda spoke at anti-war marches and headlined "Free the Army," a traveling review performed for stateside troops. Her most controversial action came in her decision to broadcast her anti-war views from a radio station in Hanoi, North Vietnam. This action earned Fonda the long-lasting enmity of many Vietnam veterans.

Hollywood dissent against the Vietnam War set a pattern for divisions over the Gulf War in 1991 and later the Iraq War in 2003. After Iraq invaded Kuwait in 1991, President George H. W. Bush asked for congressional authorization for the United States to work with the United Nations to expel Iraqi forces from Kuwait. Democrats in Congress opposed this intervention. The debate over this possible intervention spilled over into Hollywood. Charlton Heston and a few others in Hollywood publicly supported the intervention.

If division over the first Gulf War in 1991 was fierce, debate over the United States invasion of Iraq to overthrow the regime of Saddam Hussein was even fiercer. Many celebrities in Hollywood opposed the U.S. invasion and as the war continued, their opposition became increasingly vehement. Anti-war activists in Hollywood formed Artists for Winning without War, an anti-war group that worked with MoveOn.org., a national anti-war organization. Over a thousand celebrities signed an open letter to President George W. Bush protesting the invasion. Public statements by actors such as Sean Penn and others denouncing the Iraq War generated inordinate media attention. Similarly, Natalie Maines, the lead singer for the country-rock band the Dixie Chicks, set off a firestorm when she criticized Bush during a concert on the eve of the invasion. The band refused to apologize, leading some country radio stations to ban their songs.

Hollywood anti-war sentiment became a focal point for both the Left and the Right in America, as anti-war activists welcomed the leadership of

Hollywood celebrities willing to use their public visibility to voice their opinions, while supporters of the Iraq War denounced actors for voicing what was seen as ill-considered opinion. Whatever the case, such controversies revealed the important role celebrity had come to play in American culture and politics.

CHAPTER 10

Lock and Load: World War II

10.1 TESTIMONY OF DARRYL F. ZANUCK, U.S. CONGRESS SENATE SUBCOMMITTEE OF THE COMMITTEE ON INTERSTATE COMMERCE, HEARINGS REGARDING MOVING PICTURE SCREEN AND RADIO PROPAGANDA, SEPTEMBER 1941

Before the Japanese attack on Pearl Harbor, Americans disagreed on to what extent the U.S. should aid the Allies for fear of the country being dragged into another European war, but Hollywood films generally promoted a pro-British, anti-German message. In 1941, John T. Flynn, a journalist and member of the isolationist America First Committee, had become convinced that the Hollywood studio chiefs were trying to influence public sentiment for war and persuaded Republican Senator Gerald T. Nye to investigate the movie industry for pro-war propaganda. In the testimony that follows, Darryl F. Zanuck from Twentieth Century Fox defends Hollywood against the pro-censorship forces.

Senator Clark of Idaho:	Mr. Zanuck, will you please be sworn? Do you solemnly swear that the evidence you are about to give will be the truth, the whole truth, and nothing but the truth, so help you God?
Mr. Zanuck:	I do.
Senator Clark of Idaho:	Mr. Zanuck, will you please state, for the record, your full name?
Mr. Zanuck:	Darryl F. Zanuck.
Senator Clark of Idaho:	Do you have a prepared statement, Mr. Zanuck?
Mr. Zanuck:	I do, sir.
Senator Clark of Idaho:	Would you prefer to make your statement without interruption?

Mr. Zanuck:	I would, sir.
Senator Clark of Idaho:	I am sure the committee will be happy to have you proceed on that basis.
Mr. Zanuck:	Thank you.

At the outset, it seems necessary to state my personal background. I was born in Wahoo, Nebraska on September 5, 1802. At the date of my birth, Wahoo had a population of approximately 891 people. It has become famous as the birthplace of one of baseball's immortals—"Wahoo" Sam Crawford. My mother and father were both born in the United States of America. My grandparents, on both my mother's and father's side, were born in the United States of America. My parents and grandparents were regular attendants and lifelong members of the Methodist Church.

I left Wahoo at the age of 15 years and enlisted as a private in the United States Army, in the First World War. I served overseas during that conflict and rose to the rank of private, first class. [Laughter.]

Senator Nye, I am sure, will find no cause for suspicion or alarm in that background.

Various charges have been made and published in the course of this inquiry. In order to avoid misunderstanding. I would like to make my position clear on a number of these points.

In respect to my personal opinion regarding the entry of the United States into the war at the present time: I want to say first that no man who was in France during the last war can look upon war with anything but the deepest abhorrence. I wish our country would never have to fight another war. I want this country to go to war only if that is an absolute necessity either to defend ourselves now or to prevent a future attack.

In this time of acute national peril. I feel that it is the duty of every American to give his complete cooperation and support to our

President and our Congress. To do everything to defeat Hitler and to preserve America. If this course of necessity leads to war I want to follow my President along that course.

It has been further charged that Hollywood has been asked to make propoganda pictures designed to arouse a war spirit in the United States. This is not so. I assure you that no representative of the Government has asked me directly or indirectly to make pictures for the purpose of getting this country into war.

We have been asked by the Government to make training pictures for the United States Army. We have made these pictures at cost and without profit as a matter of patriotic duty. I am happy to say that the Chief of Staff, General Marshall, has told me that these films have done an immeasurable amount of good in saving manpower, material, and time in organizing the defense of America. As this committee doubtless knows, these pictures are of a strictly educational nature. I cannot believe it is an offense either for the Government to ask for this service from the industry, or for the industry to comply with such a request.

Senator Nye has charged that several pictures made by Twentieth Century-Fox are so-called propaganda pictures. I presume he refers to Man Hunt and The Man I Married. The first, Man Hunt, appeared in book form under the title of "Rogue Male," which was published by Little, Brown & Co. It also was serialized in the Atlantic Monthly. As for The Man I Married, it was published under the title "I Married a Nazi," in Liberty Magazine and in book form under the title of "Swastika." Both were widely read.

To condemn the motion-picture industry for dealing with subjects as timely, as vital, and as important as the current upheaval in the world is to subject the industry to an impossible

Mr. Zanuck: (cont.)

censorship. It would deny us access to the same vital developments which today fill our newspapers, magazines, books, the radio, and the stage. It would prevent us from giving to the people of America subjects that fill their newspapers, their books and their minds. It would leave the American motion picture as worthless and sterile as those made in Germany and Italy.

The daily newspaper has always furnished me and my associates ideas for motion pictures. I made the first gangster pictures which helped uncover the rottenness of the underworld in our various cities. Perhaps some of you saw Public Enemy No. 1, which was the first exposé on the screen of the underworld. We received many protests against that film. I suppose the underworld thought this was unfair propaganda against the gangster, just so some now feel our war pictures are unfair propaganda against Hitler. [Applause.]

Hollywood didn't create the underworld, nor did it create Hitler and the Nazis. We have portrayed them no differently than they are pictured daily in newspapers, magazines, books, and all other mediums of expression. In fact, we have merely portrayed them as they are.

The pictures regarding which so many reckless and unfounded charges have been made represent only a very small fraction of the Hollywood picture output. It is indeed strange that much effort and public money is being spent at such a crucial time over such a minor part of the industry's program. Nothing at all has been said by this committee about the vast number of historical, patriotic, and religious films the industry has been turning out each year. No word of praise is given for a service that should fill every American heart with pride.

Senators Clark and Nye have both made the charge that Twentieth Century-Fox deliberately sabotaged a picture called The Great

Commandment because this film preached peace and good will. The fact that both Senators Nye and Bennett Clark have taken pains to put this charge into the record, without the slightest attempt to secure the facts, easily available to them, which utterly refute their charge, indicates the unfairness of the methods being used in this hearing. In reply to this charge let me give you the uncontrovertible facts:

We purchased this picture because we felt it had a message—the message of peace and good will—in which the American people would be interested. We paid the Reverend Fredrick and his clerical associates $150,000, which included a profit to them. We planned to remake the picture as a great feature and at great cost. About this time we had released another picture based on a religious theme. Brigham Young. Our experience with that production convinced us that the public was not in the mood to patronize a religious picture. This despite the fact that Brigham Young had the endorsement and official sponsorship of the Mormon Church. We made some changes in The Great Commandment and then engaged in a vigorous and expensive campaign to sell it to exhibitors.

The Great Commandment has played to date in 1,087 theaters in the United States. Last week it played in 49 theaters in 49 different communities, and it is now being booked regularly in an average of 30 theaters per week. We staged an elaborate world premiere at the Uptown Theater in Kansas City, and we secured the sponsorship of almost all of the religious organizations in that city. The box-office result of this showing was the most pitiful in the history of the Uptown Theater. On Friday, Saturday, and Sunday we played to a total admission of $1,010. An ordinary film will

Mr. Zanuck: (cont.)

usually play to this amount in one day alone without any special exploitation.

To cover the Kansas City premiere we sent a special exploitation man, who worked there in advance of the opening, and we spent, in addition to the usual theater advertising, $30 for additional company-paid advertisements. The theater lost money, and we ended up by receiving only $350 as our entire share for the engagement at the Uptown Theater.

If you will look at the review of the opening in the Kansas City Times, you will see that we treated the picture with utmost care and exploitation, the same as we gave to any of our pictures.

We have an investment of $200,000 in The Great Commandment. Despite unusual efforts, we have received back from the American showing less than $33,000. Any statement that we have suppressed this film or the theme it presents is unqualifiedly false.

I would like also to call attention to Senator Bennett Clark's testimoney before this committee. He said that our industry was determined to wreak vengeance on Adolf Hitler by plunging this Nation into war on behalf of another ferocious beast, referring to Stalin.

Undoubtedly Senator Clark has overlooked the fact that Stalin and Hitler were pals, joined in a nonaggression pact, at the very time all of the pictures belaboring the totalitarian ideology were being made.

The Twentieth Century-Fox Film Corporation is exceedingly proud of its record of picture making and cooperation with its Government. I am here to represent it in all of its production phases. I also offer myself as a personal exhibit of one who was able to make among the best of motion pictures as an independent producer. I shall be happy to answer your questions. [Applause.]

Senator Clark of Idaho: Mr. Zanuck, in my own behalf and in behalf of the committee, I want to thank you for your very excellent statement.

It is now 10 minutes of 12. Before we recess I want to give a sort of outline of our future plans. I anticipate that the questions that will be asked you, Mr. Zanuck—I cannot tell for certain—will probably take not more than an hour. Then, if Mr. Balahan is here, we could probably examine him or hear his statement, if he has one, and probably finish, without doubt, this afternoon.

Mr. Willkie: He will be available.

Senator Clark of Idaho: Thank you, Mr. Willkie.

The committee has had under discussion, both here and in executive sessions, the seeing of some of these moving pictures. Last week or earlier this week we all agreed in executive session to arrange to see some of the pictures during the coming week. Senator Tobey is going to be away, but he has advised us that he has seen most of the pictures. However, Senator McFarland was discussing with me yesterday the possibility of taking next week off entirely.

The people who are here from New York and from other places have got to catch up on their work, and I know that a great many members of the committee must have neglected some of their work; I know that I have. I discussed that question with the other members of the committee, and apparently it is agreeable to take the week off.

Am I stating the situation correctly?

Senator McFarland: That is agreeable to me, Mr. Chairman. I feel that the pictures should be shown when Senator Tobey is here, anyway, so that he might see such pictures again if he wanted to or such pictures as he has not seen.

To be honest with you I am behind in my work; then furthermore, I want to go to South

Senator McFarland: (cont.)	Bend tomorrow afternoon to see Arizona and Notre Dame play football.
Senator Clark of Idaho:	I want to say in all frankness that I want to see some of these pictures. There have been about 18 listed here, but it is perfectly obvious that the committee cannot see 18 feature pictures. However, by the time we convene again we will have heard from Mr. Schenck, Mr. Warner, and Mr. Zanuck, and will know the way the testimony has developed, so that we will have a pretty good idea about picking out a number— maybe 6 or 7, to use a figure—of those pictures. Arranging to have them shown is a mechanical problem, and I am more than anxious to help work it out, as I am sure the committee also is. Senator McFarland has been very gracious in that respect. So, when we adjourn this evening, we will adjourn until 10:30 o'clock a week from Monday.
Mr. Zanuck:	May I make a suggestion?
Senator Clark of Idaho:	Yes.
Mr. Zanuck:	I realize that time and certain technical requirements may possibly prevent it, but I think it would be a great thing if in addition to the seven or eight pictures that you would like to see, you would also see seven or eight other pictures, so that you would have a balanced viewpoint upon what moving-picture producers have done for the past 20 years.
Senator Clark of Idaho:	I quite agree with your suggestion; it had not occurred to me before. I will tell you what we might do. We might leave it up to the industry to select a few pictures that they think, in their judgment, will balance the seeing of the other six or seven. I say six or seven; perhaps it will be only three, four, or five; or it may be eight, depending on how we agree.

I think that your suggestion is an eminently fair one, Mr. Zanuck. I think it will give the committee a better viewpoint as to the attitude of the industry as a whole. |

Mr. Willkie:	May I ask that you just give us about 3 days' notice?
Senator Clark of Idaho:	Oh, yes; certainly; it will all be worked out with the industry.
Mr. Willkie:	It is purely mechanical.
Senator Clark of Idaho:	With that, unless there is something else from the committee, we will recess until 2 o'clock this afternoon and will finish this afternoon.
Mr. Zanuck:	Thank you.

[At 11:55 a. m. a recess was taken until 2 p. m. of the same day.]

Afternoon Session

The subcommittee resumed at 2 p. m. upon the expiration of the recess.

Senator Clark of Idaho:	The subcommittee will please come to order. Senator Tobey I am sure will be here very shortly. Mr. Zanuck, if you will resume your position at the witness stand.

TESTIMONY OF DARRYL F. ZANUCK, VICE PRESIDENT IN CHARGE OF PRODUCTION, TWENTIETH CENTURY-FOX FILM CORPORATION—Resumed

Senator Clark of Idaho:	Mr. Zanuck, I want to get, first, just a little outline of your company. Can you tell me something about it? How are the stock interests held in Twentieth Century-Fox Film Corporation?
Mr. Zanuck:	The stock interests are held, to the best of my knowledge, by the public owning the stock, and Chase National Bank of the City of New York is a large stockholder, and there are a number of individuals who are large stockholders. The stock can be purchased on the board.
Senator Clark of Idaho:	You mean it is listed on the New York Stock Exchange?
Mr. Zanuck:	Yes, sir.

Senator Clark of Idaho: Would you say the Chase National Bank owns sufficient stock to have control?

Mr. Zanuck: As to voting control, I am not sure. I would say that I think they with their various affiliates probably have voting control, control.

Senator Clark of Idaho: There is no particular point in it. I am simply looking for information.

Mr. Zanuck: I understand.

Senator Clark of Idaho: You have some stock in Twentieth Century-Fox Film Corporation, have you?

Mr. Zanuck: I do.

Senator Clark of Idaho: Your company was formed by a merger of the old Fox Co. and the Twentieth Century Co., was it not?

Mr. Zanuck: It was known as the plan of reorganization.

Senator Clark of Idaho: As I understand it you were interested in Twentieth Century Co.

Mr. Zanuck: Yes.

Senator Clark of Idaho: And then when the reorganization of the Fox Co. occurred, I mean when the two were merged into one, you went with the merged company?

Mr. Zanuck: Yes.

Senator Clark of Idaho: And who is the president of your company?

Mr. Zanuck: Sidney Kent.

Senator Clark of Idaho: Are your duties as vice president of the company largely in the production end?

Mr. Zanuck: Entirely in the production end.

Senator Clark of Idaho: So there won't be much point in my asking you about the set-up. You can tell me, though, about how many theaters your company owns, can you not?

Mr. Zanuck: We do not own any theaters.

Senator Clark of Idaho: The company does not?

Mr. Zanuck: No.

Senator Clark of Idaho: What is the arrangement then between Fox theaters and the Twentieth Century Fox Film Corporation?

Mr. Zanuck: Well, the Fox theaters were divorced long before the reorganization or so-called merger, from the Fox Corporation, the old William Fox

	Corporation. As I understand the set-up, at the present time we have 42 percent in National Theaters Corporation. The National Theaters Corporation in turn have a number of subsidiary companies, known as Fox West Coast, Fox Rocky Mountain, and Fox this-and-that. We have 42 percent.
Senator Clark of Idaho:	So that your interest in the theaters, that is, the interest of Twentieth Century-Fox, comes through a stock ownership of about 42 percent, or whatever you said it was, in another company, which in turn owns the theaters.
Mr. Zanuck:	That is right.
Senator Clark of Idaho:	Approximately how many theaters does this subsidiary company own or have a partnership interest in, if you know?
Mr. Zanuck:	I do not know.
Senator Clark of Idaho:	It is not vitally important but I would simply like to get the set-up.
	If you do not know this just say so, but I am reading from Monograph. No. 43 of the Temporary National Economic Committee, wherein I find a tabulation entitled "Number of theaters operated by each of the major companies, 1940," and your group, if I may use that term, is listed as owning 538. Would that square somewhat with your knowledge of the situation?
Mr. Zanuck:	I would say that the National Theaters Corporation owns or partially owns about 500 or 600 theaters, but I think that I should make it very clear we have nothing to do with the operation or ownership of these theaters. We merely own stock. They are not controlled by Mr. Kent or anybody in our company.
Senator Clark of Idaho:	I understand that. But through your stock ownership, which would amount to virtual control, you indirectly own the theaters, do you not?
Mr. Zanuck:	No. We only have 42 percent of the stock.

Senator Clark of Idaho:	Is the stock on the market, and are there quite a number of shareholders?
Mr. Zanuck:	I am not sure of that.
Senator Clark of Idaho:	Of course, you are not a financial man and I am not trying to trip you on anything like that, and could not if I wanted to, but usually ownership of 42 percent of the stock of any corporation, where the stock is diversified, amounts to virtual control. I am not inferring that that is true in your case either. I am just trying to find out the situation.
	Now, as to your statement. I do not think anybody can quarrel seriously with it. You have presented the situation as you view it. One might differ with you as the method of procedure as to foreign policy and that sort of thing, but certainly there is no fundamental quarrel with your principles of Americanism and your own views as outlined in that statement.
	Now, as regards the pictures you produce, particularly so-called Nazi films, do you think that those films represent the facts as they exist?
Mr. Zanuck:	I believe that they very fairly represent the facts. I believe that, but would like to say that I made pictures out of published stories.
Senator Clark of Idaho:	What do you do in that regard? Do you take a story and then do you always follow the story more or less accurately?
Mr. Zanuck:	Well, we do that as accurately as we possibly can. Sometimes it is necessary to make changes in order to so place a book that it can become a successful motion picture. Sometimes it is very necessary for us to eliminate characters, or to add characters. But the reason why we buy a story is that we believe it will make very good entertainment on the screen after it has been adapted to the screen.
Senator Clark of Idaho:	But, apart from adapting a story to your necessary mechanical screen problems, you do not

	distort or change the story completely; is that what you mean?
Mr. Zanuck:	We do not change the story completely.
Senator Clark of Idaho:	Did you produce a picture called Four Sons, with Don Ameche as the leading character?
Mr. Zanuck:	I did.
Senator Clark of Idaho:	Are you familiar with Harrison's Reports?
Mr. Zanuck:	I have had been for a number of years. In silent picture days I do recall reading Harrison's Reports. I am not a subscriber and have not read his reports in years.
Senator Clark of Idaho:	Would you say from your general knowledge of the motion-picture industry that his is a rather fair and important trade service or book?
Mr. Zanuck:	I do not know whether it is impartial or not because I have not been able in recent years—or at least I have not subscribed to it and do not know its viewpoint on any of its subjects.
Senator Clark of Idaho:	Other witnesses have testified it is a standard trade publication. Let me read to you what Harrison's Reports in the analysis of Four Sons with Don Ameche says, bearing in mind your testimony, of course, that you do not change or distort a story:

Extremely depressing, and since it deals with conditions with which almost every person is familiar it is unlikely that it will be liked by many. The Fox Film Corporation, predecessor of Twentieth Century-Fox, produced a picture with the same title once before, in 1931—

Now, that was the first picture—

It was founded on the novel by I. A. R. Wylie; but the present version even though the publicity matter says that it was suggested by the same story, has almost no resemblance to it, except that it deals with four sons and a mother. In the old version they were a German family and presented the German side of the World War—that a German mother had suffered as much by the loss of her sons in the war as

Senator Clark of Idaho: (cont.) did any other mother. In the present version the family is made Czechoslovaks, a sort of makeshift treatment. The picture is so harrowing that it can in no way be classed as entertainment. The story idea is unpleasant, for it pits a brother against a brother.

If that statement is true then the story has been completely changed, has it not?

Mr. Zanuck: I would not say completely changed. It still remains the story of a mother and her four sons. This was the remaking of the old story; a story written around World War No. 1. We have transferred the story and brought it up to date. Having produced the picture this time we wanted to make it about the present situation, believing it would be timely.

Senator Clark of Idaho: Yes believing it would be timely. But what you did was to take a story that was set in Germany and using the character I suppose according to this of a German mother but transforming it into an entirely different setting in Czechoslovakia. You characterized Czechoslovakia when the story portrayed them as Germans.

Mr. Zanuck: No; you are reading something that is not correct. The family was a German family in our picture, the Four Sons, in the recent one living in Sudetenland.

Senator Clark of Idaho: But this says—just let me read it again:

It was founded on the novel by I. A. R. Wylie—

Mr. Zanuck [interposing]: Oh, I believe you have read it correctly. I believe Mr. Harrison's viewpoints are so strained that he, perhaps, would look at a Shirley Temple picture and make it propaganda.

Senator Clark of Idaho: One witness after another has testified here that these things are facts, and that they are based upon the story and that the story is accurately portrayed. You have said the same thing. Mr.

Harrison has no idea in life except to present these views for the theater people throughout the country. Here is what he says—and we will see the picture and want to see the picture to verify it:

It was suggested by the same story, has almost no resemblance to it, except that it deals with four sons and a mother. In the old version, they were a German family, and presented the German side of the World War—that a German mother had suffered as much by the loss of her sons in the war as did any other mother. In the present version, the family is made Czechoslovaks, a sort of makeshift treatment.

Then he says:

The picture is so harrowing that it can in no way be classed as entertainment. The story idea is unpleasant, for it pits a brother against a brother.

Then he goes ahead and tells the whole story. You say they were Germans?

Mr. Zanuck:	I say it was a German family. I would like to prove it if I can. The father in the family as the story opens—well, the mother shows the iron cross that she has on the wall, that her husband received in the last World War. One brother in this family starts going to Nazi meetings. Another brother happens to be a loyal subject of Sudetenland. They clash, brother against brother, and as the film goes on we do show, just as we did orginally, that the mother in the film suffers just as any mother in the world would suffer as she sees her sons go from her.
Senator Clark of Idaho:	That is right. Did you transfer the whole scene of action?
Mr. Zanuck:	We modernized the book, as is always done with a remaking.
Senator Clark of Idaho:	Oh, yes; I know you modernized it. Let us listen to what Mr. Harrison says again:

Senator Clark of Idaho: (cont.)	The story unfolds in a town in the Sudetenland, and deals with Eugenie Leontovitch—
	Is that a German name?
Mr. Zanuck:	That is one of the great Russian actresses.
Senator Clark of Idaho:	I read again:
	The story unfolds in a town in the Sudetenland, and deals with Eugenie Leontovitch and her four sons—
Mr. Zanuck:	That is one of the great Russian actresses.
Senator Clark of Idaho:	Is that a German family?
Mr. Zanuck:	No; that is her real name. Eugenie Leontovitch is one of the great actresses of all time. [Applause.]
Senator Clark of Idaho:	Does the story deal with her?
Mr. Zanuck:	No; she is a great Russian actress who was engaged to play the role. [Applause.]
Senator Clark of Idaho:	Listen a minute, and I want you to point out where this is incorrect. What I am trying to do is to find out whether Mr. Harrison is telling the truth here. I am reading from his reports:
	The story unfolds in a town in the Sudetenland, and deals with Eugenie Leontovitch and her four sons. Don Ameche, Robert Lowery, Alan Curtis, and George Ernest. Lowery's dream of going to America comes true unexpectedly.
	I assume they are using these characters in their real names:
	Don Ameche is shocked when Alan informs him that he had joined a German social club; he could not understand how a Czechoslovak could become a Nazi—
	Now, if Mr. Harrison is right that is a Czechoslovakian family, is it not?
Mr. Zanuck:	Yes; it is. But it is not changed. You are reading from him, and I am telling you what is in the picture. [Applause.]

Senator Clark of Idaho:	Surely. And, Mr. Zanuck, I am not disputing you. I am taking one of your standard trade journals and am endeavoring to find out if it is accurate, and you tell me it is not accurate.
Mr. Zanuck:	I should not place too much confidence on saying that that is a standard trade journal. I mean, I do not think that Mr. Harrison even pretends that he comes within the realm of what we recognize us our great trade papers. It has a very limited circulation.
Senator Clark of Idaho:	He says it has, and if there is any question about it we will look into it later. You say it is not accurate in that respect, but the story has been changed around some, has it not?
Mr. Zanuck:	It certainly has.
Senator Clark of Idaho:	You referred to Man Hunt this morning, did you not, in your statement?
Mr. Zanuck:	Yes.
Senator Clark of Idaho:	Mr. Harrison was not very hard on Man Hunt. Let me read you what he says about it:

This melodrama is not cheerful entertainment, but it is intensely gripping. Its appeal, however, may be directed more to men than to women, for the story may prove a little bit harrowing for them. Some of the situations are thrilling and hold one in tense suspense. The fact that the hero is innocent of the crime of which the Nazis had accused him and is hunted and hounded by them, makes one feel deep sympathy for him. Likewise, it intensifies one's interest in his welfare. The action takes place just before the outbreak of the war.

	I think that is a picture that we want to see, too. I would like to see it myself.
Mr. Zanuck:	If you would like me to comment on Mr. Harrison's review, I think he is again wrong. In the story the leading role, portrayed by Walter Pidgeon, admits toward the end of the picture that he really intended to shoot Hitler.
Senator Clark of Idaho:	That is right. That is in here. Do you want me to read it to you?

Mr. Zanuck: The only point I am making is that he said that sympathy should be given to the man because he was innocent. He was not innocent.

Senator Clark of Idaho [reading]: Exasperated, Saunders offers Pidgeon his freedom on condition that he sign a confession stating that it had been his intention to kill Hitler, and that he had been acting on instructions from his Government—

Mr. Zanuck: What is that last line again? Acting on what?

Senator Clark of Idaho [reading]: Exasperated, Saunders offers Pidgeon his freedom on condition that he sign a confession stating that it had been his intention to kill Hitler, and that he had been acting on instructions from his Government. Pidgeon naturally refuses to sign it. Pidgeon miraculously escapes and manages to elude his captors and get back to England, but he is followed by Gestapo agents who are determined to kill him.

And then it goes on further. Is that right?

Mr. Zanuck: Yes; that is right. He does not say that Pidgeon admits in the film that he was guilty. It is of no importance, but I just point out a correction.

Senator Clark of Idaho: It is important. If he is inaccurate in some things he is liable to be inaccurate in many things; and I as one member of the committee would like to know those inaccuracies, whether some people believe it or not. I am just as anxious that you should correct any inaccuracy that comes to your attention. I have not seen these pictures. I inquired around as to the standard trade document, or whatever you want to call it, and I was told that this was standard in the industry. So I went and got it and had it photostated. I am very happy to have any corrections that there may be. I suggested to the other witnesses that if there were inaccuracies in any of these things I would be happy to have the record show the correction.

Mr. Zanuck: I think it is also important that you consider the Film Daily, a daily newspaper of motion pictures for 22 years. Here is a summary of the replies of leading United States film critics and reviewers to questions posed by the Senate subcommittee's film inquiry. The first question is:

In your opinion, are the ____ listed pictures collectively designed to influence the public mind in the direction of participation in the European war?

The answers were: Yes, 7. No, 103.
The second question is:

Do you believe pictures such as Confessions of a Nazi Spy, Sergeant York, Escape, Underground, The Man I Married, Man Hunt, and The Great Dictator have the effect of creating a greater appreciation of our democracy and American liberties?

The answers were: Yes, 103. No, 9.
The third question was:

Do you believe it is improper for American-made motion pictures to portray conditions in Germany under the Nazi regime?

The answers were: Yes, 4. No, 109.
The fourth question was:

Do you believe Congress should take any action which would make impossible the production of pictures such as those listed?

The answers were: Yes, none; No, 113.

Senator Clark of Idaho: I am very happy to have that. Of course, you notice that there is no question asked there whether they thought pictures being produced today have the effect of inciting to war the minds of many of those who see them?

Mr. Zanuck:	No: that question is not directly asked.
Senator Clark of Idaho:	You produced Night Train, too?
Mr. Zanuck:	No, I did not produce Night Train.
Senator Clark of Idaho:	It was released by Twentieth Century-Fox?
Mr. Zanuck:	It was released by Twentieth Century-Fox, and it was produced by a subsidiary company in England and released through the releasing channels of Twentieth Century-Fox.
Senator Clark of Idaho:	I am going to quote from Mr. Harrison again, and I want you to correct him if he is in error:

This British-made espionage melodrama is a pretty exciting fare. Set against the present war background, with the locale shifting from Germany to England, the action is fast moving and, even though farfetched, it is for the most part exciting. In spite of the fact that the picture was produced in England and naturally favors the British, it does not resort to too much propaganda; it concentrates instead on the melodramatic angle. There is also some good comedy; it is handled by two droll characters who worry more about losing their golf clubs than about the fact that their country is at war. The romance is developed in a natural way.

	Is that a very fair review or analysis of it, would you say?
Mr. Zanuck:	Yes; I would say that. I have only seen it once in my life and I would not really know if that would be an accurate review of the plot of the film. I have just seen it once.
Senator Clark of Idaho:	Those are the only three pictures which have been called to my attention, Mr. Zanuck, as having possible propaganda value, produced by your company. That is the only reason I referred to them. There may have been some others mentioned in some of the other testimony. Yes; there was one mentioned, as you explained this morning—I Married a Nazi. Was that yours?
Mr. Zanuck:	The Man I Married.

Senator Clark of Idaho:	What is your notion of propaganda pictures?
Mr. Zanuck:	Well, that is a most difficult question. I usually find that when someone produces something that you do not like, you call it propaganda. [Applause.]
Senator Clark of Idaho:	I think that that is probably a pretty fair statement of the situation. Of course that would not apply if a picture was, let us say, vulgar, and I did not like it. That would not be propaganda. But what you have in mind is that if there are two sides to a question and one side thinks the picture favors the other side and does not like it for that reason, they call it propaganda. That is about it; is it not?
Mr. Zanuck:	Yes.
Senator Clark of Idaho:	Would you produce a picture, or do you think you have produced any pictures which tend to make one race of people hate another race?
Mr. Zanuck:	I certainly do not feel that I have produced any film that would suddenly reveal something to the world that would cause one race or one nation to hate another nation or another race. I do not believe I have ever entertained that thought. I believe that the celluloid record will bear me out. I do believe, however, that it is my right, as long as I stay within the laws of decency and the laws of the Nation, and as long as I remain within the provisions of our self-imposed production code, that I can produce anything that I like.
Senator Clark of Idaho:	I agree with you, Mr. Zanuck. Don't you think, though, that you ought to go a step further? I think a producer has the right—I agree with you thoroughly—to produce anything that he likes. We want equal rights. That is the only reason this inquiry is going on. We want equal rights. But where the distribution and the exhibition of what is produced is so tied up, if it be so tied up, that it can be forced en masse, not by "subterfuge"— I don't like that term—but on people who do not exactly know what they

Senator Clark of Idaho: (cont.)	are seeing, if that be true! I think you have a perfect right to produce anything you want to. If the moving picture industry were given over to completely free competition, and if those pictures that you produce did not go out under block booking and all that sort of thing. I would say you were absolutely correct.
	And I still say you are correct as to your right to produce anything you want. But it is part of a much larger pattern. Do I make myself halfway clear?
Mr. Zanuck:	Yes; you do. Here is what worries me, though—this large pattern. I don't presume that you feel that most picture producers sit down and decide, "Well, we will make this type or that type," or "We will all go this way or go that way," because I can tell you frankly I am not a member of the Producers Association. I have attended, as a guest, only one meeting in the last 3 years, and yet I am directly charged with making 52 feature pictures a year. Furthermore, on the basis of competition I would not sit down in a room with a group of my fellow producers and discuss anything that I intended to make. [Applause.]
Senator Clark of Idaho:	I think you are thoroughly right. I think that is true. You are a creative artist.
Mr. Zanuck:	Thank you.
Senator Clark of Idaho:	Whether you like to be so designated or not. You produce pictures. That is your business. That is what you are skilled in and have a knack for. But your company is represented in the Motion Picture Producers Association; is it not?
Mr. Zanuck:	Oh, yes.
Senator Clark of Idaho:	In other words, the men who determine the trade policies and handle the business end sit in the meetings of the Producers Association?
Mr. Zanuck:	Yes. My contract provides that the selection of material shall be up to me. By "material" I mean screen stories. I do not consult with any

of my associates, my executive associates, meaning the president of the company—well, I do consult with them, but I do not consult always on what type of story I will make. I don't believe I have talked to Sydney Kent about a story or whether I should make it or not make it, more than three times a year. If our material has been bad and if our pictures have not been entertaining, then the blame must be entirely mine. If they have incited people to war, then the blame is entirely mine. I stand responsible.

Senator Clark of Idaho: You are the production man. I am glad to hear that; I really am. In other words, the policy of producing pictures as determined by you is largely as a creative artist, if I may use that term. I am very happy to hear that.

Now, Mr. Zanuck. I do not want you or Mr. Balaban to think that you are favored witnesses, but I do not want to go back over all this stuff that I went into with Mr. Schenck and Mr. Warner, because of the fact that you are fundamentally interested in the artistry and the creation of these pictures, and I am looking forward to seeing them.

Mr. Zanuck: Thank you.

Senator Clark of Idaho: Unless you have something now that you would like to present in connection with any testimony that has been presented heretofore that you have heard——

Mr. Zanuck [interposing]: I do have one thing, and I shall be brief.

Senator Clark of Idaho: You do not need to be brief; but I am not going to grill you on this whole fundamental set-up just to be killing time this afternoon. So I would like to have you make any further statement that you care to make, as far as I am concerned.

Mr. Zanuck: I would like to say this, and I say it in all sincerity, and I know that you will realize that I mean no offense to anyone; because I do not. When I first read and heard of this proposed investigation or inquiry I was deeply resentful,

Mr. Zanuck: (cont.)

naturally. After a while, in thinking it over, my anger cooled a bit. It gives me an opportunity to say what I am going to say now.

I am proud to be a part of the moving-picture business. I go back and I think of what this little nickelodeon business has grown to, and I cannot help but be proud, although I was certainly not one of the originators. But I recall the hours and hours and weeks and months and years—actually years of entertainment that the people of the world have received from this industry, and it makes me proud.

I look back and I can see Henry Walthall as the "little colonel" in The Birth of a Nation. I look back and I see those covered wagons going across the plains in The Covered Wagon. I look back and see John Gilbert in The Big Parade. I see that girl on the truck when he kissed her good-bye—Réné Adoree—and went away to the war. I look back and it gives me a thrill when I think of Al Jolson in The Jazz Singer—the first time that sound came to the moving pictures. I see George Arliss as Disraeli, and I look back and recall picture after picture, pictures so strong and powerful that they sold the American way of life, not only to America but to the entire world. They sold it so strongly that when dictators took over Italy and Germany, what did Hitler and his flunky, Mussolini, do? The first thing they did was to ban our pictures, throw us out. They wanted no part of the American way of life.

And I come down right now to the last minute. I remember that great picture Gone with the Wind. I remember a picture of my own, Grapes of Wrath, and I remember the last speech in the Joad family. They had been kicked out and bounced around and the whole world was against them; they were on the spot; and I remember Ma Joad turning to the old man in the flivver, and she said: "Well, things look mighty bad and everything is going wrong, Pa. But that's the way it is with the world. You have got to take the good with the bad. But we don't ever have to worry, because we are the people."

I remember those things and I remember the enjoyment they have given. I remember the laughter and all that, and I am very proud. And, Senator, you do not have to investigate us, if you will look at all the pictures, our whole record—not just these Nazi pictures. This industry has stood for a lot. By that I mean it has been the American way of life, and it has been abused in other countries; but I am sure that when the whole celluloid record is put before the world—the whole world—you are going to agree with the people of America who patronize us when they wish to and who stay away when they do not wish to see the pictures; and we have grown only because the people have let us.

Thank you. [Applause.]

Senator Clark of Idaho: You are not only a creative artist, Mr. Zanuck, but you are a rather skillful salesman. Maybe I will see those pictures. You see, despite all of the vituperation that has been heaped upon this committee, this committee actually, whether you believe it or not, is trying to sit here and ascertain facts; and if I have been cross-examining, the only reason is because I want to get at the facts. No one on this committee has suggested—and it should be emphasized again—no one has suggested any form of censorship that would restrict your creative ability from flowing so magnificently in the future as it has in the past, into the pictures and onto the American screen. As a matter of fact, you and your associates are probably the greatest trustees of culture in this country. There is one thing on which we agree, and that is that we shall never come to that point that has so

Senator Clark of Idaho: (cont.) horribly engulfed the countries of Europe to which you refer. As to the means of evading that, we differ. Some people think the thing to do to prevent a dictatorship and the destruction of democracy in this country is to get into this war, or at least to pursue a belligerent policy: Others feel and, I think quite sincerely, that if we engage in a major war it will bring about ultimately in this country the very conditions of which you complain. That is a matter that we will not go into. I just wanted to make that statement to you. Some of the other members of the committee may have some questions. But let me say, further, that no one can take exception to what you have said.

I think you got applause from everybody that time, and I am sure there are two sides here. So you got almost unanimous applause.

We think the moving-picture industry is a great industry. No one has suggested making it a "whipping boy." But these things have come up because of a very crucial situation which has arisen in this country. I am sure that, by and large, if it is left in your hands it will probably be in pretty good hands. You are quite a trustee, you know, a trustee of expression and culture and everything that goes to mold opinions and feelings in the United States, and I am sure that you realize those responsibilities.

Have any other members of the committee anything to say?

Senator Brooks: In your testimony this morning, Mr. Zanuck, you told us that you had served as a private, first class, in the United States Army, at the age of 15, during the last war. In what capacity are you serving the United States Government at the present time?

Mr. Zanuck: Senator, I am a lieutenant colonel in the Signal Corps of the United States Army. [Applause.]

Senator Brooks: Will you tell the committee the circumstances of how you got into the Signal Corps of

	the Army, and the work you have done in connection with it?
Mr. Zanuck:	I would be very glad to. First, I might say that I am fortunate in being the chairman of the research council of the Academy of Motion Picture Artists and Scientists. The research council is a technical nonprofit organization. Nine years ago the United States Government decided that they would have to improve the photographic division of the United States Army. They sent us, 9 years ago, Army officers to train in the motion-picture business, in a phase of the motion-picture business that might be valuable at some time to this country. For 9 years we have continued to train Regular Army officers. We have had them at the rate of two or three at a time, sometimes as long as 6 to 8 months. About 2 years ago—I think I am correct in the date—we reviewed and made a survey for the War Department on training films, and the War Department at that time realized that they would have to improve the quality of these purely training films. So they came, naturally, to the research council of the academy, and as chairman of the research council of the academy I was very proud to accept a commission. I now serve approximately 1 week in each 5 weeks on active service in the production of these films which are made, of course, for the War Department on a nonprofit basis.
Senator Brooks:	There is only one other question about your testimony this morning. You mentioned the unfair investigation. This committee has not been in any sense unfair, has it?
Mr. Zanuck:	No; it certainly has not.
Senator Brooks:	That is all.
Senator McFarland:	I have just one or two questions.
	First, I would like to say to you that it would be my hope that the screen put your little speech in the moving pictures and present it throughout the United States—and I wish it

Senator McFarland: (cont.)	could go throughout the world. I think it would do everyone good.
Mr. Zanuck:	Thank you.
Senator McFarland:	That is one of the best that I ever heard. Who is Aubrey Blair?
Mr. Zanuck:	I have heard of him for a number of years. I received this telegram which I would like to read, if I may. It is addressed to me, and it is dated September 26, 1941 [reading]:

Since the first meeting of the Screen Actors Guild in 1933 I have been executive secretary. For several years Aubrey Blair was an assistant working on matters affecting the junior or extra player membership of the guild. Mr. Blair was discharged by the guild in 1939. In 1940 he was employed by Central Casting Corporation and was employed there for several months. He was discharged by Central Casting Corporation. I understand that Mr. Blair recently has been employed in some capacity by the American Federation of Labor. Mr. Blair has not been connected with the Screen Actors Guild since 1939 and no officer or employee of the guild has forwarded to the Senate committee any such statement as that attributed to Mr. Blair.

Kenneth Thomsons, *Executive Secretary, Screen Actors Guild.*

Senator McFarland:	Thank you. If you started out to produce a picture as an independent producer, how would you go about it?
Mr. Zanuck:	Having been faced with that problem once before in my career, I would naturally start to see what stories I could buy. I would read stories and get the backbone of my company together, with some material, and then I would go on the free lance market and find out what actors and actresses I could engage. And it is really amazing—if I can find a paper here in a moment—I am sorry to cause this delay—
Senator McFarland:	That is all right.
Mr. Zanuck:	I think it might be interesting. If I were to

start producing pictures tomorrow, without borrowing a sou from any company of the so-called big five or big eight, if I had the money, I could hire the following: Brian Aherne, Fred Astaire, Marlene Dietrich, Joan Blondell, Claudette Colbert, Warren William, Shirley Temple, Jack Benny—I could go on with a list of 300 names. That is the type of people that I could borrow tomorrow. I could go ahead and rent stage space. That is one thing we have a lot of in Hollywood—empty stages. The only thing I would have to have would be the money.

Senator McFarland: Don't misunderstand me; I am not contemplating going into the business, because I would be lacking in that last requirement. That is all.

Senator Clark of Idaho: I am not going into it, but let me observe this. I agree with you that if you had the money you could go out and produce a picture. The question is vastly different, however. Even if it was a good picture, its ultimate success, assuming certain conditions—but I will not go into that now.

Senator Tobey has a question.

Senator Tobey: Mr. Zanuck, if you please, you were here yesterday when I asked questions with reference to charges about the use of United States troops and the putting of United States troops into German uniforms and the commissary of the Government paying the movie men; you heard the statements made yesterday?

Mr. Zanuck: Yes.

Senator Tobey: I infer that my colleague has introduced this letter or telegram, relative to Mr. Aubrey Blair, into the record for the purpose of discrediting Mr. Blair to some extent.

Senator McFarland: I did not introduce any letter; but go ahead.

Senator Tobey: I never saw Mr. Blair, but whether or not he was discharged in 1936, the fact remains that for quite a time he was secretary of this guild, and I have in my possession a letter from Mr.

Senator Tobey: (cont.)	Blair, over his signature, with a list of artists similar to what you have suggested——
Mr. Zanuck:	He was never secretary.
Senator Tobey:	Well, assistant secretary, whichever it was. The point I make is that at that time he was in an official capacity in the actors' guild, and over his signature he makes these statements. We always say with reference to anything of that kind, "Important, if true." Provided it is true, I state and affirm again that it is reprehensible and it is something that we ought to know about and will know about. But in connection with the statement about Warner Bros. and the picture which you said they did make, as to which of these statements which I have just referred to were made, in his letter also he says:

In West Point of the Air for Metro-Goldwyn-Mayer, Metro-Goldwyn-Mayer deliberately wrecked six or more Government planes.

	Did M-G-M produce that picture, West Point of the Air?
Mr. Zanuck:	I am not sure about it, but I believe they did. I would have to consult the Film Guide.
Senator Tobey:	You did not produce it?
Mr. Zanuck:	No, sir.
Senator Tobey:	Was it before your incumbency?
Mr. Zanuck:	No. I am with Twentieth Century-Fox.
Senator Tobey:	I beg your pardon. Can you tell me anything about this picture, West Point of the Air?
Mr. Zanuck:	I am not positive whether I have seen the picture or not; but I do know that there is a regulation, a War Department regulation, that prohibits the putting of American soldiers into the uniform of another nation.
Senator Tobey:	I thought there was. I should not have bothered you about this.
Senator Clark of Idaho:	Thank you very much for your patience in staying around here and for your courtesy in helping us out.

Mr. Zanuck: Thank you very much.
[The witness withdrew from the committee table.]

10.2 RECOMMENDATION FOR AWARD OF THE SILVER STAR MEDAL TO CAPTAIN JOHN HAMILTON [STERLING HAYDEN] FROM HANS V. TOFTE TO THE DIRECTOR OF THE STRATEGIC SERVICES UNIT, FEBRUARY 28, 1946

The actor Sterling Hayden is well known for roles in such movies as *Asphalt Jungle, Dr. Strangelove: Or, How I Learned to Stop Worrying and Love the Bomb*, and *The Godfather*. He arrived in Hollywood in 1940 and had only made two films when America entered World War II. Hayden left Hollywood to serve as an undercover agent known as John Hamilton in what would become known as the Office of Strategic Services (OSS). The letter below describes Hayden's espionage activities for which he is being recommended for the Silver Star Medal (and would receive). Although a number of Hollywood celebrities would become involved in the war effort through such activities as war bond drives, United Service Organizations (USO) tours, and military service, Hayden's service was particularly extensive and dangerous.

28 February 1946
Subject: Recommendation for Award of the Silver Star Medal to
Captain John Hamilton, USMCR
To: The Director, Strategic Services Unit, Washington, D.C.

1. It is recommended that Captain John Hamilton, 0–22085, USMCR, be awarded the Silver Star Medal for exceptional meritorious service and gallantry in action while assigned to a Strategic Services operational unit in MEDTO from December 1943 to February 1944, inclusive.
2. Captain John Hamilton (then a 1st Lieutenant) was assigned to the OSS, SO Shipping Operation based at Bari and Monopoli, Italy, in December 1943. This unit established the initial American contact with Marshal Tito's National Liberation Army in Yugoslavia by landing from small naval surface craft on the German-occupied coast of Dalmatia and penetrating through enemy lines to several of the most important headquarters of Tito's forces. After negotiations with Tito and his staff and after having obtained the necessary authority from

the Allied Commander-in-Chief, the unit established shipping bases on the coast of Italy, collected a fleet of some 40 Yugoslav steamships and sailing vessels, procured cargoes of arms, ammunition, food and clothing as well as medical supplies, and organised a clandestine supply line across the Adriatic Sea, penetrating the German sea and air blockade along the Balkan coastline and landing in all some 7,000 tons of vitally needed war supplies for the National Liberation Army of Yugoslavia.

3. Owing to the timing as well as the local conditions in connection with the military situation in this particular area, the immediate results of this operation placed the German forces in Dalmatia at a great disadvantage and served to enhance the activities of Tito's forces in Dalmatia to a very considerable degree. The unit made 70 sailings altogether across the Adriatic, losing only four ships in spite of intensified enemy action on land, at sea and in the air along the clandestine supply line. Furthermore, the few American officers engaged in commanding and supervising the above-mentioned supply operations made more than a dozen armed reconnaissance penetrations deep into enemy territory in Yugoslavia and collected a substantial amount of original and at that time exceedingly valuable intelligence covering both German order of battle and the complete order of battle of Tito's Partisans in Yugoslavia.

4. On 24 December 1943, Captain John Hamilton (then lst Lieutenant) was ordered to proceed by surface craft to the Islands of Korcula, Vis, Hvar and Brac, then reportedly under German attack. The object of his mission was to find out on the spot whether the islands in question had actually been occupied by German landing forces and to make contact with staff officers of Tito's Headquarters in charge of the coastal area of Dalmatia, situated on the Island of Hvar.

Owing to exceedingly bad weather, Captain Hamilton's ship stranded and sank during the night of the 24th and 25th of December on the coast of Italy. However, Captain Hamilton managed to get ashore and returned to Bari, from where he proceeded on board another ship on the morning of the 25th.

After an extremely rough crossing, he landed on the Island of Korcula during the night of the 25th and 26th of December and made contact with units of Tito's forces. The island was under German attack. However, in order to acquaint himself with the situation, Captain Hamilton made a reconnaissance tour in a jeep accompanied by a Yugoslav staff officer and two Partisans. During the drive the car was ambushed, and the Yugoslav driver sitting next to Captain Hamilton was killed by enemy gunfire. However, Captain Hamilton and the remaining Partisans managed to shoot their way out of the ambush and escaped with the jeep.

After having ascertained the fact that the Island of Korcula was lost to the enemy, Captain Hamilton escaped with the remnants of the Partisan garrison during the night of the 26th and 27th of December, and after a hazardous sea voyage through waters patrolled by enemy E boats and landing craft, he arrived on the Island of Hvar on the morning of 27 December. He established contact with the Partisan Headquarters and had a six-hour conference with the Partisan staff officers, from whom he collected exact information as to the immediate military situation on the Dalmatian islands as well as on the mainland. The conference took place in the open outside the buildings of the said headquarters which were constantly subjected to enemy attacks from the air including Stuka dive-bombing.

Captain Hamilton remained on the Islands of Hvar and Brac until 30 December, taking an active part in the defense of the islands and the repulsion of a number of German attacks. As the only American in the area, he gave a magnificent account of himself and received the unanimous admiration and respect of the fighting Yugoslavs.

In accordance with his orders which directed him to return to his base in Italy not later than 2400 hours, New Year's Eve, Captain Hamilton boarded a small local vessel on the night of the 30th and 31st of December, again sailed through waters patrolled by enemy naval craft and proceeded to Italy across the open Adriatic through a severe winter storm. Captain Hamilton returned with complete information concerning the situation in the Dalmatian coastal areas, on the basis of which immediate steps were taken to bring aid and relief to the threatened islands. Furthermore, Allied naval operations were initiated without delay and obtained extremely favorable results against German naval craft. Also, Allied air operations were at once undertaken against German occupation forces in Dalmatia, causing the German military operation to come to a temporary standstill.

5. While stationed in Italy at the OSS shipping bases, Captain Hamilton did outstanding work and was for a period of time in command of all operations out of the port of Monopoli, working day and night with his Partisan crews totalling some 400 men, organising maintenance and repairs of ships, loading cargoes of guns, ammunition, mines, food, clothing and medical supplies, attending to the legion details in connection with the collection of cargoes, transportation, fueling,

watering and clearing of the ships, as well as providing for housing and feeding his Yugoslav crews, all under a rigid system insuring the strictest security. Captain Hamilton conducted himself at all times in a manner which commanded the greatest respect from everyone who served with him and which reflected honor to the Allied military forces in the Middle East.

HANS V. TOFTE,
Major, AUS.
(formerly Chief OSS/SO Shipping Operations in the Adriatic)

CHAPTER 11

The Red Menace: The Cold War

11.1 "STATEMENT OF PRINCIPLES," MOTION PICTURE ALLIANCE FOR THE PRESERVATION OF AMERICAN IDEALS, 1944

The Motion Picture Alliance was formed in the early 1940s by some of Hollywood's high-profile conservatives, including the directors Sam Wood and King Vidor and the producer and animator Walt Disney, and had the support of the actors John Wayne and Gary Cooper. In its "Statement of Principles," the Alliance denounced the influence of communists and other "crackpots" in the motion picture industry and promised to resist Leftist messages in film.

Statement of Principles

We believe in, and like, the American way of life: the liberty and freedom which generations before us have fought to create and preserve; the freedom to speak, to think, to live, to worship, to work, and to govern ourselves as individuals, as free men; the right to succeed or fail as free men, according to the measure of our ability and our strength.

Believing in these things, we find ourselves in sharp revolt against a rising tide of communism, fascism, and kindred beliefs, that seek by subversive means to undermine and change this way of life; groups that have forfeited their right to exist in this country of ours, because they seek to achieve their change by means other than the vested procedure of the ballot and to deny the right of the majority opinion of the people to rule.

In our special field of motion pictures, we resent the growing impression that this industry is made of, and dominated by, Communists, radicals, and crackpots. We believe that we represent the vast majority of the people who serve this great medium of expression. But unfortunately it has been an unorganized majority. This has been almost inevitable. The very love of freedom, of the rights of the individual, make this great majority reluctant to organize. But now we must, or we shall meanly lose "the last, best hope on earth."

As Americans, we have no new plan to offer. We want no new plan, we want only to defend against its enemies that which is our priceless heritage; that freedom which has given man, in this country, the fullest life and the richest expression the world has ever known; that system which, in the present emergency, has fathered an effort that, more than any other single factor, will make possible the winning of this war.

As members of the motion-picture industry, we must face and accept an especial responsibility. Motion pictures are inescapably one of the world's greatest forces for influencing public thought and opinion, both at home and abroad. In this fact lies solemn obligation. We refuse to permit the effort of Communist, Fascist, and other totalitarian-minded groups to pervert this powerful medium into an instrument for the dissemination of un-American ideas and beliefs. We pledge ourselves to fight, with every means at our organized command, any effort of any group or individual, to divert the loyalty of the screen from the free America that give it birth. And to dedicate our work, in the fullest possible measure, to the presentation of the American scene, its standards and its freedoms, its beliefs and its ideals, as we know them and believe in them.

11.2 TESTIMONY OF WALT DISNEY, U.S. CONGRESS HOUSE UN-AMERICAN ACTIVITIES COMMITTEE, HEARINGS REGARDING THE COMMUNIST INFILTRATION OF THE MOTION PICTURE INDUSTRY

When the House Un-American Activities Committee (HUAC) investigated Hollywood regarding communist infiltration in 1947, some Hollywood luminaries served as "friendly witnesses" by testifying about communist activity in Hollywood and even "naming names." One such friendly witness was the producer and animator Walt Disney who, amongst other things, testified to the power of films as propaganda and about what he believed was a communist-driven labor strike at his studio.

Monday, October 20, 1947

House of Representatives, Committee on Un-American Activities, Washington, D.C.

The committee met at 10:30 a. m., Hon. J. Parnell Thomas (chairman) presiding.

The CHAIRMAN. The meeting will come to order. The record will show that the following members are present: Mr. McDowell, Mr. Vail, Mr. Nixon, Mr. Thomas. A subcommittee is sitting.

Staff members present: Mr. Robert E. Stripling chief investigator; Messrs. Louis J. Russell, Robert B. Gaston, H. A. Smith, and A. B. Leckie, investigators; and Mr. Benjamin Mandel, director of research. Before this hearing gets under way, I would like to call attention to some of the basic principles by which the Committee on Un-American Activities is being guided in its investigation into alleged subversive influence in America's motion-picture industry.

The committee is well aware of the magnitude of the subject which it is investigating. The motion-picture business represents an investment of billions of dollars. It represents employment for thousands of workers, ranging from unskilled laborers to high-salaried actors and executives. And even more important, the motion-picture industry represents what is probably the largest single vehicle of entertainment for the American public—over 85,000,000 persons attend the movies each week.

However, it is the very magnitude of the scope of the motion-picture industry which makes this investigation so necessary. We all recognize, certainly, the tremendous effect which moving pictures have on their mass audiences, far removed from the Hollywood sets. We all recognize that what the citizen sees and hears in his neighborhood movie house carries a powerful impact, on his thoughts and behavior.

With such vast influence over the lives of American citizens as the motion-picture industry exerts, it is not unnatural—in fact, it is very logical—that subversive and undemocratic forces should attempt to use this medium for Un-American purposes.

I want to emphasize at the outset of these hearings that the fact that the Committee on Un-American Activities is investigating alleged Communist influence and infiltration in the motion-picture industry must not be considered or interpreted as an attack on the majority of persons associated with this great industry. I have every confidence that the vast majority of movie workers are patriotic and loyal Americans.

This committee, under its mandate from the House of Representatives, has the responsibility of exposing and spotlighting subversive elements wherever they may exist. As I have already pointed out, it is only to be expected that such elements would strive desperately to gain entry to the motion-picture industry, simply because the industry offers such a tremendous weapon for education and propaganda. That Communists have made such an attempt in Hollywood and with considerable success is already evident to this committee from its preliminary investigative work.

The problem of Communist infiltration is not limited to the movie industry. That even our Federal Government has not been immune from the menace is evidenced by the fact that $11,000,000 is now being spent to rid the Federal service of Communists. Communists are also firmly entrenched in control of a number of large and powerful labor unions in this country. Yet simply because there are Communist union leaders among the longshoremen or seamen, for example, one does not infer that the owners of the shipping industries are Communists and Communist sympathizers, or that the majority of workers in those industries hold to an un-American philosophy. So it is with the movie industry.

I cannot emphasize too strongly the seriousness of Communist infiltration, which we have found to be a mutual problem for many, many different fields of endeavor in the United States. Communists for years have been conducting an unrelentless "boring from within" campaign against America's democratic institutions. While never possessing a large numerical strength, the Communists nevertheless have found that they could dominate the activities of unions or other mass enterprises in this country by capturing a few strategic positions of leadership.

This technique, I am sorry to say, has been amazingly profitable for the Communists. And they have been aided all along the line by non-Communists, who are either sympathetic to the aims of communism or are unwilling to recognize the danger in Communist infiltration.

The ultimate purpose of the Communists is a well-established fact. Despite sporadic statements made to the contrary for reasons of expediency, the Communist movement looks to the establishment of Soviet-dominated, totalitarian governments in all of the countries of the world, and the Communists are willing to use force and violence to achieve this aim if necessary.

The United States is one of the biggest obstacles to this movement. The fact was startlingly illustrated recently by the open announcement of the Communist International—a world-wide party organization dedicated to promoting world-wide Communist revolution, which previously operated underground.

The vituperation leveled at the United States by this new international Communist organization clearly indicated that America is considered the chief stumbling block in the Soviet plans for world domination and is therefore the chief target in what we might call the Soviet Union's ideological war against non-Soviet governments.

There is no question that there are Communists in Hollywood. We cannot minimize their importance there, and that their influence has already made itself felt has been evidenced by internal turmoil in the industry over the Communist issue. Prominent figures in the motion-picture business have been engaged in a sort of running battle over Communist infiltration for the last 4 or 5 years and a number of anti-Communist organizations have been set up within the industry in an attempt to combat this menace.

The question before this committee, therefore, and the scope of its present inquiry, will be to determine the extent of Communist infiltration in the Hollywood motion-picture industry. We want to know what strategic positions in the industry have been captured by these elements, whose loyalty is pledged in word and deed to the interests of a foreign power.

The committee is determined that the hearings shall be fair and impartial. We have subpenaed witnesses representing both sides of the question. All we are after are the facts.

Now, I want to make it clear to the witnesses, the audience, the members of the press, and other guests here today that this hearing is going to be conducted in an orderly and dignified manner at all times. But if there is anyone here today or at any of the future sessions of this hearing who entertains any hopes or plans for disrupting the proceedings, he may as well dismiss it from his mind.

. . .

Testimony of Walter E. Disney

Mr. Stripling:	Mr. Disney, will you state your full name and present address, please?
Mr. Disney:	Walter E. Disney, Los Angeles, Calif.
Mr. Stripling:	When and where were you born, Mr. Disney?
Mr. Disney:	Chicago, Ill., December 5, 1901.
Mr. Stripling:	December 5, 1901?
Mr. Disney:	Yes, sir.
Mr. Stripling:	What is your occupation?

Mr. Disney:	Well, I am a producer of motion-picture cartoons.
Mr. Stripling:	Mr. Chairman, the interrogation of Mr. Disney will be done by Mr. Smith.
The Chairman:	Mr. Smith.
Mr. Smith:	Mr. Disney, how long have you been in that business?
Mr. Disney:	Since 1920.
Mr. Smith:	You have been in Hollywood during this time?
Mr. Disney:	I have been in Hollywood since 1923.
Mr. Smith:	At the present time you own and operate the Walt Disney Studio at Burbank, Calif?
Mr. Disney:	Well, I am one of the owners. Part owner.
Mr. Smith:	How many people are employed there, approximately?
Mr. Disney:	At the present time about 600.
Mr. Smith:	And what is the approximate largest number of employees you have had in the studio?
Mr. Disney:	Well, close to 1,400 at times.
Mr. Smith:	Will you tell us a little about the nature of this particular studio, the type of pictures you make, and approximately how many per year?
Mr. Disney:	Well, mainly cartoon films. We make about 20 short subjects, and about 2 features a year.
Mr. Smith:	Will you talk just a little louder, Mr. Disney?
Mr. Disney:	Yes, sir.
Mr. Smith:	How many, did you say?
Mr. Disney:	About 20 short subject cartoons and about 2 features per year.
Mr. Smith:	And some of the characters in the films consist of—
Mr. Disney:	You mean such as Mickey Mouse and Donald Duck and Snow White and the Seven Dwarfs, and things of that sort.
Mr. Smith:	Where are these films distributed?
Mr. Disney:	All over the world.
Mr. Smith:	In all countries of the world?
Mr. Disney:	Well, except the Russian countries.
Mr. Smith:	Why aren't they distributed in Russia, Mr. Disney?
Mr. Disney:	Well, we can't do business with them.
Mr. Smith:	What do you mean by that?
Mr. Disney:	Oh, well, we have sold them some films a good many years ago. They bought the Three Little Pigs and used it through Russia. And they looked at a lot of our pictures, and I think they ran a lot of them in Russia, but

	then turned them back to us and said they didn't want them, they didn't suit their purposes.
Mr. Smith:	Is the dialogue in these films translated into the various foreign languages.
Mr. Disney:	Yes. On one film we did 10 foreign versions. That was Snow White and the Seven Dwarfs.
Mr. Smith:	Have you ever made any pictures in your studio that contained propaganda and that were propaganda films?
Mr. Disney:	Well, during the war we did. We made quite a few—working with different Government agencies. We did one for the Treasury on taxes and I did four anti-Hitler films. And I did one on my own for Air Power.
Mr. Smith:	From those pictures that you made have you any opinion as to whether or not the films can be used effectively to disseminate propaganda?
Mr. Disney:	Yes, I think they proved that.
Mr. Smith:	How do you arrive at that conclusion?
Mr. Disney:	Well, on the one for the Treasury on taxes, it was to let the people know that taxes were important in the war effort. As they explained to me, they had 13,000,000 new taxpayers, people who had never paid taxes, and they explained that it would be impossible to prosecute all those that were delinquent and they wanted to put this story before those people so they would get their taxes in early. I made the film and after the film had its run the Gallup poll organization polled the public and the findings were that 29 percent of the people admitted that had influenced them in getting their taxes in early and giving them a picture of what taxes will do.
Mr. Smith:	Aside from those pictures you made during the war, have you made any other pictures, or do you permit pictures to be made at your studio containing propaganda?
Mr. Disney:	No; we never have. During the war we thought it was a different thing. It was the first time we ever allowed anything like that to go in the films. We watch so that nothing gets into the films that would be harmful in any way to any group or any country. We have large audiences of children and different groups, and we try to keep them as free from anything that would offend

Mr. Disney: (cont.)	anybody as possible. We work hard to see that nothing of that sort creeps in.
Mr. Smith:	Do you have any people in your studio at the present time that you believe are Communist or Fascist, employed there?
Mr. Disney:	No; at the present time I feel that everybody in my studio is 100 percent American.
Mr. Smith:	Have you had at any time, in your opinion, in the past, have you at any time in the past had any Communists employed at your studio?
Mr. Disney:	Yes; in the past I had some people that I definitely feel were Communists.
Mr. Smith:	As a matter of fact, Mr. Disney, you experienced a strike at your studio, did you not?
Mr. Disney:	Yes.
Mr. Smith:	And is it your opinion that that strike was instituted by members of the Communist Party to serve their purposes?
Mr. Disney:	Well, it proved itself so with time, and I definitely feel it was a Communist group trying to take over my artists and they did take them over.
The Chairman:	Do you say, they did take them over?
Mr. Disney:	They did take them over.
Mr. Smith:	Will you explain that to the committee, please?
Mr. Disney:	It came to my attention when a delegation of my boys, my artists, came to me and told me that Mr. Herbert Sorrell—
Mr. Smith:	Is that Herbert K. Sorrell?
Mr. Disney:	Herbert K. Sorrell, was trying to take them over. I explained to them that it was none of my concern, that I had been cautioned to not even talk with any of my boys on labor. They said it was not a matter of labor, it was just a matter of them not wanting to go with Sorrell, and they had heard that I was going to sign with Sorrell, and they said that they wanted an election to prove that Sorrell didn't have the majority, and I said that I had a right to demand an election. So when Sorrell came I demanded an election.

Sorrell wanted me to sign on a bunch of cards that he had there that he claimed were the majority, but the other side had claimed the same thing. I told Mr. Sorrell |

that there is only one way for me to go and that was an election and that is what the law had set up, the National Labor Relations Board was for that purpose. He laughed at me and he said that he would use the Labor Board as it suited his purposes and that he had been sucker enough to go for that Labor Board ballot and he had lost some election—I can't remember the name of the place—by one vote. He said it took him 2 years to get it back. He said he would strike, that that was his weapon. He said, "I have all of the tools of the trade sharpened," that I couldn't stand the ridicule or the smear of a strike. I told him that it was a matter of principle with me, that I couldn't go on working with my boys feeling that I had sold them down the river to him on his say so, and he laughed at me and told me I was naive and foolish. He said, you can't stand this strike, I will smear you, and I will make a dust bowl out of your plant.

The Chairman:	What was that?
Mr. Disney:	He said he would make a dust bowl out of my plant if he chose to. I told him I would have to go that way, sorry, that he might be able to do all that; but I would have to stand on that. The result was that he struck.

I believed at that time that Mr. Sorrell was a Communist because of all the things that I had heard and having seen his name appearing on a number of Commie front things. When he pulled the strike the first people to smear me and put me on the unfair list were all of the Commie front organizations. I can't remember them all, they change so often, but one that is clear in my mind is the League of Women Voters, the Peoples World, the Daily Worker, and the PM Magazine in New York. They smeared me. Nobody came near to find out what the true facts of the thing were. And I even went through the same smear in South America, through some Commie periodicals in South America, and generally throughout the world all of the Commie groups began smear campaigns against me and my pictures.

Mr. McDowell:	In what fashion was that smear, Mr. Disney, what type of smear?
Mr. Disney:	Well, they distorted everything, they lied; there was no

Mr. Disney: (cont.)	way you could ever counteract anything that they did: they formed picket lines in front of the theaters, and, well, they called my plant a sweat-shop, and that is not true, and anybody in Hollywood would prove it otherwise. They claimed things there were not true at all and there was no way you could fight it back. It was not a labor problem at all because—I mean, I have never had labor trouble, and I think that would be backed up by anybody in Hollywood.
Mr. Smith:	As a matter of fact, you have how many unions operating in your plant?
The Chairman:	Excuse me just a minute. I would like to ask a question.
Mr. Smith:	Pardon me.
The Chairman:	In other words, Mr. Disney, Communists out there smeared you because you wouldn't knuckle under?
Mr. Disney:	I wouldn't go along with their way of operating. I insisted on it going through the National Labor Relations Board. And he told me outright that he used them as it suited his purposes.
The Chairman:	Supposing you had given in to him, then what would have been the outcome?
Mr. Disney:	Well, I would never have given in to him, because it was a matter of principle with me, and I fight for principles. My boys have been there, have grown up in the business with me, and I didn't feel like I could sign them over to anybody. They were vulnerable at that time. They were not organized. It is a new industry.
The Chairman:	Go ahead, Mr. Smith.
Mr. Smith:	How many labor unions, approximately, do you have operating in your studies at the present time?
Mr. Disney:	Well, we operate with around 35—I think we have contacts with 30.
Mr. Smith:	At the time of this strike you didn't have any grievances or labor troubles whatsoever in your plant?
Mr. Disney:	No. The only real grievance was between Sorrell and the boys within my plant, they demanding an election, and they never got it.
Mr. Smith:	Do you recall having had any conversations with Mr. Sorrell relative to communism?
Mr. Disney:	Yes, I do.
Mr. Smith:	Will you relate that conversation?

Mr. Disney:	Well, I didn't pull my punches on how I felt. He evidently heard that I had called them all a bunch of Communists—and I believe they are. At the meeting he leaned over and he said, "You think I am a Communist, don't you," and I told him that all I knew was what I heard and what I had seen; and he laughed and said, "Well, I used their money to finance my strike of 1937," and he said that he had gotten the money through the personal check of some actor, but he didn't name the actor. I didn't go into it any further. I just listened.
Mr. Smith:	Can you name any other individuals that were active at the time of the strike that you believe in your opinion are Communist?
Mr. Disney:	Well, I feel that there is one artist in my plant, that came in there, he came in about 1938, and he sort of stayed in the background, he wasn't too active, but he was the real brains of this, and I believe he is a Communist. His name is David Hilberman.
Mr. Smith:	How is it spelled?
Mr. Disney:	H-i-l-b-e-r-m-a-n, I believe. I looked into his record and I found that, No. 1, that he had no religion and, No. 2, that he had spent considerable time at the Moscow Art Theater studying art direction, or something.
Mr. Smith:	Any others, Mr. Disney?
Mr. Disney:	Well, I think Sorrell is sure tied up with them. If he isn't a Communist he sure should be one.
Mr. Smith:	Do you remember the name of William Pomerance, did he have anything to do with it?
Mr. Disney:	Yes, sir. He came in later. Sorrell put him in charge as business manager of cartoonists and later he went to the Screen Actors as their business agent and in turn he put in another man by the name of Maurice Howard, the present business agent. And they are all tied up with the same outfit.
Mr. Smith:	What is your opinion of Mr. Pomerance and Mr. Howard as to whether or not they are or are not Communists?
Mr. Disney:	In my opinion they are Communists. No one has any way of proving those things.
Mr. Smith:	Were you able to produce during the strike?
Mr. Disney:	Yes, I did, because there was a very few, very small

Mr. Disney: (cont.)	majority that was on the outside, and all the other unions ignored all the lines because of the set-up of the thing.
Mr. Smith:	What is your personal opinion of the Communist Party, Mr. Disney, as to whether or not it is a political party?
Mr. Disney:	Well, I don't believe it is a political party. I believe it is an un-American thing. The thing that I resent the most is that they are able to get into these unions, take them over, and represent to the world that a group of people that are in my plant, that I know are good, 100-percent Americans, are trapped by this group, and they are represented to the world as supporting all of those ideologies, and it is not so, and I feel that they really ought to be smoked out and shown up for what they are, so that all of the good, free causes in this country, all the liberalisms that really are American, can go out without the taint of communism. That is my sincere feeling on it.
Mr. Smith:	Do you feel that there is a threat of communism in the motion-picture industry?
Mr. Disney:	Yes, there is, and there are many reasons why they would like to take it over or get in and control it, or disrupt it, but I don't think they have gotten very far, and I think the industry is made up of good Americans, just like in my plant, good, solid Americans. My boys have been fighting it longer than I have. They are trying to get out from under it and they will in time if we can just show them up.
Mr. Smith:	There are presently pending before this committee two bills relative to outlawing the Communist Party. What thoughts have you as to whether or not those bills should be passed?
Mr. Disney:	Well, I don't know as I qualify to speak on that. I feel if the thing can be proven un-American that it ought to be outlawed. I think in some way it should be done without interfering with the rights of the people. I think that will be done. I have that faith. Without interfering, I mean, with the good, American rights that we all have now, and we want to preserve.
Mr. Smith:	Have you any suggestions to offer as to how the industry can be helped in fighting this menace?
Mr. Disney:	Well, I think there is a good start toward it. I know that

I have been handicapped out there in fighting it, because they have been hiding behind this labor set-up, they get themselves closely tied up in the labor thing, so that if you try to get rid of them they make a labor case out of it. We must keep the American labor unions clean. We have got to fight for them.

Mr. Smith: That is all of the questions I have, Mr. Chairman.

The Chairman: Mr. Vail.

Mr. Vail: No questions.

The Chairman: Mr. McDowell.

Mr. McDowell: No questions.

Mr. Disney: Sir?

Mr. McDowell. I have no questions. You have been a good witness.

Mr. Disney: Thank you.

The Chairman: Mr. Disney, you are the fourth producer we have had as a witness, and each one of those four producers said, generally speaking, the same thing, and that is that the Communists have made inroads, have attempted inroads. I just want to point that out because there seems to be a very strong unanimity among the producers that have testified before us. In addition to producers, we have had actors and writers testify to the same. There is no doubt but what the movies are probably the greatest medium for entertainment in the United States and in the world. I think you, as a creator of entertainment, probably are one of the greatest examples in the profession. I want to congratulate you on the form of entertainment which you have given the American people and given the world and congratulate you for taking time out to come here and testify, before this committee. He has been very helpful.

Do you have any more questions, Mr. Stripling?

Mr. Smith: I am sure he does not have any more, Mr. Chairman.

Mr. Stripling: No; I have no more questions.

The Chairman: Thank you very much, Mr. Disney.

11.3 TESTIMONY OF RING LARDNER, JR., U.S. CONGRESS HOUSE UN-AMERICAN ACTIVITIES COMMITTEE, HEARINGS REGARDING THE COMMUNIST INFILTRATION OF THE MOTION PICTURE INDUSTRY

During the 1947 House Un-American Activities Committee investigations of communist infiltration in Hollywood, some "unfriendly witnesses" refused to testify. Known as "the Hollywood Ten," this group of writers, directors, and producers were jailed in contempt of Congress and blacklisted. Below is the testimony of the writer Ring Lardner, Jr., one of the Hollywood Ten, who refused to answer the question: Are you or have you ever been a member of the Communist Party? An investigator for HUAC then testified that he had obtained evidence that, indeed, Lardner was a communist.

Testimony of Ring Lardner, Jr., Accompanied by Counsel, Mr. Kenny and Mr. Crum

Mr. Stripling:	Mr. Lardner, will you please state your full name and present address?
Mr. Lardner:	Ring W. Lardner, Jr., 325 Georgina Avenue, Santa Monica, Calif.
Mr. Stripling:	When and where were you born, Mr. Lardner?
Mr. Lardner:	On August 19, 1915, in Chicago, Ill.
Mr. Stripling:	What is your occupation?
Mr. Lardner:	A writer.
Mr. Stripling:	How long have you been a writer?
Mr. Lardner:	I have been a writer about 10 years.
	Mr. Chairman, I have a short statement I would like to make.
The Chairman:	Have you completed the identification?
Mr. Stripling:	That is sufficient.
	[The witness hands statement to the chairman.]
Mr. Crum:	Have you a copy for Mr. Stripling?
Mr. Lardner:	Yes.
	[The witness hands statement to Mr. Stripling.]
The Chairman:	Mr. Lardner, the committee is unanimous in the fact that after you testify you may read your statement.
Mr. Lardner:	Thank you.
Mr. Stripling:	Mr. Lardner, you are here before the committee in

Screenwriter Ring Lardner and attorney Robert Kenny during their appearance before the House UnAmerican Activities Committee in Washington, D.C., on October 30, 1947. Lardner had won an Academy Award in 1942 and by 1947 was one of Hollywood's highest paid screenwriters. Known for his left-wing political associations, HUAC called Lardner as a witness during its investigations of communism in Hollywood. Lardner, like nine other directors and screenwriters, refused to answer questions and was found guilty of contempt of Congress. Lardner was sentenced to twelve months in prison, fired by Fox, and blacklisted by the studios. AP Photo/Byron Rollins.

	response to a subpena served upon you on September 22; is that correct?
Mr. Lardner:	Yes.
Mr. Stripling:	Mr. Lardner, are you a member of the Screen Writers Guild?
Mr. Lardner:	Mr. Stripling, I want to be cooperative about this, but there are certain limits to my cooperation. I don't want to help you divide or smash this particular guild, or to infiltrate the motion-picture business in any way for the purpose which seems to me to be to try to control that business, to control what the American people can see and hear in their motion-picture theaters.

The Chairman:	Now, Mr. Lardner, don't do like the others, if I were you, or you will never read your statement. I would suggest—
Mr. Lardner:	Mr. Chairman, let me—
The Chairman:	You be responsive to the question.
Mr. Lardner:	I am—
The Chairman:	The question is, and I will ask it; I will repeat the question.
Mr. Lardner:	All right.
The Chairman:	The question is: Are you a member of the Screen Writers Guild?
Mr. Lardner:	But I understood you to say that I would be permitted to read the statement, Mr. Chairman.
The Chairman:	Yes; after you are finished with the questions and answers—
Mr. Lardner:	Yes.
The Chairman:	But you certainly haven't answered the questions.
Mr. Lardner:	Well, I am going to answer the questions but I don't think you qualified in any way your statement that I would be allowed to read this statement.
The Chairman:	Then I will qualify it now. If you refuse to answer the questions then you will not read your statement.
Mr. Lardner:	Well, I know that is an indirect way of saying you don't want me to read the statement.
The Chairman:	Then you know right now you are not going to answer the question; is that correct?
Mr. Lardner:	No; I am going to answer the question.
The Chairman:	All right, then; answer that question.
Mr. Lardner:	All right, sir. I think these points I am bringing out are relevant to the question because I have to consider why the question is asked—
The Chairman:	We will determine why the question was asked. We want to know whether you are a member of the Screen Writers Guild.
Mr. Lardner:	Yes—
The Chairman:	That is a very simple question. You can answer that "yes" or "no." You don't have to go into a long harangue or speech. If you want to make a speech you know where you can go out there.
Mr. Lardner:	Well, I am not very good in haranguing, and I won't try it, but it seems to me that if you can make me answer

	this question, tomorrow you could ask somebody whether he believed in spiritualism.
The Chairman:	Oh no; there is no chance of our asking anyone whether they believe in spiritualism, and you know it. That is just plain silly.
Mr. Lardner:	You might—
The Chairman:	Now, you haven't learned your lines very well.
Mr. Lardner:	Well—
The Chairman:	I want to know whether you can answer the question "yes" or "no."
Mr. Lardner:	If you did, for instance, ask somebody about that you might ask him—
The Chairman:	Well, now, never mind what we might ask him. We are asking you now. Are you a member of the Screen Writers Guild?
Mr. Lardner:	But—
The Chairman:	You are an American—
Mr. Lardner:	But that is a question—
The Chairman:	And Americans should not be afraid to answer that.
Mr. Lardner:	Yes; but I am also concerned as an American with the question of whether this committee has the right to ask me—
The Chairman:	Well, we have got the right and until you prove that we haven't got the right then, you have to answer that question.
Mr. Lardner:	As I said, if you ask somebody, say, about spiritualism—
The Chairman:	You are a witness, aren't you? Aren't you a witness?
Mr. Lardner:	Mr. Chairman—
The Chairman:	Aren't you a witness here?
Mr. Lardner:	Yes: I am.
The Chairman:	All right, then a congressional committee is asking you: Are you a member of the Screen Writers Guild? Now you answer it "yes" or "no."
Mr. Lardner:	Well, I am saying that in order to answer that—
The Chairman:	All right, put the next question. Go to the $64 question.
The Witness:	I haven't—
The Chairman:	Go to the next question.
Mr. Stripling:	Mr. Lardner, are you now or have you ever been a member of the Communist Party?
Mr. Lardner:	Well, I would like to answer that question, too.

Mr. Stripling: Mr. Lardner, the charge has been made before this committee that the Screen Writers Guild which, according to the record, you are a member of, whether you admit it or not, has a number of individuals in it who are members of the Communist Party. This committee is seeking to determine the extent of Communist infiltration in the Screen Writers Guild and in other guilds within the motion-picture industry.

Mr. Lardner: Yes.

Mr. Stripling: And certainly the question of whether or not you are a member of the Communist Party is very pertinent. Now, are you a member or have you ever been a member of the Communist Party?

Mr. Lardner: It seems to me you are trying to discredit the Screen Writers Guild through me and the motion-picture industry through the Screen Writers Guild and our whole practice of freedom of expression.

Mr. Stripling: If you and others are members of the Communist Party you are the ones who are discrediting the Screen Writers Guild.

Mr. Lardner: I am trying to answer the question by stating first what I feel about the purpose of the question which, as I say, is to discredit the whole motion-picture industry.

The Chairman: You won't say anything first. You are refusing to answer this question.

Mr. Lardner: I am saying my understanding is as an American resident—

The Chairman: Never mind your understanding. There is a question: Are you or have you ever been a member of the Communist Party?

Mr. Lardner: I could answer exactly the way you want, Mr. Chairman—

The Chairman: No—

Mr. Lardner [continuing]: But I think that is a—

The Chairman: It is not a question of our wanting you to answer that. It is a very simple question. Anybody would be proud to answer it—any real American would be proud to answer the question, "Are you or have you ever been a member of the Communist Party"—any real American.

Mr. Lardner: It depends on the circumstances. I could answer it, but if I did I would hate myself in the morning.

The Chairman:	Leave the witness chair.
Mr. Lardner:	It was a question that would—
The Chairman:	Leave the witness chair.
Mr. Lardner:	Because it is a question—
The Chairman [pounding gavel]:	Leave the witness chair.
Mr. Lardner:	I think I am leaving by force.
The Chairman:	Sergeant, take the witness away.
	[Applause.]
The Chairman:	Mr. Stripling, next witness.
Mr. Stripling:	Mr. Russell, will you take the stand, please?

Testimony of Louis J. Russell

Mr. Stripling:	Mr. Russell, you are an investigator for the Committee on Un-American Activities?
Mr. Russell:	I am, sir.
Mr. Stripling:	You have previously been sworn in this hearing?
Mr. Russell:	I have.
Mr. Stripling:	You were detailed to make an investigation to determine whether or not Ring Lardner, Jr., was ever a member of the Communist Party?
Mr. Russell:	I was.
Mr. Stripling:	Will you give the committee the benefit of your investigation?
Mr. Russell:	During the course of my investigation I obtained information regarding the Communist Party registration card of Ring Lardner, Jr. This card bears the number 47180. It is made out in the name of Ring L., which, during the course of the investigation, developed to be the name of Ring Lardner, Jr., as contained on his Communist Party registration card.

This card contains a notation: "1944 Card No. 46806."

The address of Ring Lardner is given as 447 Loring, L-o-r-i-n-g; city, Los Angeles; county, Los Angeles; State, California.

The card contains a notation, "New card issued on November 30, 1944."

The description of Ring Lardner as contained on the card is as follows: "Male; occupation, writer; industry, M. picture." |

Mr. Russell: (cont.)	The question is then asked: "Member of CIO. A. F. of L., independent union, no union"? "Independent union" is checked.
	Another question asked is: "Is member club subscriber for Daily Worker"? The answer, "Yes" is checked.
Mr. Stripling:	That is all, Mr. Russell.
	Mr. Chairman, the committee has prepared a memorandum concerning the Communist affiliations of Ring Lardner, Jr.

According to the International Motion Picture Almanac and other sources, Ring Lardner, Jr., has written the following films: Meet Dr. Christian, RKO, 1939; The Courageous Dr. Christian, RKO, 1940; Arkansas Judge, Republic, 1941; Woman of the Year, MGM, 1942; The Cross of Lorraine, MGM, 1944; Tomorrow the World, United Artists, 1944; Cloak and Dagger, Warner Bros., 1946.

The files, records, and publications of the Committee on Un-American Activities contain the following information concerning the Communist-front affiliations of Ring Lardner, Jr.:

1. Under date of August 22, 1946, the Hollywood Reporter, a publication in Los Angeles, Calif., carried an editorial headed "More Red Commissars?" This editorial is quoted, in part, as follows:

Now let us take a look at another member of the Screen Writers Guild's executive board—Ring Lardner, Jr. As chairman of the Guild's powerful original materials committee Lardner incubated and sponsored the James M. Cain plan for literary dictatorship through the so-called American Authors Authority.

The Reporter has this to ask Ring Lardner, Jr.: "Are you a member of the Communist Party? Are you at present assigned to the Party's Northwest (propaganda) section? Do you hold Party Book No. 25109?" The article continues: "Lardner has a long record of activity in Communist front organizations. The March 1937 issue of The Western Worker listed him as one of the signers of an open letter which denounced the demands of the American Committee for the Defense of Trotsky for an investigation of the Russian "purge" trials. This letter contended that such an investigation would constitute political interference in the internal affairs of the Soviet Union.

Lardner and his fellow signers at that time were acting in accordance with the directives of the Stalin dictatorship which was attempting to silence the Communist faction that was loyal to Trotsky. Trotsky later was murdered in Mexico by an assassin who allegedly was a member of the Communist Party.

Mr. Chairman, this memorandum continues for 4 pages, listing 12 separate affiliations of Mr. Lardner.

The Chairman:	We would like to have it read.
Mr. Stripling:	Have it read?
The Chairman:	Yes.
Mr. Stripling:	Would it be all right if Mr. Gaston reads it?
The Chairman:	Yes.

Mr. Gaston [reading]:

In 1941 Lardner resigned his official position in the Screen Writers Guild, after James K. McGuinness and Howard Emmett Rogers had conducted a vigorous campaign against the Communist activities of that organization. But this was only a temporary retreat made necessary by the searchlight which Mr. McGuinness and Mr. Rogers had turned on the Guild's leadership. At present, Lardner in addition to being chairman of the original materials committee, is a member of the editorial committee, which is responsible for the editorial policies of the Guild's magazine.

In 1942, Lardner was on the editorial board of Communique, published by the Hollywood Writers Mobilization, a Communist-front organization, and a member of the mobilization's minority committee, a smaller group also actively engaged in party line work.

2. The American Youth for Democracy is the new name for the Young Communist League. The Committee on Un-American Activities, in its report of April 17, 1947, called upon the governors or legislatures of the various States and the administrative heads of the colleges and universities "to thoroughly expose the Communist connections of the American Youth for Democracy, as, well as the inimical objectives of the Communist Party in America." The American Youth for Democracy was also cited as a Communist front by the Special Committee on Un-American Activities in the report on March 29, 1944. The People's World of December 1, 1944, reveals that Ring Lardner, Jr., was a

Mr. Gaston:
(cont.)

sponsor of the American Youth for Democracy. The People's World is the organ of the Communist Party on the west coast.

People's World, on August 17, 1944, contained an article setting forth the winners in a contest sponsored by the American Youth for Democracy. This was a letter-writing contest held in connection with a play entitled "Tomorrow the World," and had for its theme Why Democracy Is Better Than Fascism. The article announced that judges for the contest were Ring Lardner, Jr., Franklin Fearing, William O. Oliver, Rev. J. Raymond Henderson, and Mayer Friedon. It should be noted that this was during the period when Russia was our ally.

The American Youth for Democracy, room 701, 542 South Broadway, Los Angeles, Calif., published a pamphlet setting forth the work for the American Youth for Democracy. This pamphlet listed a committee which would sponsor the American Youth for Democracy first anniversary dinner in Los Angeles in November 1944. Among those listed as sponsors were Ring Lardner, Jr., John Howard Lawson, Mrs. Charlotta A. Bass, Mrs. Dalton Trumbo, and Edward Dmytryk.

3. George Dimitroff, the former general secretary of the Communist International, was honored by a declaration issued by the Reichstag Fire Trial Anniversary Committee. According to the New York Times of December 22, 1943, page 40, Ring Lardner, Jr., was a signer of this declaration which paid honor to Dimitroff. The Reichstag Fire Trial Anniversary Committee was cited as a Communist front by the Special Committee on Un-American Activities in the report of March 29, 1944.

4. The California Action Conference for Civil Rights was cited by the California Joint Fact-Finding Committee as being "Communist inspired and dominated." The People's Daily World of September 27, 1941, lists Ring Lardner, Jr., as a sponsor of the California Action Conference for Civil Rights.

In the spring of 1946, the Civil Rights Congress, 205 East Forty-second Street, New York City, issued a pamphlet entitled "Urgent Summons to a Congress on Civil Rights." This pamphlet called upon civil rights, labor, religions, racial, and other organizations and individuals to attend a Congress on Civil Rights in Detroit on April 27–28, 1946, to formulate and agree upon a national program to defeat the offensive and reactionary and Fascist forces and to assure the maximum unification of effort to advance that program. The summons contained a partial list of sponsors. This list included the name of Ring W. Lardner, Jr.

The Civil Rights Congress is the successor to the International Labor Defense legal arm of the Communist Party.

5. The American Friends of Spanish Democracy and the Veterans of the Abraham Lincoln Brigade were a part of the Communist Party program, to provide aid and assistance to the Spanish Loyalists in response to instructions received from the Communist International at the Seventh Communist International Congress held in 1935 in Moscow. The American Friends of Spanish Democracy was cited as a Communist front by The Special Committee on Un-American Activities in the report of March 29, 1944, and by the Committee on Un-American Activities in the reports of June 12, 1947, and September 2, 1947. The Daily Worker of April 8, 1939, page 4, states that Ring Lardner, Jr., was affiliated with this organization as a signer of a petition to lift the arms embargo which the American Friends of Spanish Democracy sponsored. His affiliation with the Veterans of the Abraham Lincoln Brigade is shown by the New Masses of April 2, 1940, page 21, which lists him as a signer of a letter which that organization sent to the President of the United States. The Veterans of the Abraham Lincoln Brigade was cited as a Communist front by the Special Committee on Un-American Activities in the report of March 29, 1944, and as "under Communist control" by Professor John Dewey, chairman of the Committee for Cultural Freedom, April 1940.

6. The League of American Writers was affiliated with the International Union of Revolutionary Writers, with headquarters in Moscow, and has been pledged to the defense of the Soviet Union and the "Use of art as an instrument of the class struggle." The Special Committee on Un-American Activities cited it as a Communist front in the reports of January 3, 1940, June 25, 1942, and March 29, 1944. It was also cited by former Attorney General Francis Biddle in these words: "The overt activities of the League of American Writers in the last 2 years leave little doubt of its Communist control." (Congressional Record, September 24, 1942, page 7686). Ring Lardner, Jr., according to the Daily Worker of September 14, 1942, page 7, and People's World of September 23, 1942, page 5, was a signer of a statement of the League of American Writers on behalf of a second front. He

Mr. Gaston:
(cont.)

was also affiliated with the Hollywood chapter of the League of American Writers as a signer of the cable sent to Leon Blum, President Roosevelt, and Secretary Hull for supplies to Loyalist Spain, as shown by the New Masses of March 29, 1938, page 21.

7. The Writers Congress was sponsored by the Hollywood Writers Mobilization which is the successor to the Hollywood branch of the League of American Writers. The program of the Writers Congress, 1943, lists Ring Lardner, Jr., as the chairman of the panel on minority groups.

8. The Open Letter to American Liberals was a denunciation of the efforts made to defend Leon Trotsky and a reaffirmation of faith in the Soviet Union. It also defended the Moscow trials which were characterized by forced confessions and were staged as political demonstrations rather than trials, in our sense of the term. The Open Letter to American Liberals, of which Ring Lardner, Jr., was a signer, according to Soviet Russia Today, March 1937, pages 14 and 15 was cited as a Communist-front project by the Special Committee on Un-American Activities in the report of June 25, 1942. Soviet Russia Today was formerly the publication of the Friends of the Soviet Union and has been cited as a Communist-front publication by the Special Committee on Un-American Activities on June 25, 1942, and March 29, 1944, and by the Committee on Un-American Activities on June 12, 1947, and September 2, 1947.

9. The Progressive Citizens of America has been described as an "allegedly liberal organization which believes in cooperating with Communists" by the Committee on Un-American Activities in its report of June 12, 1947. It was formed by the pro-Communist group of the Independent Citizens Committee of the Arts, Sciences, and Professions which dissolved because of the issue of communism. According to the Daily Worker of May 16, 1947, page 11, a manuscript by Ring Lardner, Jr., was sold at auction for the benefit of the literature division of the Progressive Citizens of America.

10. According to the Daily Worker of March 31, 1947, page 11, Ring Lardner. Jr., collaborated with John Hubley and Phil Eastman in the writing of the screen version of the Brotherhood of Man, an animated color cartoon produced in United Productions of America for the Auto Workers Union. This film was based on the pamphlet, The Races of Mankind, coauthored by Ruth Benedict and Gene Weltfish, which the

War Department banned. Gene Weltfish heads the Congress of American Women which is the American affiliate of the Women's International Democratic Federation. One of the agencies through which the Brotherhood of Man can be booked is the International Workers Order film division. The International Workers Order was cited by Attorney General Francis Biddle as "One of the strongest Communist organizations" (Congressional Record, September 24, 1942, page 7688), and as a Communist front by the Special Committee on Un-American Activities in the reports of January 3, 1940, and June 25, 1942.

11. The Artists' Front to Win the War, which was cited as a Communist front by the Special Committee on Un-American Activities in the report of March 29, 1944, supported the then current Communist demand for a second front. Sponsors of the organization included many writers for the Communist press who had opposed the war during the Stalin-Hitler pact such as Alvah Bessle, Angelo Herndon, Alfred Kreymborg, Albert Maltz, Ruth McKenney, and Dalton Trumbo. The program of the Artists Front to Win the War, October 16, 1942, page 5, lists Ring Lardner, Jr., as a sponsor.

12. The Voice of Freedom Committee, according to PM of May 19, 1947, page 19, was formed by Dorothy Parker, whose record of affiliation with Communist-front organizations is set forth in a separate report. According to a news release of the organization, dated June 16, 1947, Langston Hughes, Paul Robeson, and Donald Ogden Stewart, all of whom have lengthy records of Communist-front affiliations, are sponsors of the Voice of Freedom Committee, whose function is the support of commentators who have received the acclaim of the Communist press. Ring Lardner, Jr., is listed by a leaflet of the organization as a signer of a petition which the Voice of Freedom Committee sponsored.

The Chairman: Mr. Stripling, the next witness.

11.4 THE WALDORF DECLARATION, 1947

In an effort to distance the movie industry from the Hollywood Ten and to prevent future investigations, the studios adopted the Waldorf Declaration in 1947.

Printed below, this pledge led to a blacklist of any actors, writers, or directors associated with communism, and remained in place until the early 1960s.

Members of the Association of Motion Picture Producers deplore the action of the ten Hollywood men who have been cited for contempt. We do not desire to prejudge their legal rights, but their actions have been a disservice to their employers and have impaired their usefulness to the industry.

We will forthwith discharge or suspend without compensation those in our employ and we will not re-employ any of the ten until such time as he is acquitted or has purged himself of contempt and declares under oath that he is not a Communist.

On the broader issues of alleged subversive and disloyal elements in Hollywood, our members are likewise prepared to take positive action.

We will not knowingly employ a Communist or a member of any party or group which advocates the overthrow of the Government of the United States by force or by illegal or unconstitutional methods. In pursuing this policy, we are not going to be swayed by hysteria or intimidation from any source. We are frank to recognize that such a policy involves dangers and risks. There is the danger of hurting innocent people. There is the risk of creating an atmosphere of fear. Creative work at its best cannot be carried on in an atmosphere of fear. We will guard against this danger, this risk, this fear. To this end we will invite the Hollywood talent guilds to work with us to eliminate any subversives, to protect the innocent, and to safeguard free speech and a free screen wherever threatened.

CHAPTER 12

Good Morning, Vietnam: The Vietnam War

12.1   JOHN WAYNE

John Wayne was one of several Hollywood actors, including Charlton Heston, Jimmy Stewart, Bob Hope, Sammy Davis, Jr., and Jane Fonda, to make multiple visits to Vietnam during the war. In this picture, he is signing Private First Class Fonsell Wofford's helmet during his visit to the 3rd Batallion, 7th Marines, at Chu Lai in June 1966. Earlier that year, Wayne had begun his plans for making *The Green Berets*, the only pro-intervention film to be made by Hollywood during the Vietnam War.

12.2 TRANSCRIPT OF JANE FONDA'S RADIO HANOI BROADCAST, U.S. CONGRESS HOUSE COMMITTEE ON INTERNAL SECURITY, TRAVEL TO HOSTILE AREAS, SEPTEMBER, 1972 [EXCERPT]

Although the actor John Wayne's visits to Vietnam led him to support American intervention there, the actress Jane Fonda came to the opposite conclusion and publicly condemned the war. By far the most controversial of her actions was her decision to broadcast her views from a radio station in Hanoi, North Vietnam. Not only did these speeches earn her the long-lasting enmity of many Vietnam War soldiers and veterans, but she also won the attention of Congress, which held hearings to investigate the travel of American citizens to "hostile areas." Excerpts from these hearings detail Fonda's movements in North Vietnam and her remarks to U.S. servicemen and pilots and to the Army of the Republic of Vietnam (the South Vietnamese) soldiers.

Re Activities of Jane Fonda in North Vietnam

(Mr. Ichord asked and was given permission to address the House for 1 minute, to revise and extend his remarks and include extraneous matter.)

Mr. Ichord. Mr. Speaker, late last week the Committee on Internal Security discussed, at some length, the question of whether or not to issue a subpena to the actress, Jane Fonda, with respect to broadcast statements she made over the Communist Radio Hanoi to our troops in Vietnam.

It was agreed by the committee that it would be best, at this time, to give the Justice Department time to complete its announced inquiry into the Fonda affair before considering any further course by the committee.

At the request of my colleagues on the committee, I addressed a letter which was hand-delivered Friday afternoon to Attorney General Kleindienst setting forth the committee's concern with this matter and our desire to have a report from the Justice Department by September 14 or an explanation from a representative of the Department on that date regarding what can and should be done with respect to Miss Fonda's activities in the capital of our enemy.

For the benefit of my colleagues in the House, Mr. Speaker, I include the contents of my letter to the Attorney General in the Record at this point:

Congress of the United States, House of Representatives,
Committee on Internal Security,
Washington, D.C., August 10, 1972,
Hon. Richard G. Kleindienst,
Attorney General of the United States, Department of Justice,
Washington, D.C.

Dear Mr. Attorney General: The Committee on Internal Security met this morning in executive session to consider a request that a subpoena be issued to require Jane Fonda to appear before the Committee in regard to her travel to North Vietnam and radio broadcasts to U.S. military forces during July 1972. During the meeting a number of reasons were expressed as a basis for opposition to the issuance of a subpoena. Important factors in the ultimate determination of the Committee were that the facts seemed to be already rather well-known, that the matter was under study by the Department of Justice and Fonda would be entitled to the full protection of the Fifth Amendment, that any such hearing might work to the prejudice of the Government in the event prosecution is undertaken and that the Committee's overriding interest is not in what additional information might be secured from Fonda, but rather in any insufficiency in the terms of the law or in its enforcement.

I am sure that you recognize the pernicious nature of Miss Fonda's statements to our servicemen, and the seriousness with which nearly all Members of Congress view her conduct. Although it might be fairly said that public support for American involvement in the Vietnam conflict is steadily declining, such aid and comfort to a nation with which we are engaged in hostilities is nevertheless condemned by the public. But whatever political or public reaction might obtain under the circumstances, I am sure you agree that the Department of Justice has a most solemn obligation to engage the full weight of the law against conduct which the Congress has made criminally punishable.

The Committee has reviewed the treason, sedition and other relevant statutes. It has also been informed of Fonda's travel itinerary, and has studied the transcripts of her broadcasts while recently in Hanoi. It is not difficult to perceive why a cry of treason has been raised. But if the burden of proof is too great for treason, would not a prima facie case exist under Section 2387 of Title 18, United States Code or even Section 2388, notwithstanding the jurisdictional limitation?

In discharging its responsibility to the Congress to insure that statutes within its oversight jurisdiction are being duly enforced by the Executive Branch, the Committee resolved that the staff investigation of

Fonda's activities will continue, and in the event the Justice Department determines that the broadcasts of Jane Fonda from Hanoi during July 1972 do not constitute treason or sedition, or that her conduct cannot be reached by existing statute for any other reason, then the Department is requested to furnish a report to the Committee with recommendations for legislation which would be effective to impose criminal sanctions under similar circumstances in the future. Desiring to resolve the questions at an early date, but hoping to avoid an unreasonable burden upon the Department, the Committee voted to request that the report be submitted by September 14, or in the alternative, that a representative of the Department appear before the Committee on that date.

Your cooperation and assistance in providing an analysis of the federal criminal law vis-a-vis the recent conduct of Jane Fonda will indeed be appreciated. Would you please advise me as soon as possible whether the Department will furnish a report on or before the above date or will provide for the appearance of a representative so that arrangements can be made for a meeting of the Committee.

Sincerely,
Richard H. Ichord, Chairman

Bill to Restrict Travel to Countries Engaged in Armed Conflict with the United States

(Mr. Ichord asked and was given permission to address the House for 1 minute and to revise and extend his remarks and include extraneous matter.)

Mr. Ichord. Mr. Speaker, in July of this year the actress Jane Fonda traveled to North Vietnam. She did so without a passport validated for travel to that country, without informing the State Department of her intention to travel to North Vietnam after first going to Russia, and without seeking any official authorization for the trip. Her actions, of course, were not the first we have witnessed in this vein. North Vietnam seems to be becoming a popular destination. It certainly is a means for guaranteeing publicity for the junketeer. These journeys to North Vietnam have been for a variety of purposes. The most recent ones have served to spread the enemy propaganda about dike bombing, they have aided the enemy's design in releasing prisoners of war in a dribble, they have falsely publicized the kind of treatments being afforded to the prisoners of war, and they have endeavored to sap the will and morale of our servicemen in Southeast Asia. Jane Fonda, serving as a tool of the Hanoi propagandists, made more than 20 broadcasts to American troops. Her statements are of a most pernicious nature. In my judgment they were clearly designed to engender doubts in the minds of our servicemen concerning their loyalty to the United States and their willingness to carry out military orders. This is the stuff of which sedition is made.

Over Radio Hanoi, directing her remarks to American servicemen, Jane Fonda said for example:

> Please think of what you are doing—have you any idea what your bombs are doing when you pull the levers and push the buttons?—how does it feel to be used as pawns?—tonight when you are alone ask yourselves: what are you doing? Accept no ready answers fed to you by rote from basic training—I know that if you saw and if you knew the Vietnamese under peaceful conditions, you would hate the men who are sending you on bombing missions—if they told you the truth, you wouldn't fight, you wouldn't kill—you have been told lies so that it would be possible for you to kill.

It would require a gross distortion of logic to conclude that these statements were not intended to create doubt in the mind of the listener. Is it not obvious that these remarks were intended to serve as a stimulus for diminished morale and loyalty, or for refusal of duty? It was the purpose of the sedition statute to prohibit such conduct. Regardless of how we may feel about the war in Indochina, we must not sanction efforts to destroy the morale and discipline of our troops.

. . .

In considering the applicability of the treason or sedition statutes to activities of U.S. citizens within North Vietnam it does not take a great deal of imagination to recognize that witnesses are not readily available to prove the conduct in a court of law. If we can generally agree that the activities of U.S. citizens in North Vietnam have been overwhelmingly adverse to our national interests, then the solution is to simplify the evidentiary requirements by making unlawful all travel to countries with which we are engaged in armed conflict, except insofar as deemed necessary by the President in the national interest.

In analyzing the Fonda broadcasts, as well as the activities of others who preceded her, it has appeared to me that a new statute is needed which would authorize the President to restrict travel to countries whose military forces are engaged in armed conflict with ours. The President would be empowered to make exceptions in the national interest, but all other travel to such countries would be unlawful. I think it is fair to say that the general attitude of the committee's witnesses is supportive of this legislation.

In introducing this bill today, the text of which follows, I am joined by 5 other Members of the Committee on Internal Security, Mr. Ashbrook, Mr. Davis, Mr. Thompson, Mr. Zion and Mr. Schmitz.

Mr. Speaker, I feel very strongly that Miss Fonda violated the criminal laws of the United States when she travelled to North Vietnam and made the foregoing propaganda broadcasts to American troops. I also feel very strongly that she will never be prosecuted by the Department of Justice. However, I cannot fault the Department of Justice altogether. There are very serious evidentiary difficulties as well as the consideration that prosecution will result in making a martyr out of a person who does not deserve to be a martyr and also the probability of projecting a trial into the political arena much like the Chicago Seven conspiracy trial.

Therefore I firmly believe that the only way to obviate the controversy that has raged over the heads of Fonda, Ramsey Clark and others is to effectively forbid travel by any American citizen to a country with which the United States is having hostilities without prior permission.

I have no doubt about the constitutionality of the measure. It is constitutional. I can think of no legitimate reason why any American citizen should be permitted to travel to a hostile country without proper authorization. This measure represents one of the many realistic choices that this free society must begin to make between freedom and anarchy and license if we are to remain a free society.

A Bill to Amend Section 4 of the Internal Security Act of 1950

Be it enacted by the Senate and House of Representatives of the United States of America in Congress assembled, That (a) section 4 of the Internal Security Act of 1950 (50 U.S.C. 763) is amended by adding immediately following subsection (c) of such section the following new subsection:

"(d) The President may restrict travel by citizens and nationals of the United States to, in, or through any country or area whose military forces are engaged in armed conflict with the military forces of the United States. Such restriction shall be announced by public notice which shall be published in the Federal Register. Travel to such restricted country or area by any person may be authorized by the President when he deems such travel to be in the national interest. It shall be unlawful for any citizen or national of the United States willfully and without such authorization to travel to, in, or through any country or area to which travel is restricted pursuant to this subsection."

(b) Section 4 of such Act is further amended by redesignating existing subsections (c) through (f), as (d) through (g).

July Travel Itinerary of Jane Fonda

From various descriptions of her visit in the media, along with her own statements at press conferences held in Hanoi (July 20), Paris (July 25), and New York (July 27), it is possible to describe an approximate sequence to Fonda's activities between July 8 and 22:

July 8   – Arrival in Hanoi.

July 9/11 – Visit to Hanoi "War Museum" (containing alleged specimens of U.S. fragmentation and alleged "chemical" bombs) and Bach Mai (suburb of Hanoi which also reportedly has a jet fighter field) to view alleged bomb damage to the hospital there.

July 12   – Visits to Nam Sach District ("60 kilometers east of Hanoi") and Hong Phong Village to view bomb damage to dikes and populated areas.

July 13/16 – Unknown activities, but Fonda later claimed to have "traveled hundreds of miles throughout the bombed regions" in the days preceding her Hanoi press interview of July 19 with Jean Thoraval (a French AFP reporter who with several other Western correspondents, has promoted allegations that the U.S. is deliberately bombing the dikes and areas with non-military targets).

July 14   – First taped Fonda broadcast to GIs via Radio Hanoi.

July 17/18 – Visits Nam Dinh district, described as a main textile center of North Vietnam, to observe alleged bomb damage to "non-military" targets.

July 17   – Second broadcast to GIs via Radio Hanoi in which she described previous visits to Bach Mai Hospital and Hanoi War Museum.

July 18   – Interview with captured U. S. Airmen in Hanoi.

July 19   – Interview with AFP correspondent Jean Thoraval (cf. above) which is mainly an anti-U.S. denunciation of the war and, conversely, a propaganda piece to stress the "determination" of the North Vietnamese to resist.

Fonda added that she was forced to take refuge at a road-side shelter during a U.S. raid of July 18.

July 19 – Third broadcast to GIs via Hanoi Radio.

July 20 – Press Conference at "Hanoi International Club" where she described her visits to the countryside since July 8, her earlier meeting with U. S. PWs and concluded with her usual anti- U.S. diatribe.

July 20 – Radio Hanoi broadcast, described as a Vietnamese translation of a Fonda statement, on the North Vietnamese "liberation" of Quang Tri Province and how the ARVN counteroffensive was doomed to failure; fourth broadcast to GIs explaining U.S.-SVN violations of the Geneva Accords of 1954.

July 21 – Fifth and sixth broadcasts to GIs, both aimed at U.S. fliers, on alleged war crimes and veiled suggestions to refuse to fly further combat missions.

July 21 – Fonda meets with North Vietnamese Nguyen Duy Trinh where she claimed to have "witnessed U.S. crimes in Hanoi . . . Hai Hung, Ha Tay and Nam Ha provinces" and expressed thanks to him for distinguishing between "U.S. imperialists" and "The American people who are friends of the Vietnamese people in the struggle for peace and democracy." Fonda also told the Vice Premier that "she was convinced that under the wise leadership of the Vietnam Workers Party and the DRV Government the Vietnamese people will certainly win brilliant victory."

July 21 – Fonda broadcast to "the Vietnamese People."

July 22 – Fonda departed Hanoi. "Seeing her off at the airport," a Radio Hanoi broadcast noted, "were members of the Vietnam Committee of Solidarity with the American People and the Vietnamese Film Artistes Association"; stopped at Vientiane, "escorted by a French photographer."

July 23 – Arrives in Paris via Moscow on Aeroflot flight; delayed tape broadcast to "South Vietnamese Youth" on alleged repressions of the Thieu government and the VC struggle against it.

July 24 – Seventh Radio Hanoi broadcast to GIs (noted as having been recorded July 16, 1972).

July 25 – Press Conference in Paris.

July 27 – Arrival in New York.

July 28 – New York Press Conference. Basically the same rhetoric as the Paris press meeting.

July 28 – Eighth broadcast to GIs (delayed tape ca. July 18–19).

July 29 – Delayed tape (in English) to "Saigon Soldiers." (In English to ARVN? Also meant for American ears with respect to desertion?)

July 29 – Arrival in Los Angeles.

July 31 – Attended Los Angeles premiere of "F.T.A." and announces she is "abandoning her career" until after the November election "in order to campaign against the Vietnam War."

Texts of Fonda's Broadcasts to U.S. Servicemen

Report on Jane Fonda's Activities,
Statement on Bombed Dikes
Hanoi VNA in English to Havana
[For Nguyen Duy Phuc,
Correspondent of Voice of Vietnam]

Hanoi—Visiting American actress Jane Fonda July 12 went to see the dikes bombed by American planes the day before in Nam Sach district, Hai Hung Province. She noted that in the area she visited, it was easy to see that there are no military targets, there is no important highway, there is no communication network and there is no heavy industry. In her assessment, the U.S. has made deliberate attacks on dikes to jeopardise life and terrorise the people.

Later she visited Hong Phong village, remote locality far from major communication lines and industrial centres. On July 11, at daybreak when the villagers were about to begin farm work, U.S. war planes raced in and wantonly bombed a hamlet in the village. Many houses were blasted, fruit trees mangled and household furniture was seriously damaged. Two old persons were killed and many others wounded.

Jane Fonda felt great indignation at this U.S. attack on civilian populations. In the past few days, she had contacts with many workers, peasants and intellectuals to gather information. She called on the special representation of the RSV in Hanoi, had conversations with a number of fighters, artists and victimized people coming from South Vietnam. She was cordially received by Nguyen Phu Soai, acting head of the special representation.

Statement by Jane Fonda, After Visiting Dikes and Dams at Nam Sach
Hit by U.S. Aircraft

. . .

Yesterday morning, I went to the district of Nam Sach to see the
damage that has been done to the dikes in that district, and I wondered
what has been going on with the hands of those who are pulling the lever
and dropping the bombs on the fields and on the dikes of the Red River
Delta. Do you know, for example, that for centuries since the middle ages,
the Vietnamese peasants have built up and reinforced a great complex
network of dikes which hold back the torrential water of the rivers flowing down from the mountains in summer during the monsoon seasons?
Without these dikes 15 million people's lives would be endangered, and
would die by drowning and by starvation. Anthony Lewis from the *New
York Times* wrote an article just before I left the U.S. in which he said
that successive U.S. administrations had rejected the idea of bombing the
dikes in the Red River Delta, because they all felt the dikes are not entirely
military targets and that this was the type of terrorist tactic that is
unworthy of American people and American flags. But today, as you
know better than I, American Phantom jets are bombing strategic points
in the dike networks in this area.

I (?implore) you, I beg you to consider what you are doing. In the area
where I went yesterday it was easy to see that there are no military targets,
there is no important highway, there is no communication network, there
is no heavy industry. These are peasants. They grow rice and they rear pigs.

They are similar to the farmers in the midwest many years ago in the
U.S. Perhaps your grandmothers and grandfathers would not be so different from these peasants. They are happy people, peace-loving people.
When I went by walking on the way to the dikes to see the damage, would
it be made enough I was an American and I was afraid of the reaction
would be taken by the local people. [sentence as received] But they looked
at me curiously and I saw no hostility in their eyes. I looked very carefully.
I thought curiously. I saw the women. They seemed to be asking themselves: What kind of people can Americans be, those who would drop all
kinds of bombs, so carelessly on their innocent heads, destroying their
villages and endangering the lives of these millions of people.

All of you in the cockpits of your planes, on the aircraft carriers, those
who are loading the bombs, those who are repairing the planes, those
who are working on the 7th Fleet, please think what you are doing.

Are these people your enemy? What will you say to your children years
from now who may ask you why you fought the war? What words will
you be able to say to them?

Message to U.S. Pilots
Hanoi in English to Southeast Asia

Now here is a recorded message from actress Jane Fonda to U.S. pilots involved in the Vietnam war: [follows recorded female voice with American accent]

This is Jane Fonda. I have come to North Vietnam to bear witness to the damage being done to the Vietnamese land and to Vietnamese lives.

Just like the Thieu regime in Saigon which is sending its ARVN soldiers recklessly into dangerous positions for fear that it will be replaced by the U.S. Government if it fails to score some strategic military gains, so Nixon is continuing to risk your lives and the lives of the American prisoners of war under the bomb in a last desperate gamble to keep his office come November. How does it feel to be used as pawns? You may be shot down, you may perhaps even be killed, but for what, and for whom?

Eighty percent of the American people, according to a recent poll, have stopped believing in the war and think we should get out, think we should bring all of you home. The people back home are crying for you. We are afraid of what, what must be happening to you as human beings. For it isn't possible to destroy, to receive salary for pushing buttons and pulling levers that are dropping illegal bombs on innocent people, without having that damage your own souls.

Tonight when you are alone, ask yourselves: What are you doing? Accept no ready answers fed to you by rote from basic training on up, but as men, as human beings, can you justify what you are doing? Do you know why you are flying these missions, collecting extra combat pay on Sunday?

The people beneath your planes have done us no harm. They want to live in peace; they want to rebuild their country. They cannot understand what kind of people could fly over their heads and drop bombs on them. Did you know that the antipersonnel bombs that are thrown from some of your planes were outlawed by the Hague Convention of 1907, of which the United States was a signatory? I think that if you knew what these bombs were doing, you would get very angry at the men who invented them. They cannot destroy bridges or factories. They cannot pierce steel or cement. Their only target is unprotected human flesh. The pellet bombs now contain rough-edged plastic pellets and your bosses, whose minds think in terms of statistics not human lives, are proud of this new perfection. The plastic pellets don't show up on X-rays and cannot be removed. The hospitals here are filled with babies and women and old people who will live for the rest of their lives in agony with these pellets embedded in them.

Can we fight this kind of war and continue to call ourselves Americans? Are these people so different from our own children, our mothers, or grandmothers? I don't think so, except that perhaps they have a surer sense of why they are living and for what they are willing to die.

I know that if you saw and if you knew the Vietnamese under peaceful conditions, you would hate the men who are sending you on bombing missions. I believe that in this age of remote-controlled push-button war, we must all try very, very hard to remain human beings. [recording ends]

Hanoi in English to Southeast Asia 1000 GMT 29 Jul 72 B

We now bring you a recorded speech to Saigonese troops by American actress Jane Fonda: [follows a recorded female voice with American accent]

This is Jane Fonda from Hanoi. I'm addressing myself to the ARVN soldiers.

Many people in the United States deplore what is being done to you. We understand that Nixon's aggression against Vietnam is a rascist [sic] aggression, that the American war in Vietnam is a rascist [sic] war, a white man's war—(?which) was very clearly indicated when Ambassador to Saigon Elsworth Bunker described the Vietnamization program as changing the color of the corpses.

We deplore that you are being used as cannon fodder for U.S. imperialism. We've seen photographs of American bombs and antipersonnel weapons being dropped, wantonly, accidentally perhaps, on your heads, on the heads of your comrades. And we note with interest that (?these) kind of accidents don't happen, at least not with as much frequency, to American soldiers, and we think this is an indication of the lack of concern that is being taken for your lives by the white American officers, both in Vietnam and in the Pentagon and in the White House—not to mention the officers in Saigon who have been bought off by the ruling class of the United States.

We've seen photographs of many of you clinging to the helicopters trying to escape from what you knew was a suicide mission. We understand that you have been pressganged, many of you, into the army because your land has been destroyed by American bombs, because there are no other jobs to be had in Saigon, perhaps because you have to support

Actress Jane Fonda and North Vietnamese soldiers and peasants near Hanoi in July 1972. Fonda, seated on an anti-aircraft gun, went there to "encourage" North Vietnamese soldiers fighting against "American Imperialist airraiders." Congress investigated her activities and travels for potential treason, but Fonda was never charged with the crime. AP Photo/Nihon Denpa News.

your family, because you will be the—you will be put in jail and beaten if you tried to avoid the draft.

We well understand the kind of situation that you are put in because American soldiers are in the same kind of situation, and we feel that—that you have much in common. You are being sent to fight a war that is not in your interests but is the interest of the small handful of people who have gotten rich and hope to get richer off this war and off the turning of your country into a neocolony of the United States.

We read with interest about the growing numbers of you who are understanding the truth and joining with your fellow countrymen to fight for freedom and independence and democracy. We note with interest, for example, that as in the case of the 56th Regiment of the 3d Division of the Saigon army, ARVN soldiers are taken into the ranks of the National Liberation Front, including officers who may retain their rank.

We think that this is an example of the fact that the democratic, peace-loving, patriotic Vietnamese people want to embrace all Vietnamese people in forgiveness, open their arms to all people who are willing to fight against the foreign invader.

We know what U.S. imperialism has done to our country in the United States, how it is affecting the working people of the United States and particularly the people of (?courage). And so we know what lies in store for any third world country that could have the misfortune of falling into the hands of a country such as the United States and becoming a colony. [pause]

We all are striving very hard, the peace loving people of the United States, to end this war as soon as possible so that you can all return to your families in the condition of freedom and independence. We understand that the only way to end the war is for the United States to withdraw all its troops, all its airplanes, its bombs, its generals, its CIA advisers and to stop the support of the Thieu regime in Saigon, this man who has defiled not only his own country but the United States. The support of such a criminal is a blight on the American (?society which will take a long time to erase). [recording ends]

You've just listened to a Jane Fonda recorded speech to Saigonese troops.

CHAPTER 13

Follow That Camel: The Iraq War

13.1 PETITION LETTER FROM ARTISTS FOR WINNING WITHOUT WAR, 2003

In 2002, the U.S. invaded Iraq with the goal of overthrowing the president Saddam Hussein, based on his alleged ties to terror organizations and his human-rights abuses. Unconvinced about the need for intervention, many celebrities in Hollywood opposed the invasion. They formed the group Artists for Winning Without War in conjunction with the liberal group MoveOn.org. Over a thousand celebrities signed an open letter to President George W. Bush in which they pledged their patriotism but condemned "a pre-emptive military invasion of Iraq."

To: President Bush
Subject: Artists Say Win Without War

War talk in Washington is alarming and unnecessary.

We are patriotic Americans who share the belief that Saddam Hussein cannot be allowed to possess weapons of mass destruction. We support rigorous UN weapons inspections to assure Iraq's effective disarmament.

However, a pre-emptive military invasion of Iraq will harm American national interests. Such a war will increase human suffering, arouse animosity toward our country, increase the likelihood of terrorist attacks, damage the economy, and undermine our moral standing in the world. It will make us less, not more, secure.

We reject the doctrine—a reversal of long-held American tradition—that our country, alone, has the right to launch first-strike attacks.

The valid U.S. and UN objective of disarming Saddam Hussein can be achieved through legal diplomatic means. There is no need for war. Let us

Actors Ethan Hawke, Jessica Lange, and Steve Buscemi of Artists for Winning Without War join members of Win Without War, MoveOn.org, and the American Friends Service Committee outside the United Nations in delivering a worldwide anti-war petition to the United States Mission to the United States in New York on March 10, 2003. They were protesting President George W. Bush's threat to invade Iraq due to the country's alleged possession of nuclear weapons and harboring of terrorists. The U.S. led a multinational invasion of Iraq ten days later. AP Photo/Stuart Ramson.

instead devote our resources to improving the security and well-being of people here at home and around the world.

Signed,

Artists for Winning Without War

Mike Farrell,
  Co-Chair
Robert Greenwald,
  Co-Chair
Gillian Anderson
Edward Asner
Rene Auberjonois
David Bale
Kim Basinger
Ed Begley, Jr.
Theo Bikel
Barbara Bosson
Jackson Browne
Peter Buck (REM)
Diahann Carroll
Eugene J. Carroll, Jr.,
  Rear Adm. U.S.
  Navy (Ret.)
Kathleen Chalfant
Don Cheadle
Jill Clayburgh
David Clennon
Jack Coleman
Peter Coyote
Lindsay Crouse
Suzanne Cryer
Matt Damon
Dana Daurey
Ambassador Jonathan
  Dean (U.S. Rep.
  to NATO
  Warsaw Pact)
Vincent D'Onofrio
David Duchovny
Olympia Dukakis
Charles S. Dutton
Hector Elizondo
Cary Elwes
Shelley Fabares
Mike Farrell
Mia Farrow

Laurence Fishburne
Sean Patrick Flanery
Bonnie Franklin
John Fugelsang
Jeananne Garafalo
Larry Gelbart
Melissa Gilbert
Danny Glover
Elliott Gould
Samaria Graham
Robert Greenwald
Robert Guillaume
Paul Haggis
Robert David Hall
Ethan Hawke
Ken Howard
Helen Hunt
Anjelica Huston
LaTanya Richardson
  Jackson
Samuel L. Jackson
Jane Kaczmarek
Melina Kanakaredes
Casey Kasem
Mimi Kennedy
Jessica Lange
Tea Leoni
Wendie Malick
Camryn Manheim
Marsha Mason
Richard Masur
Dave Matthews
Kent McCord
Robert Duncan
  McNeill
Mike Mills (REM)
Janel Moloney
Esai Morales
Ed O'Neill
Chris Noth
Peter Onorati

Alexandra Paul
Ambassador Edward
  Peck (former
  U.S.
  Ambassador to
  Iraq)
Seth Peterson
CCH Pounder
David Rabe
Alan Rachins
Bonnie Raitt
Carl Reiner
Tim Robbins
Steve Robinson,
  Sgt., U.S. Army
  (Ret.)
Mitch Ryan
Susan Sarandon
Tony Shalhoub
Jack Shanahan,
  Vice Adm. U.S.
  Navy (Ret.)
William Schallert
Martin Sheen
Armin Shimerman
Gloria Steinem
Marcia Strassman
Michael Stipe (REM)
Susan Sullivan
Loretta Swit
Studs Terkel
Lily Tomlin
Blair Underwood
Dennis Weaver
Bradley Whitford
James Whitmore
James Whitmore, Jr.
Alfre Woodard
Noah Wyle
Peter Yarrow
Howard Zinn

13.2 RICH LOWRY, "LOVE YOUR COUNTRY"

While the petition signed by Artists for Winning without War generated very little controversy, when Natalie Maines, the lead signer for the country band the Dixie Chicks, criticized Bush during a concert on the eve of the American-led invasion of Iraq, she set off a firestorm. The band refused to apologize, leading some radio stations to ban their songs. In "Love Your Country," the columnist Rich Lowry discusses why the Dixie Chicks' actions provoked outrage when the protests of Hollywood celebrities did not.

For the Dixie Chicks, life just isn't fair.

Sean Penn can go on a prewar tour of Iraq that plays into the hands of Iraqi propagandist Baghdad Bob and be warmly welcomed back to Hollywood. The lead singer of the Dixie Chicks makes a stray insult of President Bush, and the group's radio playtime disappears, its album sales plummet, and the controversy lingers on seven weeks and an apology later.

What the Dixie Chicks forgot is that, as country singers, they might be "artists," but they're not entitled to the alienated self-righteousness assumed by most every other artist in the country. No, they are part of the Country Music Nation, the red-white-and-blue musical heart of America, where our enemies are evil, our cause is righteous, and comments critical of the commander in chief on foreign soil on the eve of a war are, uh, shall we say, not appreciated.

At a London concert on March 10, Texan Natalie Maines told the audience, "We're ashamed that the president of the United States is from Texas."

In response to the resulting outrage, the group has adopted the sense of victimization favored by all celebrities when they're criticized. One Dixie Chick says the controversy is a sign that people are "scared to speak up, scared to question." Actually, people are speaking up—driving a tractor over Dixie Chick CDs is a rather robust act of free expression.

The Chicks have also borrowed from the m.o. of female rock stars: When in doubt, take off your clothes. The group appears naked with various slogans related to the brouhaha on their bodies on the cover of Entertainment Weekly. "It's not about the nakedness," says Maines. Uh-huh.

The flap will further convince urban sophisticates that country music is hopelessly simplistic. Actually, country is the deepest and most realistic of all popular music genres. Its audience is not just kids, so its themes and emotional pitch, in contrast to rock, don't have to be aimed perpetually at snotty 16-year-olds.

Country songs deal with the eternal theme of love, but also single fatherhood, alcoholism, prayer, death, fishing, loneliness, the whole gamut of adult life, including its burdens of responsibility, such as having trouble paying the bills. The last is a worry rarely expressed by rock artists whose audience isn't old enough to have thought of it.

As cultural critic Stanley Kurtz has pointed out, country music represents a slice of American life still relatively untouched by the cultural upheaval of the 1970s, including its poisonous distrust of American power. So, country music features the kind of patriotic anger that would have been utterly unremarkable, say, in the America of the 1940s.

A small parade of 9–11 songs are heard on country stations. Most of them are similar in tone to Darryl Worley's "Have You Forgotten?"— "Some say this country's just out looking for a fight/After 9–11 man I'd have to say that's right."

You wouldn't necessarily want U.S. policy-makers to act on this sentiment, but neither would you want to live in a country that didn't sometimes feel it. It too represents a sort of realism, the hard fact that we have to choose between getting murdered by our enemies and aggressively thwarting them.

The Dixie Chicks have instead resorted to the easy artistic pose of righteousness that condemns the country's "warmongering" president without offering any alternative of how to respond to the threats of the post-9–11 world.

It might be that the Dixie Chicks leave the country format altogether, or—more likely—that they perversely benefit from their heightened notoriety. In the meantime, they can at least show the willingness to shoulder individual responsibility that is at the heart of country.

As a famous lyric from the historic country group The Carter Family has it: "Everybody's got to walk that lonesome valley/We've got to walk it by ourselves/There's nobody here can walk it for us/We've got to walk it by ourselves."

CHAPTER 14

Fahrenheit 9/11: The War on Terror

14.1 "STATEMENT OF CONSCIENCE," NOT IN OUR NAME

Not in Our Name (NION) was founded in 2002 in order to resist the United States government's course in the wake of the September 11, 2001, terrorist attacks. As its "Statement of Conscience" illustrates, the organization considered many of the elements of the American "War on Terror," including the invasion of Afghanistan, the passage of the Patriot Act, and the establishment of detention centers at Guantanamo, to be violations of human rights at best and war crimes at worst. Hollywood celebrities, like the directors Robert Altman and Spike Lee and the actors Ed Asner and Ruby Dee, were involved in NION's founding, but it closed its doors in March 2008.

As George W. Bush is inaugurated for a second term, let it not be said that people in the United States silently acquiesced in the face of this shameful coronation of war, greed, and intolerance. He does not speak for us. He does not represent us. He does not act in our name.

No election, whether fair or fraudulent, can legitimize criminal wars on foreign countries, torture, the wholesale violation of human rights, and the end of science and reason.

In our name, the Bush government justifies the invasion and occupation of Iraq on false pretenses, raining down destruction, horror, and misery, bringing death to more than 100,000 Iraqis. It sends our youth to destroy entire cities for the sake of so-called democratic elections, while intimidating and disenfranchising thousands of African American and other voters at home.

In our name, the Bush government holds in contempt international law and world opinion. It carries out torture and detentions without trial around the world and proposes new assaults on our rights of privacy, speech and assembly at home. It strips the rights of Arabs, Muslims and

South Asians in the U.S., denies them legal counsel, stigmatizes and holds them without cause. Thousands have been deported.

As new trial balloons are floated about invasions of Syria, or Iran, or North Korea, about leaving the United Nations, about new "lifetime detention" policies, we say not in our name will we allow further crimes to be committed against nations or individuals deemed to stand in the way of the goal of unquestioned world supremacy.

Could we have imagined a few years ago that core principles such as the separation of church and state, due process, presumption of innocence, freedom of speech, and habeas corpus would be discarded so easily? Now, anyone can be declared an "enemy combatant" without meaningful redress or independent review by a President who is concentrating power in the executive branch. His choice for Attorney General is the legal architect of the torture that has been carried out in Guantánamo, Afghanistan, and Abu Ghraib.

The Bush government seeks to impose a narrow, intolerant, and political form of Christian fundamentalism as government policy. No longer on the margins of power, this extremist movement aims to strip women of their reproductive rights, to stoke hatred of gays and lesbians, and to drive a wedge between spiritual experience and scientific truth. We will not surrender to extremists our right to think. AIDS is not a punishment from God. Global warming is a real danger. Evolution happened. All people must be free to find meaning and sustenance in whatever form of religious or spiritual belief they choose. But religion can never be compulsory. These extremists may claim to make their own reality, but we will not allow them to make ours.

Millions of us worked, talked, marched, poll watched, contributed, voted, and did everything we could to defeat the Bush regime in the last election. This unprecedented effort brought forth new energy, organization, and commitment to struggle for justice. It would be a terrible mistake to let our failure to stop Bush in these ways lead to despair and inaction. On the contrary, this broad mobilization of people committed to a fairer, freer, more peaceful world must move forward. We cannot, we will not, wait until 2008. The fight against the second Bush regime has to start now.

The movement against the war in Vietnam never won a presidential election. But it blocked troop trains, closed induction centers, marched, spoke to people door to door—and it helped to stop a war. The Civil Rights Movement never tied its star to a presidential candidate; it sat in, freedom rode, fought legal battles, filled jailhouses—and changed the face of a nation.

We must change the political reality of this country by mobilizing the tens of millions who know in their heads and hearts that the Bush regime's "reality" is nothing but a nightmare for humanity. This will require creativity, mass actions and individual moments of courage. We must come together whenever we can, and we must act alone whenever we have to.

We draw inspiration from the soldiers who have refused to fight in this immoral war. We applaud the librarians who have refused to turn over lists of our reading, the high school students who have demanded to be taught evolution, those who brought to light torture by the U.S. military, and the massive protests that voiced international opposition to the war on Iraq. We affirm ordinary people undertaking extraordinary acts. We pledge to create community to back courageous acts of resistance. We stand with the people throughout the world who fight every day for the right to create their own future.

It is our responsibility to stop the Bush regime from carrying out this disastrous course. We believe history will judge us sharply should we fail to act decisively.

Over 9,000 people have now signed this statement. Among the initial signers are:

James Abourezk, former U.S. senator

Janet Abu-Lughod, professor emerita, New School

As'ad AbuKhalil, California State University, Stanislaus

Michael Albert

Edward Asner

Michael Avery, president, National Lawyers Guild

Russell Banks

Amiri Baraka

Rosalyn Baxandall, chair, American Studies/Media and Communications,

State University of New York at Old Westbury

Medea Benjamin, cofounder of Global Exchange and Code Pink

Phyllis Bennis

Larry Bensky, Pacifica radio

Michael Berg

Jessica Blank and Erik Jensen

William Blum, author, US foreign policy

St. Clair Bourne

Judith Butler, author and professor, University of

California at Berkeley

Julia Butterfly, director, Circle of Life Foundation

Leslie Cagan, national coordinator, United for Peace and Justice

Kathleen & Henry Chalfant

Noam Chomsky, MIT

Ramsey Clark, former U.S. Attorney-General

Marilyn Clement, nat'l coordinator, Campaign for a National Health Program NOW

Robbie Conal, artist

Peter Coyote

Angela Davis

Diane di Prima, poet

Michael Eric Dyson

Nora Eisenberg, author of War at Home and Just the Way You Want Me

Daniel Ellsberg, former Defense and State Department official

Eve Ensler

Lawrence Ferlinghetti

Carolyn Forché

Michael Franti

Boo Froebel

Peter Gerety

Jorie Graham, Harvard University

André Gregory

Jessica Hagedorn, writer

Suheir Hammad

Sam Hamill, Poets Against the War

Danny Hoch, playwright/actor

Marie Howe

Abdeen M. Jabara, past president, American-Arab Anti-Discrimination Committee

Bill T. Jones

Rickie Lee Jones

Barbara Kingsolver

C. Clark Kissinger, Refuse & Resist!

Evelyn Fox Keller, Professor of History of Science, MIT

Hans Koning, writer

David Korn, author of Kornshell

David C. Korten

Rabbi Michael Lerner, editor, TIKKUN magazine & Rabbi, Beyt Tikkun Synagogue, SF

Phil Lesh, Grateful Dead

Staughton Lynd

Reynaldo F. Macías, chair, National Association for Chicana & Chicano Studies

Dave Marsh

Maryknoll Sisters, Western Region

Jim McDermott, Member of Congress, State of Washington

Robert Meeropol, executive director, Rosenberg Fund for Children

Robin Morgan, author and activist

Walter Mosley

Jill Nelson, writer

Odetta

Rosalind Petchesky, Distinguished Professor of Political Science, Hunter College & the

Graduate Center—CUNY

Jeremy Pikser, screenwriter (Bulworth)

Frances Fox Piven

James Stewart Polshek, architect

William Pope L

Francine Prose

Jerry Quickley, poet

Michael Ratner, president, Center for Constitutional Rights

David Riker, filmmaker

Stephen Rohde, civil liberties lawyer

Matthew Rothschild, editor, The Progressive magazine

Luc Sante

Roberta Segal-Sklar, communications director, National Gay and Lesbian Task Force

Wallace Shawn

Zach Sklar

Starhawk

Tony Taccone

Alice Walker

Naomi Wallace

Leonard Weinglass

Peter Weiss, president, Lawyers Committee on Nuclear Policy

Cornel West

C.K. Williams, poet,	director, Center for	Displaced Films
Princeton University	Advanced Visual	Zephyr
Saul Williams	Studies, MIT	Howard Zinn,
Krzysztof Wodiczko,	David Zeiger,	historian

14.2 REMARKS BY RON SILVER AS PREPARED FOR DELIVERY AT THE 2004 REPUBLICAN NATIONAL CONVENTION

The actor Ron Silver, best known for his role in the White House drama *The West Wing*, was one of the few Hollywood celebrities to staunchly support President George W. Bush. Even though Silver is a self-described liberal and a Democrat, the actor spoke at the 2004 Republican National Convention in support of Bush's "War on Terror." As his speech illustrates, Silver believes the "horrors" of September 11th necessitate the use of force and finds it "ironic" that other human-rights advocates in the entertainment community disagree.

New York, Aug. 30 /PRNewswire/—The following are remarks by Ron Silver as prepared for delivery at the 2004 Republican National Convention:

I want to thank the President and the Republican Party for holding this event in my hometown, my father's hometown, my grandfather's and great grandfather's birthplace.

Just over 1,000 days ago, 2,605 of my neighbors were murdered at the World Trade Center—men, women and children—as they began their day on a brilliantly clear New York autumn morning, less than four miles from where I am now standing.

We will never forgive. Never forget. Never excuse!

At the end of World War II, General Douglas MacArthur, Supreme Allied Commander of the South Pacific, said:

"It is my earnest hope—indeed the hope of all mankind—that from this solemn occasion a better world shall emerge out of the blood and carnage of the past, a world found upon faith and understanding, a world dedicated to the dignity of man and the fulfillment of his most cherished wish for freedom, tolerance and justice."

The hope he expressed then remains relevant today.

We are again engaged in a war that will define the future of human-kind. Responding to attacks on our soil, America has led a coalition of

Actor Ron Silver at the Republican National Convention held in Madison Square Garden, New York, on August 29, 2004. Silver gave a speech to the convention explaining his support of President George W. Bush's War on Terror. Silver was one of the few Hollywood celebrities to support President Bush's foreign policy. AP Photo/Stephen Savolia.

countries against extremists who want to destroy our way of life and our values.

This is a war we did not seek.

This is a war waged against us.

This is a war to which we had to respond.

History shows that we are not imperialists . . . but we are fighters for freedom and democracy.

Even though I am a well-recognized liberal on many issues confronting our society today, I find it ironic that many human rights advocates and outspoken members of my own entertainment community are often on the front lines to protest repression, for which I applaud them but they are usually the first ones to oppose any use of force to take care of these horrors that they catalogue repeatedly.

Under the unwavering leadership of President Bush, the cause of freedom and democracy is being advanced by the courageous men and women serving in our Armed Services.

The President is doing exactly the right thing.

That is why we need this President at this time!

I am grateful for the chance to speak tonight to express my support for our Commander-in-Chief, for our brave troops, and for the vital cause which they have undertaken.

General Dwight Eisenhower's statement of 60 years ago is true today . . .

"United in this determination and with unshakable faith in the cause for which we fight, we will, with God's help, go forward to our greatest victory."

Thank you.

Paid for by the Committee on Arrangements for the
2004 Republican National Convention
2 Penn Plaza * New York, NY 10121 * (212) 356–2004
Not authorized by any candidate or candidate committee

PART IV

Social Movements

In the 1930s, Hollywood expressed its commitment to social justice in petitions, meetings, rallies and demonstrations for various causes: the Spanish Civil War, fascism in Europe, Italy's invasion of Ethiopia, the Scottsboro boys, jailed labor leader Tom Mooney, labor strikes, the Hearst newspaper chain, among others. When Vittorio Mussolini, the son of Italy's dictator, visited Hollywood in 1937, actors and directors demonstrated against his presence.

Civil rights leaders and many in Hollywood had long called for better roles for African–Americans and other ethnic minorities. Walter White, executive secretary of the National Association for the Advancement of Colored People (NAACP) met numerous times with studio heads to express his anger at the industry's stereotyping and degrading representation of African–Americans and other ethnic minorities in Hollywood. He complained that Hollywood offered only menial roles to African–Americans portraying maids, porters, and butlers, often in comic relief. As a result of these meetings the studios pledged to take these concerns into consideration. Indeed, during the filming of *Gone with the Wind* (1939), producer David Selznick consulted with the NAACP to excise more offensive elements of the novel—particularly the valorization of the Ku Klux Klan and lynching. After the war, African–American actors gradually began to receive rewarding and leading roles in Hollywood films. Hollywood made a handful of films addressing sensitive racial issues including *Crossfire* (1947), *Gentleman's Agreement* (1947), *Pinkie* (1949), *No Way Out* (1950), and *Broken Arrow* (1950).

Despite this modest progress, some African–American actors feared that the NAACP's involvement might bring about a backlash and that the studios would stop offering roles to them entirely. Ironically, while creating new opportunities for minority actors, the NAACP's campaign hurt the careers of a few of the older African–American actors who had been popular in the 1930s. Actor Stepin Fetchit had become the poster child for playing the kinds of stereotypical roles that NAACP complained about to the studios. In 1945, Stepin Fetchit wrote a pleading letter from Chicago where he was barely getting by playing small clubs asking director John Ford to put him in a movie. Fetchit wrote "[T]he way I've been getting along—why you'd think I was the one who started this war. I've been doing awful. . . . I've never seen so much suffering with good health in all my life." In response Ford proposed giving Fetchit a small role as an orderly in a new western he was making. Darryl Zanuck opposed the idea, writing Ford, "No one has laughed longer and louder at Stepin Fetchit than I have, but to put him on the screen at this time would I am afraid raise terrible objections from colored people. Walter White, when he addressed us on the problems of colored people singled out Stepin Fetchit as I recall, as an example of the humiliation of the colored race. Stepin Fetchit always portrays the lazy, stupid half-wit, and this is the thing that the colored people are furious about." Zanuck asked Ford, "Do you really want to take a chance?" Ford declined.

New African–American stars emerged in the postwar period who brought new dignity to their roles, including Sidney Poitier, Harry Belafonte, Dorothy Dandridge, and Juanita Moore. Progress remained slow, and, in fact, roles for African–Americans decreased. Between 1945 and 1952, black membership in the Screen Actors Guild dropped from approximately 500 members to 125. Furthermore, black actors were under the same sort of pressure as their white colleagues to not appear too radical and distance themselves from causes or organizations associated with Communism. Paul Robeson, for example, was blacklisted because of his Communist affiliations and before casting Belafonte in the film *Carmen Jones,* 20th Century Fox demanded he denounce Communism. Belafonte obliged.

The growth of the civil rights movement in the 1950s and 1960s awakened activism in both black and white actors. Sammy Davis, Jr., Belafone, Poitier, Ossie Davis, and Ruby Dee all raised considerable money and publicity for the cause. Meanwhile, white actors such as Charlton Heston also took a leading role in the civil rights struggle. Heston helped organize a Hollywood contingent to join Martin Luther King, Jr.'s March on Washington in 1963, the largest celebrity political action yet seen. As the struggle for civil rights turned more militant, so did many in Hollywood. Actors including Rod Steiger, Robert Ryan, Sammy Davis, Jr., Belafonte, Dee, and Davis gave thousands of dollars to Students for a Democratic Society.

The depiction of Native American Indians also drew criticism from activists in Hollywood. Hollywood movies historically depicted Indians as savages and obstacles to civilization. There were occasional exceptions to these stereotypes. In John Ford's 1937 classic, *Drums Along the Mohawk*, the Indian character Blue Book (played by Chief Big Tree) is a Christian and loyally stands by the hero of the story throughout the film. After World War II, the image of the Indian in film began to change, albeit slowly. *Broken Arrow* (1950) told the story of an Indian agent, played by Jimmy Stewart, who becomes convinced that the Apaches have been treated unfairly and befriends an Apache leader named Cochise. The film was hailed for its "balanced portrayal of Native Americans," but the part of Cochise was played by white actor Jeff Chandler, a casting choice some Native American actors criticized. In 1971, director John Ford made one of the most sympathetic films about the plight of the American Indian when *Cheyenne Autumn* was released. It told the true story of three hundred starving Indian men, women, and children stranded in the wastelands of Oklahoma and of their 1,500-mile return to their homeland of Yellowstone. The 1970s saw numerous movies sympathetic to American Indians including the thrilling drama *Chato's Land* (1971), the low-budget smash *Billy Jack* (1971), and the hilarious *Blazing Saddles* (1974).

By this time, an Indian civil rights movement had been organized through the efforts of the American Indian Movement (AIM). A friend of AIM, actor Marlon Brando gave the cause of Indian civil rights great publicity when he sent Sacheen Littlefeather in his place to the Academy Awards ceremony to reject his Oscar for Best Actor for *The Godfather* (1972). When Brando's name was called, Littlefeather went on stage and refused to accept the award, explaining Brando's outrage about how Native Americans had been treated by the film industry. The protest divided the Hollywood Establishment and later caused Brando considerable embarrassment when it was discovered that Littlefeather was not an Apache Indian as she claimed, but a Mexican actress named Maria Cruz.

Also in the 1970s, many actors entered the fight to ratify the Equal Rights Amendment. Passed by Congress in 1972, the proposed amendment, the Equal Rights Amendment (ERA), declared succinctly: "Equality of rights under the law shall not be denied or abridged by the United States or by any State on account of sex." The amendment needed approval of three-fourths (38) of the states to become constitutional.

The ERA was also aided by an impressive list of celebrities including television actor Alan Alda, comedians Lily Tomlin and Carol Burnett, producer Norman Lear, former sitcom star and wife of Phil Donahue, Marlo Thomas, actress Candice Bergen, cartoonist Garry Trudeau ("Doonesbury"), columnists Ann Landers and Erma Bombeck, Maureen Reagan, and Christie Hefner, daughter of *Playboy* publisher Hugh

Hefner. Indeed, the list of celebrities who came out in support of ERA, contributing time and money seemed endless. Joining the celebrity list were actresses Jean Stapleton (*All in the Family*) and Patty Duke Austin. Singer Helen Reddy, whose hit song "I Am Woman" captured the mood of feminist women in the 1970s, enlisted in the ERA crusade. Stars of popular television programs of the day also were found at fundraisers and political rallies, including Tyne Daly Brown, Valerie Harper, Henry Winkler, Ed Asner, and Jack Klugman. These celebrities gave and attended fundraisers, testified at hearings, spoke at ERA rallies, and appeared in television and radio spots on behalf of ERA. Not all feminists welcomed these celebrities, however, in their ranks.

Sometimes this celebrity support backfired, as when television star and movie actor Alan Alda testified on behalf of the ERA at the Illinois hearing on ratification in 1974. The actor was ridiculed when he echoed U.S. Senator Patricia Schroeder's support for female conscription. Asked by a hostile State Senator if he would support his own daughters being drafted during a war, Alda emphatically answered, "Yes," but then added that his daughters would not enter into the military even if drafted because they were pacifists who opposed all war and would declare themselves to be conscientious objectors. He gave the appearance of saying conscription was right for everyone else except his daughters.

Ethnic awareness encouraged other groups, including Italian–Americans, to assert their own demands on the movie and television industry. The first visible appearance of organized support for changing the stereotypical Italian–American gangster came when the Italian–American Civil Rights League was founded in 1971, ironically, encouraged, if not led, by reputed New York organized crime figure Joseph Columbo. The Italian–American Anti-Defamation League soon claimed 45,000 members and gained national attention when the singer and actor Frank Sinatra held a benefit concert for the organization. The organization pressured Alka-Seltzer into dropping a commercial stereotyping an Italian–American comically complaining with a heavy accent, "Now, that's a spicy meatball." The organization also convinced the producer of *The Godfather* to remove references to "the Mafia" and "Cosa Nostra" in the dialogue. However, the assassination of Columbo at a league rally in late 1971 brought an end to the organization.

In 1975, the National Italian–American Foundation was founded as a political organization to protect the cultural image of Italian–Americans. Its annual report, *Focus,* directs attention at directors, actors, and writers who allegedly portray Italian–Americans in a poor light. Martin Scorsese, director of such films as *Mean Streets* (1973) and *Goodfellas* (1991), became a frequent target of the foundation, as did actor Robert DeNiro, who starred in a number of Scorsese films. Scorsese vehemently denied these accusations that he was stereotyping all Italian–Americans as violent, dumb, and racist.

While the film industry sought to improve its image for racial tolerance and ethnic diversity, critics charged that Hollywood celebrities were out of touch with main street America and projecting the small world of Hollywood activism on the rest of the country. These criticisms led actor and social activist George Clooney to defend Hollywood activism in his acceptance speech for Best Supporting Actor at the 2006 Academy Awards ceremony. Clooney claimed that Hollywood was often in the vanguard of social issues and civil rights, while the rest of America remained backward. Clooney's speech incited further criticism in the polarized political atmosphere of the early twenty-first century.

CHAPTER 15

Get on the Bus: The Civil Rights Movement

15.1 LETTER FROM DAVID O. SELZNICK TO WALTER WHITE, EXECUTIVE SECRETARY OF NAACP

Civil rights organizations had repeatedly criticized Hollywood for what they considered the negative portrayal of African–Americans onscreen. In the 1930s, Walter White, the executive secretary of the National Association for the Advancement of Colored People (NAACP), worked with the producer David O. Selznick during the production of *Gone with the Wind* in an effort to represent African–Americans as positively as possible within the confines of the material. As this letter between Selznick and White illustrates, even though Selznick fulfilled his promises to the NAACP, critics of his portrayal of the "loyal" slaves Mammy, Pork, Uncle Peter, and Big Sam still elicited criticism, a complaint the producer had trouble understanding.

Mr. Walter White, Secretary
National Association for the Advancement of Colored People
69 Fifth Avenue
New York City   April 2, 1940

Dear Mr. White:
I am in receipt of your letter of March 26th. I am most appreciative of your statement that we lived up to our promises, and would appreciate it if your press department could clarify your attitude for those papers which have seen fit to attack us, the names of which are no doubt known to your press and public relations departments. Having leaned over backwards on these matters, and feeling as keenly as we do in problems involving racial prejudices, I feel it is unfair that we should be attacked as being on the other side.

Your letter refers to an enclosure, but contained none.

I am more distressed than I can say that you should feel that any of the horrible instances to which you refer should in any way be traceable to motion pictures generally, even though I note that it is not "Gone With the Wind" specifically which you feel is responsible. I personally have talked to many people who have volunteered the comment that "Gone With the Wind" is a splendid tribute to the loyalty and fine character of the Negro, particularly in its delineation of Mammy, Pork, Uncle Peter and Big Sam, with literally not a single Negro character of importance on the other side; and that Mammy, as portrayed by Hattie McDaniel, is certain to win many millions of new friends for the Negro race.

Is there anything you have to suggest that I might do to be helpful to your cause? Is there, for instance, any form of membership in your organization that I might personally take out to demonstrate exactly where I stand on your issues?

I hope that all of you will understand that nothing on earth could have kept "Gone With the Wind" from the screens of this country; and it is my personal opinion that any attempt to keep it from the screens would, if anything, have reacted upon your cause rather than helped it. I like to feel, also, that there are no other auspices under which it could possibly have been made that would have been more friendly to the Negro, and that could or would have done any more with the film on behalf of the Negro, than was done by our company.

With kindest regards,

Very sincerely yours,
David O. Selznick

15.2 "REPORT ON SPECIAL GIFTS FUNDRAISING," AUGUST, 1965, NEW YORK FRIENDS OF SNCC

Even though the combined pressure of the studio system and the blacklist had discouraged political activism in the 1950s, the bourgeoning civil rights movement drew black and white film and television stars back into politics. Although all of the major civil rights organizations received celebrity support, the Student Nonviolent Coordinating Committee (SNCC) devised some of the most creative partnerships. In 1963, the New York Friends of SNCC began throwing "house parties" at which actors like Sidney Poitier, Diahann Carroll, and Theodore Bikel

Actor Charlton Heston, singer Harry Belafonte, writer James Baldwin, and actor Marlon Brando at the March on Washington on August 28, 1963. These men had supported the civil rights movement in various ways for several years. In 1963, Heston chaired a Hollywood Arts Group to recruit celebrities to participate in the March on Washington. The event's purpose was to show support for a pending civil rights bill to desegregate public accommodations and was one of the high points of the civil rights movement, due to its large and peaceful participation. AP Images.

mingled with and entertained guests. As this "Report on Special Gifts Fundraising" demonstrates, SNCC's house parties raised tens of thousands of dollars for the organization.

December 1, 1963　Host: Mr. and Mrs. Lester Avnet
Kings Point, Long Island, New York
Guests: Sidney Poitier, Diahann Carroll,
Theodore Bikel
Amt. Paid: $7425

December 8, 1963　Host: Mr. and Mrs. Max Youngstein
Guests: Sidney Poitier, Diahann Carroll,
Theodore Bikel
Amt. Paid: $5680

May 24, 1964
Host: Mr. and Mrs. Bernard Aisenberg
New Rochelle, N.Y.
Guests: Theodore Bikel, Ossie Davis, Ruby Dee
Amt. Paid: $4242   Amt. Pledges Unpaid: $75

June 7, 1964
Host: Miss Diahann Carroll
Manhattan
Guests: Harry Belafonte, Sidney Poitier, Rod Steiger,
Claire Bloom, Robert Ryan, Sammy Davis, Jr.,
William B. Williams
Amt. Paid: $7553   Amt. Pledges Unpaid: $500

August 7, 1964
Host: Mr. and Mrs. David Kaufman
Harrison, N.Y.
Guest: Harry Belafonte
Amt. Paid: $11,265   Amt. Pledges Unpaid: $200

August 8, 1964
Host: Mr. and Mrs. Robert Benjamin
Great Neck, N.Y.
Guest: Harry Belafonte
Amt. Paid: $8038   Amt. Pledges Unpaid: $1350

August 23, 1964
Host: Mr. and Mrs. Leo Nevas
Westport, Conn.
Guests: Ruby Dee, Ossie Davis
Amt. Paid: $10,966.95   Amt. Pledges Unpaid: $220

August 22, 1964
Host: Mr. and Mrs. Tony Drexel Duke
Boys' Harbor, Easthampton, N.Y.
Guest: John Killens
Amt. Paid: $8623   Amt. Pledges Unpaid: None

In the New York area the following parties have been organized by the Special Gifts fundraising Committee:

May 24
Host: Mr. and Mrs. Bernard Aisenberg
New Rochelle, N.Y.
Guests: Theodore Bikel, Ozzie Davis, Ruby Dee
Amt. paid: $4242   Amt. pledges: unpaid: $115

June 7
Host: Miss Diahann Carroll
Manhattan
Guests: Harry Belafonte, Sidney Poitier, Rod Steiger

Claire Bloom, Robert Ryan, Sammy Davis Jr.,
William B. Williams
Amt. paid: $7553   Amt. pledges unpaid $500

August 7
Host: Mr. and Mrs. David Kaufman
Harrison, N.Y.
Guest: Harry Belafonte
Amt. paid: $11,265   Amt. pledges unpaid: $200

August 8
Host: Mr. and Mrs. Robert Benjamin
Great Neck, N.Y.
Guest: Harry Belafonte
Amt. paid: $8038   Amt. pledges unpaid: $1350

August 23
Host: Mr. and Mrs. Leo Nevas
Westport, Conn.
Guests: Ruby Dee, Ozzie Davis [sic.]
Amt. paid: $10,966.95   Amt. pledges unpaid: $220

August 22
Host: Mr. and Mrs. Tony Drexel Duke
Boys' Harbor, Easthampton, N.Y.
Guest: John Killens
Amt paid: $8873   Amt. pledges unpaid:

September 13
Host: Dr. and Mrs. Herbert Rosen
Katonah, N.Y.
Guest: Robert Ryan
Amt. paid: approx. $5425   Amt. pledges unpaid: $120

15.3 "BLACKS VS. SHAFT"

In the 1970s, a genre known as "blaxploitation" burst into theaters. These films starred African–Americans who, in a series of exploits often laden with violence, action, and sex, ultimately "stuck it to Whitey." As this article from *Newsweek* illustrates, a debate ensued amongst African–Americans about the value of these films and about the wisdom of civil rights organizations becoming involved in the film industry.

Aside from the rare blockbuster film such as "The Godfather," the only gold mine left for Hollywood to tap has been the burgeoning black audience (*Newsweek*, Sept. 6, 1971) that has been gobbling up the new black films. In recent months, these movies have come under increasing fire from segments of the black community for creating false heroes who demean the black image: Melvin Van Peebles's persecuted superstud in "Sweet Sweetback's Baadasssss Song"; John Shaft, the black James Bond who is all murder and machismo; the gun-slinging hero of "The Legend of Nigger Charley," and, more recently, the cocaine-pusher protagonist of "Super Fly," a film whose staggering $150,000 gross in its first week in New York City is characteristic of the whirlwind success of these films.

Last week, the crescendo of criticism turned to action with the formation of CAB, the Coalition Against Blaxploitation, by a group of local Los Angeles civil-rights organizations—the NAACP, the Southern Christian Leadership Conference and CORE. Founded by Junius Griffin, who resigned last week as president of the Beverly Hills chapter of the NAACP, CAB plans to institute its own rating system of black movies, classifying them as superior, good, acceptable, objectionable or thoroughly objectionable. "We will not tolerate the continued warping of our black children's minds with the filth, violence and cultural lies that are all-pervasive in current productions of so-called black movies," says Griffin. "The transformation from the stereotyped Stepin Fetchit to Super Nigger on the screen is just another form of cultural genocide. The black community should deal with this problem by whatever manner necessary."

Gangsters

Conrad Smith, leader of the Los Angeles branch of CORE, told *Newsweek*'s Henry McGee: "We're prepared to go all the way with this, even to the extent of running people out of the theaters. We're definitely going to see that this thing comes to an end." As its first action, CAB will classify four black films—"The Legend of Nigger Charley," "The Final Comedown," and two new films, "Sounder," the inspirational and touching story of a sharecropping family's survival in the rural South of the 1920s, and "Melinda," an engaging if violent yarn about a disc jockey's search for the white gangsters who murdered his girl friend. But the group is known to have objections to practically every successful black film made in the past two years.

In their turn, the producers, directors and stars of these films, both black and white, attack CAB heatedly for what they regard as its elitist stance. (As currently constituted, the CAB rating board is composed of five members of the NAACP, one of whom is white, although there is talk of expanding the group to include laymen from the black community.) "I rather resent and I would think blacks resent the implication of this organization that black audiences are somehow not able to recognize something that is degrading to themselves," says Samuel Z. Arkoff, the white head of American International Pictures, whose black version of Dracula (called naturally "Blacula") promises to be the company's biggest moneymaker this year.

Adds Ron O'Neal, the handsome young black star of "Super Fly": "They're saying that they know better than the black people themselves what they should look at, that they're going to be the moral interpreters for the destiny of black people. I'm so tired of handkerchief-head Negroes moralizing on the poor black man." Walter Burrell, chairman of CAB's rating committee, answers O'Neal this way: "Black people are hungry to see the black image on the screen and they'll go and see anything. There's got to be some responsibility."

It is unlikely that CAB will enjoy any real success in its new venture, since its powers of enforcement lie largely outside the law, and the black audiences who whoop and holler with pleasure at the sex, violence and funky humor in the black films are unlikely to be significantly influenced by advisory ratings. But the formation of CAB has dramatized the larger question of the quality and influence of the new movies that are, at least in part, obvious attempts by the film moguls to exploit America's last captive movie audience.

Black critic Clayton Riley, writing in The New York Times, recently attacked the new black films for their fairy-tale treatment of black life, for creating fantasy superheroes whose omnipotence reinforces the social passivity in the black audience and for their use of worn-out Hollywood conventions: ". . . the cowboys and the sleuths, the dope traffic aristocrats and empty-headed women, the colored Keystone Cops are products of the same Hollywood minds that made millions while excluding blacks from the industry. Now they've discovered a latter-day vein of gold to rip off. That's not so surprising. The help they are getting from black artists is."

Spoofy

Black filmmakers under attack resort to the same defense as white studio chiefs of years past—that they are only giving the audience what it wants. And the traditional riposte, that an audience can only want what it is given, still obtains. But black filmmakers present a more valid argument when they contend that though their films may have the limitations of most white action films, they at least present effective heroes in the place of the downtrodden black men of films past. "People talk about black movies being exploitative," says Hugh Robertson, director of "Melinda," "and sure, a lot of them are spoofy and outrageous, but the black community has been conditioned to want fantasy in films by the movies they've seen just as white people have. The only difference now is that the black fantasy isn't totally negative."

Gordon Parks Jr., who directed "Super Fly," says: "People who come down from Harlem and plunk down their three dollars don't want to see drip 'n' drab. They want to be entertained. And if they see superheroes with fast cars and fancy clothes, well, that's the American dream—everyone's American dream. And I say to Mr. Clayton Riley that it's b------- that these people are going back home to the ghetto complaining because they aren't Shaft. White people don't go home upset because they aren't James Bond or John Wayne."

Right now, there is no question that the black audience, starved for years for films that see the world from a black point of view, is eating up just about anything that is slickly served. It is no accident that the most successful of the black films—both good and bad—invariably serve up heroes who "stick it to the Man." The intent of the new black films is not art but the commercial exploitation of the repressed anger of a relatively powerless community.

But, as with the boom of sexploitation films, the black explosion is self-regulating. In time, black moviegoers will want to know not just whether a movie is black, but whether it's any good. Bad black movies will flop, just like the bad white ones do. In the end, the answer to the problem of synthetic and second-rate black films lies in the growing discrimination and sophistication of the black audience, not in the effectiveness of any rating system.

CHAPTER 16

How the West Was Won: The American Indian Movement

16.1 SPEECH BY SACHEEN LITTLEFEATHER AT THE ACADEMY AWARDS, 1973

As the American Indian Movement (AIM) gained traction, the actor Marlon Brando, who was a longtime friend to the cause, brought it even more publicity at the 1973 Academy Awards. Nominated for Best Actor for *The Godfather* (1972), Brando sent Sacheen Littlefeather, a woman who identified herself as an Apache and an activist, in his place, and she rejected the award in his name. Littlefeather's speech, reprinted below, explains Brando's reasoning for the rejection and shows the audience's reaction to her presence.

Hello. My name is Sacheen Littlefeather. I'm Apache and I am president of the National Native American Affirmative Image Committee. I'm representing Marlon Brando this evening and he has asked me to tell you in a very long speech which I cannot share with you presently because of time but I will be glad to share with the press afterwards that he very regretfully cannot accept this very generous award. And the reasons for this being are the treatment of American Indians today by the film industry. [Some rumbling in the audience.] Excuse me . . . [boos and claps] and on television in movie reruns and also with the recent happenings at Wounded Knee.

I beg at this time that I have not intruded upon this evening and that we will, in the future, in our hearts and our understanding meet with love and generosity.

Thank you on behalf of Marlon Brando.

A woman who identified herself as Sacheen Littlefeather tells the audience at the Academy Awards ceremony in Los Angeles, California, on March 27, 1973 that Marlon Brando was declining to accept his Oscar for Best Actor for his role in *The Godfather* (1972). Littlefeather said Brando was protesting the portrayal of Native Americans in motion pictures and on television. She was later identified as Maria Cruz. AP Photo.

Although the Sacheen Littlefeather episode led some in Hollywood to question Marlon Brando's tactics, few questioned his sincerity. Indeed, in this picture taken in December 1974, Brando is donating 40 acres of land to Hank Adams, head of the Survival of American Indians Association. The ceremony took place on the site, near Augora, California. United Press International.

16.2 ROBERT E. THOMPSON, "BRANDO'S REJECTION OF OSCAR SCORED"

Marlon Brando's rejection of the Academy Award for Best Actor in 1973 divided the Hollywood Establishment. The actress Jane Fonda thought it was "wonderful," whereas Charlton Heston said it was "childish." Most agreed with Robert E. Thompson, a journalist for the *Los Angeles Herald-Examiner*, who explains below that he admires Brando's stance but disagrees with his tactics, especially when Brando made two million dollars playing an Italian–American gangster, another ethnic group that considered itself maligned by the film industry.

Back on top after a decade of mediocre acting in mediocre films, Marlon Brando has written his own sequel to "I Buried My Heart at Wounded Knee." Its title is: "I Abandoned My Oscar at The Music Center."

And what a pow wow it has generated!

Those who bleed profusely at the mere mention of the word "cause" have suddenly defied Brando his accorded sainthood to his comely Apache stand-in Sacheen Littlefeather. Those whose only cause is making money and costuming themselves in the Stars and Stripes have all but likened the actor to Benedict Arnold.

As for myself, I am of two minds about Brando's conduct. I admire his dedication to social justice for American Indians. I think his rejection of the Academy Award for best actor in "The Godfather" was pretentious and demeaning to an industry that has made him a millionaire and an international star.

The Indian has suffered great hardship in this land that once was his private domain. He wants to reside with his fellow Indians on reservations, but finds it practically impossible to earn a living. He suffers from social and economic deprivation and he deserves far better from this nation.

It also must be noted that Brando is not a Johnny-Come-Lately to the cause of Indian justice. He has been active in this movement for a number of years.

Indeed, the talented actor may be quite sincere in believing that "the motion picture community has been responsible as any for degrading the Indian and making a mockery of his character."

Yet . . . Brando has accepted the huge amounts of money paid him by the leaders of the community he seems to detest. Nor has he turned down roles in films replete with violence, vulgarity and obscenity that degrade other ethnic groups.

Conditions among American Indians may have been even worse in 1951 than they are in 1973. But Brando had no hesitation that year in appearing before the Academy Awards ceremony to accept an Oscar for "On the Waterfront."

For these reasons, Brando's action last Tuesday night appears to have been a grandstand play, cloaked in hypocrisy.

Hollywood and the annual Oscar pageant are easy targets. The first is hardly an exemplary community. The second carries the stigma of producers, performers, directors and other contenders advertising for honor—the Oscar—that should be awarded strictly on the basis of achievement.

But the motion picture community also demonstrated taste and courage in voting its top acting award two years ago to George C. Scott when he made it clear in advance he would not accept the Oscar.

Despite the fact that members of the Motion Picture Academy of Arts and Sciences knew they would be rebuffed, they gave Scott their award because his performance as George Patton was one of the finest ever recorded on film.

A similar incident happened last year, when the Academy named Jane Fonda as best actress, although her anti-war activities had made her one of the most unpopular figures in the nation. Art prevailed over politics.

In fact, Miss Fonda, an emotional radical, exhibited far greater style than Brando. Accepting her Oscar, she merely noted that although she had much to say, the Academy Award ceremony was not the forum in which to say it.

But Brando had to make a theatrical production of his rejection of the Oscar. Rather than appear himself, he sent Miss Littlefeather and, unfortunately, there were some in the audience who had the bad taste to boo her.

Why did Brando not have the courage to do it himself? He presumably was back from a long sojourn in the South Pacific, which, of course, was made possible by the hundreds of thousand of dollars paid him whenever he makes a movie for a decadent Hollywood film maker.

He claimed he was needed at Wounded Knee, but he was not there the night of the Oscar Awards nor for three days afterward. If there was to be abuse, he was willing to let Miss Littlefeather take it.

How can an actor become a martyr when he [refused] personally to face fire?

CHAPTER 17

Workin' 9 to 5: The Women's Movement

17.1 MIKE LAWRENCE, "SENATORS M*A*S*H 'HAWKEYE': ERA-BACKING STAR LOSES SOME SHINE"

A number of high-profile celebrities, including men, supported the feminist movement in the 1970s. Alan Alda was a particularly strong supporter, and he campaigned tirelessly for the Equal Rights Amendment. However, as this article from the *Quad City Times* explains, his involvement also showed how a celebrity endorsement could actually backfire for a particular cause.

Springfield, Ill.—After his first encounter with the Illinois General Assembly, actor Alan Alda probably will be more than happy to return to the Korean "battlefield" of his smash television show, M*A*S*H.

Alda, who stars as Hawkeye, was greeted with a round of boos and accused of being a "carpetbagger" when he appeared before the House to thank members for approving ratification of the Equal Rights Amendment.

Then, in a Senate committee hearing at which ERA was rejected, Alda's integrity was called into question.

When Alda climbed onto the House rostrum, he received a cordial reception, but the anti-ERA forces began showing their disapproval as he began discussing the subject.

Alda said, "A great wave of electricity was felt all over the country when you approved this issue."

But a red-faced Rep. Philip Collins, R-Calumet City, rose as Alda was concluding to say, "I resent the fact that the rostrum of the House of Representatives was used on one side of an issue."

He said, "I resent carpetbaggers telling us how to vote."

Alda was later grilled by members of the Senate Executive Committee.

He said he was speaking on behalf of ERA in his role as a member of the national commission for the observance of international women's year.

Actor Alan Alda with his wife Arlene and daughters Eve, Elizabeth, and Beatrice, circa 1973. Alda was a member of the National Organization for Women and testified in favor of the ratification of the Equal Rights Amendment. Motion Picture and Television Archive/Chester Maydole.

CHAPTER 18

You Talkin' to Me? Ethnic Assertions

18.1 POSITION STATEMENT OF THE NATIONAL ITALIAN AMERICAN FOUNDATION

Founded in 1975, the National Italian American Foundation (NIAF) has emerged as the biggest Italian–American political and cultural group in the United States. Part of the NIAF's agenda is to improve the image of Italian–Americans in the media. As this *Focus* report from 2002 illustrates, the group pressures media outlets to resist portraying Italian–Americans in stereotypical ways and promotes "the best of Italian–American culture."

Fighting the Negative

NIAF has recently responded to several media items including radio and television advertisements, television programs, newspaper columns, and even cartoons, which were perceived as offensive and/or unflattering to Italian–Americans. These items demonstrated the media's "usual" proclivity for stereotyping Italian–Americans as criminals, the association of Italian–Americans with organized crime, the stereotyping of Italian–Americans as buffoons, and the portrayal of Italian–Americans as uneducated, crude, and/or excitable. The impact of these stereotypes was reflected in a Zogby survey of U.S. teenagers taken last year where 44 percent of the respondents identified Italian–Americans as the most likely to play a crime boss or gang member in a movie or on television. Moreover, the overall findings of this study suggest that teens learn the less admirable aspects of their heritage from the entertainment industry's stereotyping and that teens' perceptions of other ethnic, religious, and racial groups are shaped by the entertainment industry's stereotypes.

The item which roused the greatest turmoil was the beginning of a new season of *The Sopranos* program on HBO. NIAF Chairman Frank

Guarini immediately issued a statement which reaffirmed NIAF's "disappointment that the show's success is on the backs of Italian–Americans who continue to be stereotyped and portrayed negatively in this fictional series." Both NIAF President Joseph Cerrell and NIAF Executive Director John Salamone did several media interviews and made statements reiterating the Chairman's statement.

NIAF's Executive Director will meet with HBO executives in November to discuss the network's programming choices and its incessant use of negative depictions of Italian–Americans. NIAF will propose that:

1. HBO place a disclaimer either before or after airing an episode of *The Sopranos* saying that this program is fictional and its characters in no way resemble the estimated 25 million Americans of Italian descent who are honest and law-abiding people. In addition, the disclaimer should convey that the program is not intended to defame any particular ethnic group.
2. HBO should provide NIAF with an open line of communication where NIAF could make programming suggestions. Through this dialogue, NIAF would encourage more balanced portrayals of Italian–Americans in HBO programming. NIAF would have a means through which it could refer scripts and projects that positively portray Italian–Americans.
3. HBO celebrate Italian–American Heritage Month (October) by showing films and programs that positively portray Italian–Americans and accurately reflect the Italian–American experience. HBO, in addition to other stations, celebrates African–American History Month in February and Hispanic Heritage month each fall.
4. HBO arrange public service announcements where prominent Italian–Americans talk about the positive aspects of their heritage.

Emphasizing the Positive

Outside of the HBO initiative, NIAF believes that a proactive measure to curb the defamation and discrimination of Italian–Americans is through the promotion of the best of Italian–American culture and heritage. Italian–Americans are a highly accomplished and educated group. We need to share this with others. As you are aware, the promotion of the best of Italian–American culture and heritage is being accomplished through NIAF's grants and cultural/educational programs, however, more work needs to be done.

A new initiative in promoting the best of Italian–American culture and heritage is by institutionalizing it at American colleges and universities. This can be achieved through the teaching of courses in Italian–American history and literature and the developing of programs in Italian–Americans Studies. Young people need to be taught the *real* Italian–American experience. The media has severely distorted what it means to be Italian–American. Negative stereotyping and images are fueled through ignorance and misunderstanding of Italian–Americans. How many times have we watched with bewilderment a movie or commercial with an offensive and demeaning Italian–American stereotype and turned to our wives and husbands and said, "We're not anything like that." Let's not only educate ourselves but the public as well.

In an effort to promote the study of Italian–American courses at American colleges and universities, NIAF held a conference on May 30 in New York City to discuss this topic. Assembling a panel of professors, writers, journalists, and a college president, NIAF first tackled this topic. NIAF then continued this dialogue with a conference on October 26 in Washington, DC. Moderated by U.S. Supreme Court Justice Antonin Scalia, the conference featured another impressive panel that addressed the issue. Aside from sponsoring conferences and encouraging discussion in this area, the NIAF Grants program has awarded a number of grants to schools which have either developed or are developing Italian–American Studies courses and programs. This impressive list of schools includes the City University of New York, SUNY Stony Brook, Montclair State University, Central Connecticut State University, and the University of Minnesota at Morris.

The institutionalization of Italian–American Studies in American colleges and universities will be a long and difficult process; however, it is definitely an objective that is achievable. Open any college catalog and notice the number of courses offered in African–American history, Jewish Studies, and Latino Studies. Our goal is to have Italian–American Studies courses listed alongside these other courses.

Proud Americans, Proud Italian–Americans

The finding of the 2000 Census reaffirmed what many of us already knew, that Italian–Americans are a group that continues to maintain a strong ethnic identity. According to the 2000 Census, an increased number of people are identifying themselves as simply "American" rather than as a member of a specific ethnic group. This was especially evident with

Actor Robert DeNiro playing Travis Bickle in Martin Scorsese's *Taxi Driver* (1976). The actions of the psychotic and murderous Bickle led critics to condemn the film's graphic violence. Some Italian–American groups also criticized DeNiro's and Scorsese's portrayals of Italians as violent, racist, mob-connected criminals in *Taxi Driver*, as well as in other films on which the two collaborated. Motion Picture and Television Archive/1976 Columbia Photo by Josh Weiner.

individuals of European decent with the one notable exception, Americans of Italian ancestry. While other European groups, including German, Irish, English, and Polish, witnessed their numbers decline significantly since the 1990 Census, the number of people reporting to be Americans of Italian decent in the 2000 Census increased by seven percent.

Italian–Americans continue to embrace their heritage and culture. As Chairman Guarini noted, "Organizations like NIAF are thriving because ethnicity remains vitally important to the Italian–American community." This was echoed by NIAF President Cerrell who stated, "Italian–Americans are a highly visible group of professionals in business, politics, sports, entertainment, and the arts, who continue to contribute a great deal to the U.S. while never forgetting their heritage."

Together let's spread the good news of what Italian–Americans are doing.

18.2 DAVID RENSIN, *"PLAYBOY* INTERVIEW: MARTIN SCORSESE" [EXCERPT]

The director Martin Scorsese has often been targeted by the National Italian American Foundation (NIAF) for the violent gangster activity and psychotic behavior he emphasizes in many of his films. The NIAF fears the consequences of such themes on moviegoers' perceptions of Italian–Americans. However, as he explains in this *Playboy* interview, Scorsese believes that since he is an Italian–American who grew up in a violent neighborhood, it is his right to explore "the things he knows about" and to try to understand "how those organized-crime figures are interlaced into the Italian–American lifestyle."

Playboy: It's a letter to the editor from the *Los Angeles Times Magazine*, in response to an article about you when *GoodFellas* was released. It reads, in part, "Like other hack directors, Scorsese uses mayhem to excite audiences, not reveal meaning."

Scorsese: Oh, the violence question. It comes up.

Playboy: Obviously, this is a criticism you're familiar with. Does it upset you?

Scorsese: Only because, as I've said many times, the violence comes out of the things that I really know about. It would be very difficult for me to do a war picture. Take Oliver Stone and *Platoon*. He saw war. You get that sense of absolute horror and panic. Maybe it's no justification that these things come from *my* experience. But that's why I make personal movies. I make them about what I think I understand.

I grew up in the tenements. I lived only half a block away from the Bowery. We saw the dregs, the poor vagrants and the alcoholics. I saw everything. Most mornings on the way to grammar school, I'd see two bums fighting each other with broken bottles. Blood all over the ground. I had to step around the blood and the bottles—and I'm just eight years old. Or I'd be sitting in the derelicts' bar across the way. We'd go in—we were only kids, nine years old—and sit there. We'd watch guys get up and struggle over to another table and start hallucinating and beating up someone.

The first sexual thing I ever saw was at night: two derelicts performing fellatio on each other and then vomiting it up. I was about thirteen then. But I'll never forget the images. Never forget them. The first aspect of life I remember

Scorsese: seeing was the death of it. You don't even have to go to
(cont.)   the Bowery now to see it. In Manhattan, it's all over the
             streets.

             . . .

Playboy: And these are the experiences you've embraced on film. Why?
Scorsese: Violence is just a form of how you express your feelings to
             someone. Take this situation: Let's say you're growing up in
             this area and you want to be a gangster. Well, you can get into
             somebody's crew, and you start working, but you've got to
             prove yourself. And what you have to do, you know, is very
             clear. For instance, an old friend who got into that lifestyle for
             a while told me this incredible story.

             He had to go collect money—because it's always about
             money. He's told by the man running his crew, "You go to the
             guy in the store, take this bat and break it over his head. Get
             the money." The guy says, "Why?" And he says, "Well,
             because he's been late a few weeks and he owes me the vig.
             He should be hit. Get the money if you can." So he gets there.
             He also takes a younger guy with him. They get in the store
             and he sees there are a lot of people waiting to buy things. So
             he takes the owner in the back and threatens the guy for
             money.

             The guy says, "Oh, I have it. I have it here. Glad you came.
             Here's the money." So he takes it and leaves. On the way out,
             the young guy who was learning from him says, "You were
             supposed to hit him." "No, he had the money. We don't have
             to hit him; he gave us the money." So he went back to his boss
             and said, "Here's the money." The boss said, "Did you hit
             him? Did you break his head?" "No." "Why not?" "He *had*
             the money. And there were people there." "That's the point.
             He's late, isn't he? Take the bat and break his head. Even when
             he *gives* you the money, *especially* if there's people there.
             That's how you do it."

             And not only do you have to do it, you have to learn to
             enjoy it. And that's what I think people started to get upset
             about again lately, with *GoodFellas*.
Playboy: In stories about you, there's always the suggestion that
             although you were too sickly to join in, you *wanted* to be a
             wise guy—much like Henry Hill in *GoodFellas*.
Scorsese: I *couldn't* do it personally, but as a boy of thirteen or fourteen,
             I had to harden my heart against the suffering. I had to take it.

My friends go to beat up somebody, I went with them. I didn't jump in, but I watched or set it up.

Playboy: Really?

Scorsese: Oh, of course. Sure, you do all that. It's part of growing up there. So it's *my* experience. I don't expect this person who wrote the letter you read to have the same experience. Maybe he had experience with violence in another way. I don't know, but that's for him to make a film or write about; I have no argument.

. . .

Playboy: Does violence in films cause violence in the streets?

Scorsese: It depends on the person. I don't believe any one movie or any one book makes people *in their right mind*, whatever that is, go out and act some way because they saw it in a movie. [But I can't satisfy] America's need for quick, one-statement answers here. American readers seem to want to read a clear statement and say, "You know, they're right." As simple as that, like taking polls on CNN. It's crazy. That's not a one-statement answer, it's a very complicated question.

Playboy: Roger Ebert said he didn't think you could make *Taxi Driver* today, because it had the wrong kind of violence. He said it was meaningful, well-thought-out violence, as opposed to random violence.

Scorsese: I suppose the kind of random violence he's talking about is in films like *Total Recall*—which I haven't seen—which are really the action-adventure B films from the Thirties and Forties taken to another level. That violence confuses me and perplexes me. I really don't understand it. Violence in films today is so abstract. Horror films and the disemboweling of people. Maybe that satisfies a need in human beings that was satisfied by real blood lust two thousand years ago. I don't know what's happened to our society. I don't know why we have to see our entrails being dragged out. I don't get it.

Playboy: What about *Taxi Driver*? The film is perhaps the pre-eminent example of how the public associates you with violence.

Scorsese: Well, I didn't do the violence scenes in *Taxi Driver* for titillation, for instance, or for an audience to have *fun* with. It was just a natural progression of the character in the story. And the total tragedy of it.

. . .

Playboy: One person who got it wrong was John Hinckley. He used

Playboy:
(cont.) having seen *Taxi Driver*, and having become obsessed with Jodie Foster, as part of his defense.

Scorsese: To use the film as a defense is such an oversimplification. A horror. But attempted assassinations are so horrible, and the country is so frightened by this phenomenon, that using the film as a defense kind of sedates the public. It makes them feel, "It's OK, we've got everything under control. It was the fault of these guys who made this picture, and it was the fault of *Catcher in the Rye*." Does this then mean it has really nothing to do with his *family*, it has nothing to do with *maybe* there's something wrong physically with his brain?

Playboy: When did you hear the news linking the film and the assassination attempt?

Scorsese: We were in Los Angeles for the Academy Awards. Afterward—Bob won the Academy Award for *Raging Bull*—at a party at Ma Maison, someone said, "Didn't you hear the news?"

Playboy: How did you feel at that moment?

Scorsese: I said it was absurd. Then they explained the details about Hinckley.

. . .

Playboy: Let's start wrapping this up, with one of your favorite subjects. Why did you once say you hated the phrase Italian–American sensibility?

Scorsese: Did I say that? [*Laughs*] I get upset about the happy, dancing, singing peasants, organ-grinder's monkey, everybody eating pasta cliché of the Italian–American. Any ethnic group would be a little annoyed by the stereotypes.

Playboy: Italian–Americans seem to be annoyed at you for stereotyping them as wise guys and Mobsters.

Scorsese: OK. But I want to be clear about this: It's not the experience for *all* Italian–Americans. Not everybody in my neighborhood was a wise guy. This is a very annoying area to talk about without the Italian–Americans' getting upset. I point out, and Nick Pileggi [author of the book *Wiseguy* and co-author of the screenplay *GoodFellas*] points out, that out of twenty million Italian–Americans there are only four thousand known organized-crime members. Yet there is a reality to how those organized-crime figures are interlaced into the Italian–American lifestyle. To best understand the importance and the unimportance on it is to come from that lifestyle. It's very difficult to describe.

. . .

Playboy: How would you compare your Italian–American films with *The Godfather*, *Married to the Mob*, *Prizzi's Honor?*

Scorsese: Demme was using stereotype for *Married to the Mob*, but for a farce, you can get away with it. *Prizzi's Honor?* Forget it; it's a whole different thing. Jack Nicholson and Anjelica Huston went right over the top with those accents. It was a wonderful self-parody in a way, and it's very difficult to do.

Playboy: Are you at all offended or cynical about those films?

Scorsese: Yeah. Certain films about Italian–Americans are exaggerations. They're not made by Italian–Americans. *Moonstruck*, for example, is an enjoyable picture, but it's a little exaggerated in terms of the ethnicity of it. It sometimes is disturbing. When the titles come up and you hear *That's Amore* by Dean Martin, as an Italian–American, you cringe a little bit. Or *Mambo Italiano* in the titles of *Married to the Mob*. I told Demme, "You can't do that, you're not Italian. Only Italians can play that music. Only Italians can say the bad things about ourselves."

Playboy: Have you ever gotten compliments on these kind of films from, say, Mafia types?

Scorsese: Nick Pileggi told me that Henry Hill told him that [Mafia kingpin] Paulie Vario never went to the movies. One night, they said, "Paulie, we're going to take you to see this picture." They took him to see a movie, and it was *Mean Streets*. And he loved it. It was his favorite picture. And I got the same response from Ed McDonald, who was head of the Brooklyn organized-crime strike task force.

Playboy: Why was it so appealing?

Scorsese: Because it had a truth to it. And that was the highest compliment.

CHAPTER 19

Gone with the Wind? Hollywood's Track Record

19.1 GEORGE CLOONEY, BEST SUPPORTING ACTOR ACCEPTANCE SPEECH, 2006 ACADEMY AWARDS

When accepting his Oscar for Best Actor in a Supporting Role at the 2006 Academy Awards, George Clooney responded to the frequently made critique that Hollywood is out of touch with mainstream values. In the reprinted speech below, Clooney argues that Hollywood has often been on the right side of social issues, like AIDS and civil rights, that were once unpopular.

Wow. Wow. All right, so I'm not winning director. It's the funny thing about winning an Academy Award, it will always be synonymous with your name from here on in. It will be Oscar winner, George Clooney. Sexiest Man Alive, 1997. Batman, died today in a freak accident at a—Listen, I don't quite know how you compare art. You look at these performances this year, of these actors and unless we all did the same role, everybody put on a bat suit, and we'll all try that. Unless we all did the same role, I don't know how you compare it. They are stellar performances and wonderful work, and I'm honored, truly honored to be up here. And finally, I would say that, you know, we are a little bit out of touch in Hollywood every once in a while. I think it's probably a good thing. We're the ones who talk about AIDS when it was just being whispered, and we talked about civil rights when it wasn't really popular. And we, you know, we bring up subjects. This Academy, this group of people gave Hattie McDaniel an Oscar in 1939 when blacks were still sitting in the backs of theaters. I'm proud to be a part of this Academy. Proud to be part of this community, and proud to be out of touch. And I thank you so much for this.

Actor George Clooney accepting the Best Supporting Actor honor at the 78th Annual Academy Awards on March 5, 2006, at the Kodak Theater in Hollywood, California. Clooney praised the film community for its progressive approach to political issues, a statement that set off a storm of controversy amongst pundits nation-wide. Motion Picture and Television Archive/2006 AMPAS.

19.2 JONAH GOLDBERG, "HOLLYWOOD'S EYE CONTACT WITH SOCIAL ISSUES"

When the actor George Clooney proudly boasted of "being out of touch" at the 2006 Academy Awards, he provoked a wave of criticism by liberal and conservative columnists alike. Critics, like Jonah Goldberg, argued that the film industry had actually proven itself backward on social issues and that most celebrities were too self-absorbed to understand pressing and controversial issues.

One of my favorite tidbits about Hollywood that I've gleaned from the starstruck press is that a great many of its most accomplished stars don't allow their staffs to look them in the eye. I'm not making this up. It has been reported that Barbra Streisand not only discourages eye contact among staff, but that she required hotel workers to leave her presence only by walking backward. Jennifer Lopez—who had 75 attendants help her prepare for a cameo on "Will & Grace"—is also reputed to forbid her subalterns to look into the windows of her soul. Sylvester Stallone won't stand for such effrontery, and Tom Cruise likes to ban eye contact, too, at least while he's working.

This, of course, is just the tip of the iceberg. Many of Hollywood's glitterati have staffers for every human need. Some of the biggest stars have personal aroma therapists. Mariah Carey employs someone whose only job is to hand her towels. Kim Basinger has a personal umbrella-holder charged with protecting her from the sun's aging rays. Sean Penn once made a staffer swim the icy and dangerous currents of the East River simply to get him a cigarette.

And so on.

I bring this up because when I hear a movie star boast that he's "proud to be out of touch," this is the sort of thing I think of.

George Clooney, Hollywood liberalism's best, prettiest and shiniest pony, has something different in mind. As you no doubt heard, Clooney offered an eloquent bit of self-congratulation Sunday night when he accepted his Best Supporting Actor Oscar. Responding to the notion that Hollywood is "out of touch," Clooney gushed that "We were the ones who talked about AIDS . . . about civil rights, when it wasn't really popular." He swooned over the fact that "this Academy, this group of people gave Hattie McDaniel an Oscar in 1939 when blacks were still sitting in the backs of theaters." And so, he testified, he is "proud to be 'out of touch'."

One wonders whether he shopped this little speech out to one of his staffers or if he came up with it all by his lonesome. Either way, he needs a new speechwriter.

First, let's keep in mind that it really wasn't "this group of people" who gave Hattie McDaniel the first Oscar ever awarded to an African–American for her work in "Gone with the Wind." But we all understand he was speaking figuratively.

Clooney wants to buy some grace on the cheap by getting credit for McDaniel's Oscar, and we might as well give it to him. But he should expect to carry some of the baggage as well. After all, while McDaniel's wonderful performance was certainly something to be proud of, the role she won it for—an archetypal Aunt Jemima—is hardly the sort of thing they like to encourage at the Image Awards. According to an illuminating 1999 article by Leonard Leff in The Atlantic, when McDaniel received her statue, she told the assembled Academy that she hoped she'd "always be a credit to my race."

Margaret Mitchell's book "Gone with the Wind" is hardly a staple of the progressive canon. Its black characters were either gorilla-like savages or complacent servants perfectly content with being slaves. The Ku Klux Klan, meanwhile, was a "tragic necessity." Sidney Howard, charged with making a screenplay out of the book, told Mitchell that she offered "the best written darkies, I do believe, in all literature," and hoped she might help him bring them to life on the big screen.

Of course, the same Hollywood that gave McDaniel her Oscar also produced "Gone with the Wind" and countless other films whose racism was, far, far, far less open to dispute. Al Jolson's blackface, Stepin Fetchit, "Mandingo" and, of course, Woodrow Wilson's favorite movie, "Birth of a Nation," seem like just a few examples of how "in touch" Hollywood was back then. And I'm not even going to get into all of the pro-communist and anti-American movies Hollywood has churned out over the last 60 years.

But you see, I'm simply missing the point. Not too long ago, Clooney said in an interview, "Yes, I'm a liberal, and I'm sick of it being a bad word. I don't know at what time in history liberals have stood on the wrong side of social issues." In other words, just as a Hollywood diva can never be wrong in the eyes of an underling—how could she be? they can't even make eye contact—being "out of touch" means, simply, being right. And just a little better than everyone else, too.

MARILYN MONROE
and her bosom companions
TONY CURTIS
JACK LEMMON
BILLY WILDER
production
"SOME LIKE IT HOT"
RAFT · O'BRIEN · BROWN
BILLY WILDER and I. A. L. DIAMOND · BILLY WILDER

PART V

Cultural Values

Hollywood movies express more than cultural values in modern America. Indeed, movies have become integral to defining popular culture—helping to set fashion, speech, and trends. Given the importance of movies (and television) to American popular culture it is inevitable that Hollywood and its products became center stage for culture wars beginning with the first appearance of nickelodeons at the turn of the twentieth century. The ensuing debate between critics and defenders of Hollywood centered on core issues involving free speech, social responsibility, the exact influence of film on viewers, the rights of a community to set standards of morality, and the right of artistic expression. Such issues were not easily resolved and led to acrimonious debate that continues today.

In making movies, Hollywood since its inception sought a single goal: generating profit. Studios attempted to draw audiences to their films with good story lines, artistic craft, star power, and, ultimately, entertainment. In a mass culture, this also meant titillating audiences with images of sex and violence. In the late 1920s and early 1930s, many films in Hollywood employed these devices to lure audiences into the theater. Gangster films such as *Scarface* (1932) projected graphic violence on the screen that had not been seen in earlier films. At the same time, other films presented sexual themes that had been repressed in polite American society.

Actor-comedian Mae West became notorious for her sexual banter and one-liners in her early 1930s films. After a vaudeville and stage career in which she appeared in plays such as *Sex* and *The Drag* (about homosexuality), *Pleasure Man*, and *The Constant Sinner*, West came to Hollywood in 1932 at the age of thirty-eight. Her career took off with *She Done Him Wrong* (1933) and *I'm No Angel* (1933). The sexual *double entendres* she delivered in these films gained her fame. The most enduring one came when she asked a man, "Is that a gun in your pocket or are you just glad to see me?"

Hollywood's depictions of violence and sex drew criticism from traditional Roman Catholics and evangelical Protestants who charged that these films were romanticizing and glamorizing the worst aspects of American society. Critics charged that because of Hollywood's important place in modern culture, movie producers had a special responsibility to help elevate American democratic culture. Roman Catholic priests and layman organized the especially effective Legion for Decency to pressure the studios to impose self-censorship on its products. Fearing federal intervention, the studios agreed to the Hays Code in 1934. The Hays Code remained in force formally until 1968, when it was replaced by a new rating system agreed to by the Motion Picture Producers Association (MPPA).

Even before this new rating system, however, the Hays Code had begun to break down with the rise of independent studios in the 1950s and 1960s, as well as the large influx of foreign films in this period. The Supreme Court's decision, *Joseph Burstyn, Inc. v. Wilson* (1952), marked the first signs that the Hays Code was losing its effect. The decision ruled that provisions of the New York Education Law allowing censorship of commercial showings of non-licensed motion picture films was a violation of First Amendment free speech. This decision overturned a landmark decision in *Mutual Film Corporation v. the Industrial Commission of Ohio* (1915) which determined that movies were not an art form worthy of First Amendment protections, but rather a business. The Burstyn case concerned an Italian film, *The Miracle* (1950), directed by Roberto Rossellini about a peasant who believes herself to be the Virgin Mary. When the New York Board of regents ruled that the film was sacrilegious, the distributors of the film took the board to court. This decision was the first of many that the courts undertook over the subsequent two decades, when it grappled with definitions of censorship, obscenity, pornography, free speech, and community standards.

Further evidence of the ineffectiveness of the Hays Code were apparent in the release of Billy Wilder's *Some Like It Hot* (1959) about two male musicians who, in their efforts to flee from Chicago mobsters, dress as women and join an all-female band. Wilder released the film without a certificate of approval from the Hays Code. In the 1960s, young audiences demanded that Hollywood tackle controversial themes and subjects. However, new organizations emerged to protest sex and violence on the screen. Once again fearing a public backlash or federal involvement, the MPPA tried to compromise by agreeing to a new rating system that went into effect in late 1968. This rating was subsequently refined in 1984 when a PG-13 category was created. The rating system drew criticism from civil libertarians as censorship, as well as from moralist opponents who claimed that the system was generally unenforced by movie theaters.

Such debates took place in a far-reaching discussion by public officials and the courts about pornography in the United States. In 1957, the Supreme Court ruled in *Roth v. United States* that obscenity does not fall within the First Amendment's guarantee of free speech, or under the Fourteenth Amendment's Due Process clause. Nine years later in 1966, the court reversed itself in *Memoirs v. Massachusetts* by arguing that society has no interest in "overriding the guarantees of free speech and press and establishing a regime of CENSORSHIP." In 1973, the Supreme Court reversed itself again in *Miller v. California*, which ruled that obscenity is outside the First Amendment's protections and reaffirmed *Roth*'s original test for obscenity. It differed from *Roth*, however, in that it left the determination of obscenity up to state legislatures to decide and rejected the necessity of national standards. In later decisions the Supreme Court refined this decision by allowing for communities to impose obscenity standards. It is within this context of changing court opinion that Attorney General Edwin Meese formed a Commission on Pornography that issued a report in July 1989.

The public debate and legal battle over pornography occurred in reaction to the proliferation of pornography films in American culture. The release of *Deep Throat* in 1972, a $25,000 budget film, took pornography out of the shabby down-town theater to suburban America, and many other pornographic films followed. The development of DVD players, CD technology, and the internet enabled Americans to view pornography in their homes. The growth of the pornography industry spurred anti-pornography activists including traditional religious moralists and anti-pornography feminists who believed these films encouraged sexual violence against women. At issue was the perennial debate over the influence of film on general audiences and individual viewers prone to violence, as well as film's general influence on society. Such questions ensured that Hollywood and film will continue to be debated in American politics.

These debates over the meaning of free speech and obscenity continued into the twenty-first century in a culture war over family values. The breakdown of the traditional family headed by a father and a mother, the rising out-of-wedlock birth rate, and continued violence toward women led critics to charge that Hollywood had contributed to a deteriorating culture. Defenders of the film industry answered that the industry produced movies reflecting a changing culture. It was only supplying what the American people wanted.

This was a debate that was not easily resolved.

CHAPTER 20

I'm No Angel: Family Values in the Great Depression

20.1 THE MOTION PICTURE PRODUCTION CODE OF 1930 (HAYS CODE) [EXCERPT]

A series of industry scandals, including a murder and a drug overdose in the 1920s, fed into the perception that Hollywood would be more aptly named "Sin City." In order to combat its unseemly image, an influential Republican lawyer named Will H. Hays drafted a series of topics he believed the studios should avoid, a list commonly known as "the formula." With the advent of talking pictures that same year, a Chicago newspaperman and a Catholic priest pressured the studios to enhance the list to include a moral system, and the studios officially adopted what became known as the Hays Code, included below, in 1930.

If motion pictures present stories that will affect lives for the better, they can become the most powerful force for the improvement of mankind.

A Code to Govern the Making of Talking, Synchronized and Silent Motion Pictures. Formulated and formally adopted by The Association of Motion Picture Producers, Inc. and The Motion Picture Producers and Distributors of America, Inc. in March 1930.

Motion picture producers recognize the high trust and confidence which have been placed in them by the people of the world and which have made motion pictures a universal form of entertainment.

They recognize their responsibility to the public because of this trust and because entertainment and art are important influences in the life of a nation.

Hence, though regarding motion pictures primarily as entertainment without any explicit purpose of teaching or propaganda, they know that the motion picture within its own field of entertainment may be directly responsible for spiritual or moral progress, for higher types of social life, and for much correct thinking.

During the rapid transition from silent to talking pictures they have realized the necessity and the opportunity of subscribing to a Code to govern the production of talking pictures and of reacknowledging this responsibility.

On their part, they ask from the public and from public leaders a sympathetic understanding of their purposes and problems and a spirit of cooperation that will allow them the freedom and opportunity necessary to bring the motion picture to a still higher level of wholesome entertainment for all the people.

General Principles

1. No picture shall be produced that will lower the moral standards of those who see it. Hence the sympathy of the audience should never be thrown to the side of crime, wrongdoing, evil or sin.
2. Correct standards of life, subject only to the requirements of drama and entertainment, shall be presented.
3. Law, natural or human, shall not be ridiculed, nor shall sympathy be created for its violation.

Particular Applications

I. Crimes Against the Law

These shall never be presented in such a way as to throw sympathy with the crime as against law and justice or to inspire others with a desire for imitation.

1. Murder

   a. The technique of murder must be presented in a way that will not inspire imitation.
   b. Brutal killings are not to be presented in detail.
   c. Revenge in modern times shall not be justified.

2. Methods of Crime should not be explicitly presented.

   a. Theft, robbery, safe-cracking, and dynamiting of trains, mines, buildings, etc., should not be detailed in method.

    b.   Arson must be subject to the same safeguards.

    c.   The use of firearms should be restricted to the essentials.

    d.   Methods of smuggling should not be presented.

3.   Illegal drug traffic must never be presented.

4.   The use of liquor in American life, when not required by the plot or for proper characterization, will not be shown.

II. Sex

The sanctity of the institution of marriage and the home shall be upheld. Pictures shall not infer that low forms of sex relationship are the accepted or common thing.

1.   Adultery, sometimes necessary plot material, must not be explicitly treated, or justified, or presented attractively.

2.   Scenes of Passion

    a.   They should not be introduced when not essential to the plot.

    b.   Excessive and lustful kissing, lustful embraces, suggestive postures and gestures, are not to be shown.

    c.   In general passion should so be treated that these scenes do not stimulate the lower and baser element.

3.   Seduction or Rape

    a.   They should never be more than suggested, and only when essential for the plot, and even then never shown by explicit method.

    b.   They are never the proper subject for comedy.

4.   Sex perversion or any inference to it is forbidden.

5.   White slavery shall not be treated.

6.   Miscegenation (sex relationships between the white and black races) is forbidden.

7.   Sex hygiene and venereal diseases are not subjects for motion pictures.

8.   Scenes of actual child birth, in fact or in silhouette, are never to be presented.

9.   Children's sex organs are never to be exposed.

III. Vulgarity

The treatment of low, disgusting, unpleasant, though not necessarily evil, subjects should always be subject to the dictates of good taste and a regard for the sensibilities of the audience.

IV. Obscenity

Obscenity in word, gesture, reference, song, joke, or by suggestion (even when likely to be understood only by part of the audience) is forbidden.

V. Profanity

Pointed profanity (this includes the words, God, Lord, Jesus, Christ—unless used reverently—Hell, S.O.B., damn, Gawd), or every other profane or vulgar expression however used, is forbidden.

VI. Costume

1. Complete nudity is never permitted. This includes nudity in fact or in silhouette, or any lecherous or licentious notice thereof by other characters in the picture.
2. Undressing scenes should be avoided, and never used save where essential to the plot.
3. Indecent or undue exposure is forbidden.
4. Dancing or costumes intended to permit undue exposure or indecent movements in the dance are forbidden.

VII. Dances

1. Dances suggesting or representing sexual actions or indecent passions are forbidden.
2. Dances which emphasize indecent movements are to be regarded as obscene.

VIII. Religion

1. No film or episode may throw ridicule on any religious faith.
2. Ministers of religion in their character as ministers of religion should not be used as comic characters or as villains.
3. Ceremonies of any definite religion should be carefully and respectfully handled.

IX. Locations

The treatment of bedrooms must be governed by good taste and delicacy.

X. National Feelings

1. The use of the Flag shall be consistently respectful.
2. The history, institutions, prominent people and citizenry of other nations shall be represented fairly.

XI. Titles

Salacious, indecent, or obscene titles shall not be used.

XII. Repellent Subjects

The following subjects must be treated within the careful limits of good taste:

1. Actual hangings or electrocutions as legal punishments for crime.
2. Third degree methods.
3. Brutality and possible gruesomeness.
4. Branding of people or animals.
5. Apparent cruelty to children or animals.
6. The sale of women, or a woman selling her virtue.
7. Surgical operations.

Reasons Supporting the Preamble of the Code

I. Theatrical motion pictures, that is, pictures intended for the theatre as distinct from pictures intended for churches, schools, lecture halls, educational movements, social reform movements, etc., are primarily to be regarded as ENTERTAINMENT

Mankind has always recognized the importance of entertainment and its value in rebuilding the bodies and souls of human beings.

But it has always recognized that entertainment can be a character either HELPFUL or HARMFUL to the human race, and in consequence has clearly distinguished between:

a. Entertainment which tends to improve the race, or at least to re-create and rebuild human beings exhausted with the realities of life; and
b. Entertainment which tends to degrade human beings, or to lower their standards of life and living.

Hence the MORAL IMPORTANCE of entertainment is something which has been universally recognized. It enters intimately into the lives of men and women and affects them closely; it occupies their minds and affections during leisure hours; and ultimately touches the whole of their lives. A man may be judged by his standard of entertainment as easily as by the standard of his work.

So correct entertainment raises the whole standard of a nation.

Wrong entertainment lowers the whole living conditions and moral ideals of a race.

Note, for example, the healthy reactions to healthful sports, like baseball, golf; the unhealthy reactions to sports like cockfighting, bullfighting, bear baiting, etc.

Note, too, the effect on ancient nations of gladiatorial combats, the obscene plays of Roman times, etc.

II. Motion pictures are very important as ART

Though a new art, possibly a combination art, it has the same object as the other arts, the presentation of human thought, emotion, and experience, in terms of an appeal to the soul through the senses.

Here, as in entertainment,

Art enters intimately into the lives of human beings.

Art can be morally good, lifting men to higher levels. This has been done through good music, great painting, authentic fiction, poetry, drama.

Art can be morally evil it its effects. This is the case clearly enough with unclean art, indecent books, suggestive drama. The effect on the lives of men and women are obvious.

Note: It has often been argued that art itself is unmoral, neither good nor bad. This is true of the THING which is music, painting, poetry, etc. But the THING is the PRODUCT of some person's mind, and the intention of that mind was either good or bad morally when it produced the thing. Besides, the thing has its EFFECT upon those who come into contact with it. In both these ways, that is, as a product of a mind and as the cause of definite effects, it has a deep moral significance and unmistakable moral quality.

Hence: The motion pictures, which are the most popular of modern arts for the masses, have their moral quality from the intention of the minds which produce them and from their effects on the moral lives and reactions of their audiences. This gives them a most important morality.

1. They reproduce the morality of the men who use the pictures as a medium for the expression of their ideas and ideals.
2. They affect the moral standards of those who, through the screen, take in these ideas and ideals.

In the case of motion pictures, the effect may be particularly emphasized because no art has so quick and so widespread an appeal to the masses. It has become in an incredibly short period the art of the multitudes.

III. *The motion picture, because of its importance as entertainment and because of the trust placed in it by the peoples of the world, has special MORAL OBLIGATIONS:*

A. Most arts appeal to the mature. This art appeals at once to every class, mature, immature, developed, undeveloped, law abiding, criminal. Music has its grades for different classes; so has literature and drama. This art of the motion picture, combining as it does the two fundamental appeals of looking at a picture and listening to a story, at once reaches every class of society.
B. By reason of the mobility of film and the ease of picture distribution, and because of the possibility of duplicating positives in large

quantities, this art reaches places unpenetrated by other forms of art.

C. Because of these two facts, it is difficult to produce films intended for only certain classes of people. The exhibitors' theatres are built for the masses, for the cultivated and the rude, the mature and the immature, the self-respecting and the criminal. Films, unlike books and music, can with difficulty be confined to certain selected groups.

D. The latitude given to film material cannot, in consequence, be as wide as the latitude given to book material. In addition:

  a. A book describes; a film vividly presents. One presents on a cold page; the other by apparently living people.

  b. A book reaches the mind through words merely; a film reaches the eyes and ears through the reproduction of actual events.

  c. The reaction of a reader to a book depends largely on the keenness of the reader's imagination; the reaction to a film depends on the vividness of presentation.
    Hence many things which might be described or suggested in a book could not possibly be presented in a film.

E. This is also true when comparing the film with the newspaper.

  a. Newspapers present by description, films by actual presentation.

  b. Newspapers are after the fact and present things as having taken place; the film gives the events in the process of enactment and with apparent reality of life.

F. Everything possible in a play is not possible in a film:

  a. Because of the larger audience of the film, and its consequential mixed character. Psychologically, the larger the audience, the lower the moral mass resistance to suggestion.

  b. Because through light, enlargement of character, presentation, scenic emphasis, etc., the screen story is brought closer to the audience than the play.

  c. The enthusiasm for and interest in the film actors and actresses, developed beyond anything of the sort in history, makes the audience largely sympathetic toward the characters they portray and the stories in which they figure. Hence the audience is more ready to confuse actor and actress and the characters they portray, and it is most receptive of the emotions and ideals presented by the favorite stars.

G.   Small communities, remote from sophistication and from the hardening process which often takes place in the ethical and moral standards of larger cities, are easily and readily reached by any sort of film.

H.   The grandeur of mass settings, large action, spectacular features, etc., affects and arouses more intensely the emotional side of the audience.

In general, the mobility, popularity, accessibility, emotional appeal, vividness, straightforward presentation of fact in the film make for more intimate contact with a larger audience and for greater emotional appeal.

Hence the larger moral responsibilities of the motion pictures.

Reasons Underlying the General Principles

I. *No picture shall be produced which will lower the moral standards of those who see it*

Hence the sympathy of the audience should never be thrown to the side of crime, wrongdoing, evil or sin.

This is done:

1.   When evil is made to appear attractive and alluring, and good is made to appear unattractive.

2.   When the sympathy of the audience is thrown on the side of crime, wrongdoing, evil, sin. The same is true of a film that would throw sympathy against goodness, honor, innocence, purity or honesty.

Note: Sympathy with a person who sins is not the same as sympathy with the sin or crime of which he is guilty. We may feel sorry for the plight of the murderer or even understand the circumstances which led him to his crime: we may not feel sympathy with the wrong which he has done. The presentation of evil is often essential for art or fiction or drama. This in itself is not wrong provided:

a.   That evil is not presented alluringly. Even if later in the film the evil is condemned or punished, it must not be allowed to appear so attractive that the audience's emotions are drawn to desire or approve so strongly that later the condemnation is forgotten and only the apparent joy of sin is remembered.

b. That throughout, the audience feels sure that evil is wrong and good is right.

II. Correct standards of life shall, as far as possible, be presented

A wide knowledge of life and of living is made possible through the film. When right standards are consistently presented, the motion picture exercises the most powerful influences. It builds character, develops right ideals, inculcates correct principles, and all this in attractive story form.

If motion pictures consistently hold up for admiration high types of characters and present stories that will affect lives for the better, they can become the most powerful force for the improvement of mankind.

III. Law, natural or human, shall not be ridiculed, nor shall sympathy be created for its violation

By natural law is understood the law which is written in the hearts of all mankind, the greater underlying principles of right and justice dictated by conscience.

By human law is understood the law written by civilized nations.

1. The presentation of crimes against the law is often necessary for the carrying out of the plot. But the presentation must not throw sympathy with the crime as against the law nor with the criminal as against those who punish him.
2. The courts of the land should not be presented as unjust. This does not mean that a single court may not be presented as unjust, much less that a single court official must not be presented this way. But the court system of the country must not suffer as a result of this presentation.

20.2 MOTION PICTURES CLASSIFIED BY NATIONAL LEGION OF DECENCY: FEBRUARY, 1936–NOVEMBER, 1950 [EXCERPT]

Even though the studios adopted the Hays Code, it was not aggressively enforced, and in 1934 the National Legion of Decency formed in order to "stem the flood of immorality" gushing from Hollywood. The Legion pressured the studios to add an enforcement measure to the Code, and, indeed, the studios established the Production Code Administration (PCA) to screen films and give them a certificate of approval. The Legion, however, still considered some films objectionable and began classifying films as "A" (morally unobjectionable), "B" (morally objectionable in part), or "C" (condemned). Excerpted below is an extract from a 1950s motion pictures rating booklet published by the League. Classified as "B" is the film *My Little Chickadee* (1939) starring Mae West, in which West famously asked "Is that a gun in your pocket or are you just glad to see me?"

Combining . . . the powerful effect of entertainment motion pictures with the existence of films morally objectionable in whole or in part, we can easily understand the need for the existence of such an organization as the National Legion of Decency. For the principle aim of the Legion of Decency is to discourage the production and patronizing of films which are not "worthy of the rational nature of man," which are not "morally healthy." For this reason the Legion criticizes and classifies entertainment films solely and exclusively from the viewpoint of Christian morality and decency. Support of, and cooperation with the aims of the Legion will in no small measure contribute to the salvation of souls and to the safeguarding of the principles upon which our country is founded.

WILLIAM A. SCULLY,
Coadjutor Bishop of Albany,
Chairman, Bishop's Committee on Motion Pictures.

. . .

Pursuant to policies laid down by the Episcopal Committee on Motion Pictures, the Legion reviews and classifies entertainment motion pictures solely from the viewpoint of morality and decency. The review work is in the hands of the Motion Picture Department of the International Federation of Catholic Alumnae which was selected by the bishops as the official reviewing group for the Legion. These graduates of Catholic high schools and colleges, trained in the work of reviewing motion pictures are complemented in more serious and difficult cases by a Board of Consultors composed of priests and laymen. The reviewers through the cooperation of the motion picture companies see films before they are released. Reports on the moral content of the picture are made on a printed ballot which are processed by the executive staff of the Legion. Classification of films is then made according to the weight of the opinions expressed, into one of the following categories.

A-I—Morally Unobjectionable for General Patronage. These films are considered to contain no material which would be morally dangerous to the average motion picture audience, adults and children alike.

A-II—Morally Unobjectionable for Adults. These are films which in themselves are morally harmless but which, because of subject matter or treatment, require maturity and experience if one is to witness them without danger of moral harm. While no definite age limit can be established for this group, the judgment of parents, pastors and teachers would be helpful in determining the decision in individual cases.

B—Morally Objectionable in Part for All. Films in this category are considered to contain elements dangerous to Christian morals or moral standards.

C—Condemned. Condemned films are considered to be those which because of theme or treatment are what has been described by the Holy Father as "positively bad."

Some few films have been "Separately Classified." In each case a reason has been assigned for this action.

It is to be noted that in deciding the ratings of films no consideration is given to their artistic, technical, et cetera, qualities. Only moral content is weighed.

Condemned films have often been reclassified. This has been done only when the offensive elements in them have been eliminated or substantially changed. This has always been the policy of the Legion and was adopted in the interests of the greater good for the greater number.

It is to be noted that until 1939 it was the policy of the Legion not to publish reasons for its objections.

The classification of all the films which appear in the following pages would not have been possible without the intelligent and persevering work of the members of the Motion Picture Department of the International Federation of Catholic Alumnae. These women, working on a volunteer basis, in a most trying and exacting type of Catholic Action, have given unselfishly of themselves and of their time in order that God's handiwork, the souls of human beings might not be corrupted by the blight of evil motion pictures.

REV. PATRICK J. MASTERSON,
Executive Secretary.
REV. THOMAS F. LITTLE,
Assistant Executive Secretary.
MRS. JAMES F. LOORAM,
Chairman, M.P.D., I.F.C.A.

Title and Distributor	Rating	Year of Review
My Dream Is Yours (Warners)	A-II	1948–49
My Favorite Blonde (Paramount)	A-I	1941–42
My Favorite Brunette (Paramount)	A-II	1946–47
My Favorite Spy (RKO)	A-I	1941–42
My Favorite Wife (RKO)	B	1939–40
Objection: Suggestive remarks.		
My Foolish Heart (RKO)	B	1949–50
Objection: Tends to condone immoral actions and justify divorce.		
My Friend Flicka (20th Century-Fox)	A-I	1942–43
My Friend Irma (Paramount)	A-II	1948–49
My Friend Irma Goes West (Paramount)	B	1949–50
Objection: Suggestive costuming, dialogue and situations.		
My Gal Loves Music (Universal)	A-II	1944–45
My Gal Sal (20th Century-Fox)	A-II	1941–42
My Girl Tisa (Warners)	A-I	1947–48
My Hands Are Clay (British) (Hoffberg Prod., Inc.)	A-I	1949–50
My Heart Belongs to Daddy (Paramount)	B	1942–43
Objection: Suggestive insinuations.		
My Irish Molly (John Argyle-Alliance Pictures)	A-I	1939–40
My Kingdom for a Cook (Columbia)	A-II	1942–43
My Life (formerly Ecstasy) (Pix Dist. Corp.)	C	1936–37
My Life With Caroline (RKO)	A-II	1940–41
My Little Chickadee (Universal)	B	1939–40
Objection: Suggestive lines and situations.		
My Love Came Back (Warner-First National)	A-II	1939–40
My Lucky Star (20th Century-Fox)	A-I	1937–38

Title and Distributor	Rating	Year of Review
My Man Godfrey (Universal)	A-I	1936–37
My Name Is Julia Ross (Columbia)	A-II	1945–46
My Old Kentucky Home (Monogram)	A-II	1937–38
My Own True Love (Paramount)	B	1948–49
Objection: Reflects the acceptability of divorce.		
My Pal Trigger (Republic)	A-I	1945–46
My Pal Wolf (RKO)	A-I	1943–44
My Reputation (Warners)	A-II	1945–46
My Sister Eileen (Columbia)	A-II	1941–42
My Son Is a Criminal (Columbia)	A-II	1938–39
My Son Is Guilty (Columbia)	A-II	1939–40
My Son, My Son (United Artists)	A-II	1939–40
My Son, the Hero (Producers Releasing Corp.)	B	1942–43
Objection: Suggestive lines. Reflects the acceptability of divorce.		
Mysteres de Paris, Les (French) (Franco-American Film Corp.)	A-II	1936–37
Mysterious Desperado, The (RKO)	A-I	1948–49
Mysterious Doctor, The (Warners)	A-I	1942–43
Mysterious Intruder (Columbia)	A-II	1945–46
Mysterious Miss X, The (Republic)	A-I	1938–39
Mysterious Mr. Moto (20th Century-Fox)	A-I	1937–38
Mysterious Mr. Valentine (Republic)	A-II	1945–46
Mysterious Rider, The (Paramount)	A-I	1937–38
Mystery at the Burlesque (British) (Monogram)	B	1949–50
Objection: Suggestive dialogue.		
Mystery Broadcast (Republic)	A-II	1942–43
Mystery House (Warners)	A-I	1937–38
Mystery in Mexico (RKO)	A-II	1947–48
Mystery Man (United Artists)	A-I	1943–44
Mystery of Marie Roget (Universal)	A-II	1941–42
Mystery of Mr. Wong, The (Monogram)	A-I	1938–39
Mystery of the Hooded Horsemen (Grand National)	A-I	1936–37
Mystery of the 13th Guest (Monogram)	A-I	1943–44
Mystery of the White Room (Universal)	A-II	1938–39
Mystery Plane (Monogram)	A-I	1938–39

Title and Distributor	Rating	Year of Review
Mystery Range (Mercury)	A-I	1936–37
Mystery Sea Raider (Paramount)	A-I	1939–40
Mystery Ship (Universal)	A-II	1940–41
Mystery Street (MGM)	A-II	1949–50
My Wife's Relatives (Republic)	A-I	1938–39
My Wild Irish Rose (Warners)	A-I	1947–48
Nabonga (Producers Releasing Corp.)	A-I	1943–44
Nach mit dem Kaiser, Die (German) (Tobis)	A-II	1936–37
Nail, The (Spanish) (Azteca Films)	B	1948–49

Objection: Tends to condone illicit actions.

Nais (French) (Siritzky International Pictures Corp.)	C	1947–48

Objection: This film presents justification of illicit love and condones crime.

Naked City, The (Universal-International)	A-II	1947–48
Nancy Drew and the Hidden Staircase (Warners)	A-I	1938–39
Nancy Drew, Detective (Warners)	A-I	1938–39
Nancy Drew, Reporter (Warners)	A-I	1938–39
Nancy Drew, Trouble Shooter (Warners)	A-I	1938–39
Nancy Goes to Rio (MGM)	A-II	1949–50
Nancy Steele Is Missing (20th Century-Fox)	A-II	1936–37
Naszut Felaron (Hungarian) (Lux)	A-I	1936–37
Nation Aflame (Treasure)	A-II	1936–37
National Barn Dance, The (Paramount)	A-I	1943–44
National Velvet (MGM)	A-I	1944–45
Native Land (Frontier Films)	A-II	1941–42
Naughty Arlette (British) (Eagle Lion)	B	1949–50

Objection: Suggestive costuming and situations.

Naughty But Nice (Warners)	A-II	1938–39
Naughty Marietta (Reissue) (MGM)	A-II	1944–45
Naughty Nineties (Universal)	A-II	1944–45
Navajo Kid (Producers Releasing Corp.)	A-I	1945–46
Navajo Trail, The (Monogram)	A-I	1944–45
Navajo Trail Raiders (Republic)	A-I	1948–49
Naval Academy (Columbia)	A-I	1940–41
Navy Blue and Gold (MGM)	A-I	1937–38
Navy Blues (Warner-First National)	B	1940–41

Objection: Suggestive song and scenes.

CHAPTER 21

Some Like It Hot: The Erosion of Censorship

21.1 *JOSEPH BURSTYN, INC. v. WILSON, COMMISSIONER OF EDUCATION OF NEW YORK, ET AL.* (1952)

Joseph Burstyn, Inc. v. Wilson (1952) was a landmark Supreme Court decision which largely marked the decline of motion picture censorship in the United States. It determined that certain provisions of the New York Education Law allowing a censor to forbid the commercial showing of any non-licensed motion picture film, or revoke or deny the license of a film deemed to be "sacrilegious," was a "restraint on freedom of speech" and thereby a violation of the First Amendment. In the excerpted portion below, the court explains why it was overturning *Mutual Film Corp v. Industrial Commission of Ohio* (1915) and finding that movies were an art form worthy of First Amendment protection and not merely a business.

Provisions of the New York Education Law which forbid the commercial showing of any film without a license and authorize denial of a license on a censor's conclusion that a film is "sacreligious," held void as a prior restraint on freedom of speech and of the press under the First Amendment, made applicable to the states by the Fourteenth Amendment. Pp. 497–506.

1. Expression by means of motion pictures is included within the free speech and free press guaranty of the First and Fourteenth Amendments. Pp. 499–502.

    (a) It cannot be doubted that motion pictures are a significant medium for the communication of ideas. Their importance as an organ of public opinion is not lessened by the fact that they are designed to entertain as well as to inform. P. 501.

(b) That the production, distribution and exhibition of motion pictures is a large-scale business conducted for private profit does not prevent motion pictures from being a form of expression whose liberty is safeguarded by the First Amendment. Pp. 501–502.

(c) Even if it be assumed that motion pictures possess a greater capacity for evil, particularly among the youth of a community, than other modes of expression, it does not follow that they are not entitled to the protection of the First Amendment or may be subjected to substantially unbridled censorship. P. 502.

(d) To the extent that language in the opinion in *Mutual Film Corp. v. Industrial Comm'n*, 236 U.S. 230, is out of harmony with the views here set forth, it is no longer adhered to. P. 502.

2. Under the First and Fourteenth Amendments, a state may not place a prior restraint on the showing of a motion picture film on the basis of a censor's conclusion that it is "sacrilegious." Pp. 502–506.

(a) Though the Constitution does not require absolute freedom to exhibit every motion picture of every kind at all times and all places, there is no justification in this case for making an exception to the basic principles of freedom of expression previously announced by this Court with respect to other forms of expression. Pp. 502–503.

(b) Such a prior restraint as that involved here is a form of infringement upon freedom of expression to be especially condemned. *Near v. Minnesota*, 283 U.S. 697. Pp. 503–504.

(c) New York cannot vest in a censor such unlimited restraining control over motion pictures as that involved in the broad requirement that they not be "sacrilegious." Pp. 504–505.

(d) From the standpoint of freedom of speech and the press, a state has no legitimate interest in protecting any or all religions from views distasteful to them which is sufficient to justify prior restraints upon the expression of those views. P. 505. [497]

303 N. Y. 242, 101 N. E. 2d 665, reversed.

Mr. Justice Clark Delivered the Opinion of the Court

The issue here is the constitutionality, under the First and Fourteenth

Amendments, of a New York statute which permits the banning of motion picture films on the ground that they are "sacrilegious." That statute makes it unlawful "to exhibit, or to sell, lease or lend for exhibition at any place of amusement for pay or in connection with any business in the state of New York, any motion picture film or reel [with specified exceptions not relevant here], unless there is at the time in full force and effect a valid license or permit therefor of the education department . . ."[1] The statute further provides:

> "The director of the [motion picture] division [of the education department] or, when authorized by the regents, the officers of a local office or bureau shall cause to be promptly examined every motion picture film submitted to them as herein required, and unless such film or a part thereof is obscene, indecent, immoral, inhuman, sacrilegious, or is of such a character that its exhibition would tend to corrupt morals or incite to crime, shall issue a license therefor. If such director or, when so authorized, such officer shall not license any film submitted, he shall furnish to the applicant therefor a written report of the reasons for his refusal and a description of each rejected part of a film not rejected in toto."[2]

Appellant is a corporation engaged in the business of distributing motion pictures. It owns the exclusive rights to distribute throughout the United States a film produced in Italy entitled "The Miracle." On November 30, 1950, after having examined the picture, the motion picture division of the New York education department, [498] acting under the statute quoted above, issued to appellant a license authorizing exhibition of "The Miracle," with English subtitles, as one part of a trilogy called "Ways of Love."[3] Thereafter, for a period of approximately eight weeks, "Ways of Love" was exhibited publicly in a motion picture theater in New York City under an agreement between appellant and the owner of the theater whereby appellant received a stated percentage of the admission price.

During this period, the New York State Board of Regents, which by statute is made the head of the education department,[4] received "hundreds of letters, telegrams, post cards, affidavits and other communications" both protesting against and defending the public exhibition of "The Miracle."[5] The Chancellor of the Board of Regents requested three members of the Board to view the picture and to make a report to the entire Board. After viewing the film, this committee reported to the Board that in its opinion there was basis for the claim that the picture was "sacrilegious." Thereafter, on January 19, 1951, the Regents directed appellant to show cause, at a hearing to be held on January 30, why its license to show "The Miracle" should not be rescinded on that ground. Appellant appeared at this hearing, which was conducted by the same three-member committee of the Regents which had previously viewed the picture, and challenged the jurisdiction of the committee and of the Regents to proceed with the case. With the consent of the committee, various interested persons and [499] organizations submitted to it briefs and exhibits bearing upon the merits of the picture and upon the constitutional and statutory questions involved. On February 16, 1951, the Regents, after viewing "The Miracle," determined that it was "sacrilegious" and for that reason ordered the Commissioner of Education to rescind appellant's license to exhibit the picture. The Commissioner did so.

Appellant brought the present action in the New York courts to review the determination of the Regents.[6] Among the claims advanced by appellant were (1) that the statute violates the Fourteenth Amendment as a prior restraint upon freedom of speech and of the press; (2) that it is invalid under the same Amendment as a violation of the guaranty of separate church and state and as a prohibition of the free exercise of religion; and, (3) that the term "sacrilegious" is so vague and indefinite as to offend due process. The Appellate Division rejected all of appellant's contentions and upheld the Regents' determination. 278 App. Div. 253, 104 N. Y. S. 2d 740. On appeal the New York Court of Appeals, two judges dissenting, affirmed the order of the Appellate Division. 303 N. Y. 242, 101 N. E. 2d 665. The case is here on appeal. 28 U. S. C. § 1257 (2).

As we view the case, we need consider only appellant's contention that the New York statute is an unconstitutional abridgment of free speech and a free press. In *Mutual Film Corp. v. Industrial Comm'n*, 236 U.S. 230 (1915), a distributor of motion pictures sought to enjoin the enforcement of an Ohio statute which required the prior approval of a board of censors before any motion [500] picture could be publicly exhibited in the state, and which directed the board to approve only such films as it adjudged to be "of a moral, educational or amusing and harmless character." The statute was assailed in part as an unconstitutional abridgment of the freedom of the press guaranteed by the First and Fourteenth Amendments. The District Court rejected this contention, stating that the first eight Amendments were not a restriction on state action. 215 F. 138, 141 (D. C. N. D. Ohio 1914). On appeal to this Court, plaintiff in its brief abandoned this claim and contended merely that the statute in question violated the freedom of speech and publication guaranteed by the Constitution of Ohio. In affirming the decree of the District Court denying injunctive relief, this Court stated:

"It cannot be put out of view that the exhibition of moving pictures is a business pure and simple, originated and conducted for profit, like other spectacles, not to be regarded, nor intended to be regarded by the Ohio constitution, we think, as part of the press of the country or as organs of public opinion."[7]

In a series of decisions beginning with *Gitlow v. New York*, 268 U.S. 652 (1925), this Court held that the liberty of speech and of the press which the First Amendment guarantees against abridgment by the federal government is within the liberty safeguarded by the Due Process Clause of the Fourteenth Amendment from invasion by state action.[8] That principle has been [501] followed and reaffirmed to the present day. Since this series of decisions came after the Mutual decision, the present case is the first to present squarely to us the question whether motion pictures are within the ambit of protection which the First Amendment, through the Fourteenth, secures to any form of "speech" or "the press."[9]

It cannot be doubted that motion pictures are a significant medium for the communication of ideas. They may affect public attitudes and behavior in a variety of ways, ranging from direct espousal of a political or social doctrine to the subtle shaping of thought which characterizes all artistic expression.[10] The importance of motion pictures as an organ of public opinion is not lessened by the fact that they are designed to entertain as well as to inform. As was said in *Winters v. New York*, 333 U.S. 507, 510 (1948):

"The line between the informing and the entertaining is too elusive for the protection of that basic right [a free press]. Everyone is familiar with instances of propaganda through fiction. What is one man's amusement, teaches another's doctrine."

It is urged that motion pictures do not fall within the First Amendment's aegis because their production, distribution, and exhibition is a large-scale business conducted for private profit. We cannot agree. That books, newspapers, and magazines are published and sold for profit does not prevent them from being a form of expression whose liberty is safeguarded by the First Amendment.[11] [502] We fail to see why operation for profit should have any different effect in the case of motion pictures.

It is further urged that motion pictures possess a greater capacity for evil, particularly among the youth of a community, than other modes of expression. Even if one were to accept this hypothesis, it does not follow that motion pictures should be disqualified from First Amendment protection. If there be capacity for evil it may be relevant in determining the permissible scope of community control, but it does not authorize substantially unbridled censorship such as we have here.

For the foregoing reasons, we conclude that expression by means of motion pictures is included within the free speech and free press guaranty of the First and Fourteenth Amendments. To the extent that language in the opinion in *Mutual Film Corp. v. Industrial Comm'n, supra,* is out of harmony with the views here set forth, we no longer adhere to it.[12]

To hold that liberty of expression by means of motion pictures is guaranteed by the First and Fourteenth Amendments, however, is not the end of our problem. It does not follow that the Constitution requires absolute freedom to exhibit every motion picture of every kind at all times and all places. That much is evident from the series of decisions of this Court with respect to other [503] media of communication of ideas.[13] Nor does it follow that motion pictures are necessarily subject to the precise rules governing any other particular method of expression. Each method tends to present its own peculiar problems. But the basic principles of freedom of speech and the press, like the First Amendment's command, do not vary. Those principles, as they have frequently been enunciated by this Court, make freedom of expression the rule. There is no justification in this case for making an exception to that rule.

The statute involved here does not seek to punish, as a past offense, speech or writing falling within the permissible scope of subsequent punishment. On the contrary, New York requires that permission to communicate ideas be obtained in advance from state officials who judge the content of the words and pictures sought to be communicated. This Court recognized many years ago that such a previous restraint is a form of infringement upon freedom of expression to be especially condemned. *Near v. Minnesota ex rel. Olson,* 283 U.S. 697 (1931). The Court there recounted the history which indicates that a major purpose of the First Amendment guaranty of a free press was to prevent prior restraints upon publication, although it was carefully pointed out that the liberty of the press is not limited to that protection.[14] It was further stated that "the protection even as to previous restraint is not absolutely unlimited. But the limitation has been recognized only [504] in exceptional cases." *Id.,* at 716. In the light of the First Amendment's history and of the Near decision, the State has a heavy burden to demonstrate that the limitation challenged here presents such an exceptional case.

New York's highest court says there is "nothing mysterious" about the statutory provision applied in this case: "It is simply this: that no religion, as that word is understood by the ordinary, reasonable person, shall be treated with contempt, mockery, scorn and ridicule . . . ."[15] This is far from the kind of narrow exception to freedom of expression which a state may carve out to satisfy the adverse demands of other interests of society.[16] In seeking to apply the broad and all-inclusive definition of "sacrilegious" given by the New York courts, the censor is set adrift upon a boundless sea amid a myriad of conflicting currents of religious views, with no [505] charts but those provided by the most vocal and powerful orthodoxies. New York cannot vest such unlimited restraining control over motion pictures in a censor. Cf. *Kunz v. New York*, 340 U.S. 290 (1951).[17] Under such a standard the most careful and tolerant censor would find it virtually impossible to avoid favoring one religion over another, and he would be subject to an inevitable tendency to ban the expression of unpopular sentiments sacred to a religious minority. Application of the "sacrilegious" test, in these or other respects, might raise substantial questions under the First Amendment's guaranty of separate church and state with freedom of worship for all.[18] However, from the standpoint of freedom of speech and the press, it is enough to point out that the state has no legitimate interest in protecting any or all religions from views distasteful to them which is sufficient to justify prior restraints upon the expression of those views. It is not the business of government in our nation to suppress real or imagined attacks upon a particular religious doctrine, whether they appear in publications, speeches, or motion pictures.[19]

Since the term "sacrilegious" is the sole standard under attack here, it is not necessary for us to decide, for example, [506] whether a state may censor motion pictures under a clearly drawn statute designed and applied to prevent the showing of obscene films. That is a very different question from the one now before us.[20] We hold only that under the First and Fourteenth Amendments a state may not ban a film on the basis of a censor's conclusion that it is "sacrilegious."

Reversed.

. . .

Footnotes to the Majority Opinion

1. McKinney's N. Y. Laws, 1947, Education Law, § 129.
2. *Id.*, § 122.

3. The motion picture division had previously issued a license for exhibition of "The Miracle" without English subtitles, but the film was never shown under that license.

4. McKinney's N. Y. Laws, 1947, Education Law, § 101; see also N. Y. Const., Art. V, § 4.

5. Stipulation between appellant and appellee, R. 86.

6. The action was brought under Article 78 of the New York Civil Practice Act, Gilbert-Bliss N. Y. Civ. Prac., Vol. 6B, 1944, 1949 Supp., § 1283 et seq. See also McKinney's N. Y. Laws, 1947 Education Law, § 124.

7. 236 U. S., at 244.

8. *Gitlow v. New York*, 268 U.S. 652, 666 (1925); *Stromberg v. California*, 283 U. S. 359, 368 (1931); *Near v. Minnesota ex rel. Olson*, 283 U.S. 697, 707 (1931); *Grosjean v. American Press Co.*, 297 U.S. 233, 244 (1936); *De Jonge v. Oregon*, 299 U.S. 353, 364 (1937); *Lovell v. Griffin*, 303 U.S. 444, 450 (1938); *Schneider v. State*, 308 U.S. 147, 160 (1939).

9. See *Lovell v. Griffin*, 303 U.S. 444, 452 (1938).

10. See Inglis, Freedom of the Movies (1947), 20–24; Klapper, The Effects of Mass Media (1950), passim; Note, Motion Pictures and the First Amendment, 60 Yale L. J. 696, 704–708 (1951) and sources cited therein.

11. See *Grosjean v. American Press Co.*, 297 U. S. 233 (1936); *Thomas v. Collins*, 323 U. S. 516, 531 (1945).

12. See *United States v. Paramount Pictures, Inc.*, 334 U.S. 131, 166 (1948): "We have no doubt that moving pictures, like newspapers and radio, are included in the press whose freedom is guaranteed by the First Amendment." It is not without significance that talking pictures were first produced in 1926, eleven years after the Mutual decision. Hampton, A History of the Movie (1931), 382–383.

13. E.g., *Feiner v. New York*, 340 U.S. 315 (1951); *Kovacs v. Cooper*, 336 U.S. 77 (1949); *Chaplinsky v. New Hampshire*, 315 U.S. 568 (1942); *Cox v. New Hampshire*, 312 U.S. 569 (1941).

14. *Near v. Minnesota ex rel. Olson*, 283 U.S. 697, 713–719 (1931); see also *Lovell v. Griffin*, 303 U.S. 444, 451–452 (1938); *Grosjean v American Press Co.*, 297 U.S. 233, 245–250 (1936); *Patterson v. Colorado*, 205 U.S. 454, 462 (1907).

15. 303 N. Y. 242, 258, 101 N. E. 2d 665, 672. At another point the Court of Appeals gave "sacrilegious" the following definition:

> "the act of violating or profaning anything sacred." *Id.*, at 255, 101 N. E. 2d at 670. The Court of Appeals also approved the Appellate Division's interpretation: "As the court below said of the statute in question, 'All it purports to do is to bar a visual caricature of religious beliefs held sacred by one sect or

another . . ." *Id.*, at 258, 101 N. E. 2d at 672. Judge Fuld, dissenting, concluded from all the statements in the majority opinion that "the basic criterion appears to be whether the film treats a religious theme in such a manner as to offend the religious beliefs of any group of persons. If the film does have that effect, and it is 'offered as a form of entertainment,' it apparently falls within the statutory ban regardless of the sincerity and good faith of the producer of the film, no matter how temperate the treatment of the theme, and no matter how unlikely a public disturbance or breach of the peace. The drastic nature of such a ban is highlighted by the fact that the film in question makes no direct attack on, or criticism of, any religious dogma or principle, and it is not claimed to be obscene, scurrilous, intemperate or abusive." *Id.*, at 271–272, 101 N. E. 2d at 680.

16. Cf. *Thornhill v. Alabama*, 310 U.S. 88, 97 (1940); *Stromberg v. California*, 283 U.S. 359, 369–370 (1931).

17. Cf. *Niemotko v. Maryland*, 340 U.S. 268 (1951); *Saia v. New York*, 334 U.S. 558 (1948); *Largent v. Texas*, 318 U.S. 418 (1943); *Lovell v. Griffin*, 303 U.S. 444 (1938).

18. See *Cantwell v. Connecticut*, 310 U.S. 296 (1940).

19. See the following statement by Mr. Justice Roberts, speaking for a unanimous Court in *Cantwell v. Connecticut*, 310 U.S. 296, 310 (1940):

> "In the realm of religious faith, and in that of political belief, sharp differences arise. In both fields the tenets of one man may seem the rankest error to his neighbor. To persuade others to his own point of view, the pleader, as we know, at times, reports to exaggeration, to vilification of men who have been, or are, prominent in church or state, and even to false statement. But the people of this nation have ordained in the light of history, that, in spite of the probability of excesses and abuses, these liberties are, in the long view, essential to enlightened opinion and right conduct on the part of the citizens of a democracy.
>
> "The essential characteristic of these liberties is, that under their shield many types of life, character, opinion and belief can develop unmolested and unobstructed. Nowhere is this shield more necessary than in our own country for a people composed of many races and of many creeds."

20. In the Near case, this Court stated that "the primary requirements of decency may be enforced against obscene publications." 283 U.S. 697, 716. In *Chaplinsky v. New Hampshire*, 315 U.S. 568, 571–572 (1942), Mr. Justice Murphy stated for a unanimous Court: "There are certain well-defined and narrowly limited classes of speech, the prevention and punishment of which have never been thought to raise any Constitutional problem. These include the lewd and obscene, the profane, the libelous, and the insulting or 'fighting' words—those which by their very utterance inflict injury or tend to incite an immediate breach of the peace." But see *Kovacs v. Cooper*, 336 U.S. 77, 82

(1949): "When ordinances undertake censorship of speech or religious practices before permitting their exercise, the Constitution forbids their enforcement."

21.2 TESTIMONIES OF JACK VALENTI AND STEPHEN FARBER, "MOVIE RATINGS AND THE INDEPENDENT PRODUCER," HEARINGS BEFORE THE SUBCOMMITTEE ON SPECIAL SMALL BUSINESS PROBLEMS OF THE COMMITTEE ON SMALL BUSINESS, HOUSE OF REPRESENTATIVES, NINETY-FIFTH CONGRESS, FIRST SESSION, MARCH 24, 1977, AND APRIL 14, 1977

Even after *Joseph Burstyn, Inc. v. Wilson* (1952), the studios were reluctant to embrace controversial themes for fear of offending audiences and searched for a compromise that would allow free speech but also protect audiences from potentially offending material. The Motion Picture Association of America (MPAA) film rating system went into effect on November 1, 1968 and has remained in place, with modifications, ever since, despite the complaints of its critics. Congress responded to these critiques by holding hearings in 1977 at which the longtime MPAA president Jack Valenti, who defends the rating system, and Stephen Farber, who attacks it, testified.

Testimony of Jack Valenti, President, Motion Picture Association of America

Mr. Valenti: I do.

Mr. Russo: State your name and address.

Mr. Valenti: Jack Valenti, 1600 I Street, N.W., Washington.

You speak Italian with a noble Roman accent, Ms. Fenwick. [Laughter.]

This subcommittee has asked me to give a brief exposition on the rating system, which I am pleased to do.

First, let me give you our objective. All great solutions to a problem begin with objectives. The objective of this rating system, its simple and sole objective, is to give advance information to parents so that participants can make judgments about their children's viewing habits, the films they want or do not choose their children to see.

The root and gristle of the rating system is founded on parental responsibility. The parent must care about what his or her children hear, the books they read, the people they play with, the schools they go to, the conduct of their lives and the movies they attend.

If the parent abandons or neglects that responsibility, no government, no agency, no commission, and no rating system is going to salvage his or her child's future. So I say initially that parental responsibility is linked irretrievably to our motion picture rating system and its objectives.

The rating system was born in the mid-sixties. I left the White House as Special Assistant to President Johnson in May of 1966, and became president of the Motion Picture Association. I don't have to tell any of you what those mid-sixties were all about. We had a cataclysmic change in the mores and customs of our society.

It was a radical, avalanching revision of how we lived. We had insurrection on the campus and riots in the street, women's liberation was rising, sexual permissiveness on the campus and elsewhere, an abandonment of the old guidelines. We wondered what kept the country together.

In short, we were in a hell of a fix in the sixties, and no one knew it better than President Johnson. Wherever the young were in ferment was where most of this change was taking place. It would have been absurd to think that movies, the most creative of the art forms, would have remained unaffected by this social change.

So I came to realize that I was presiding over a new motion picture industry. Frankness and candor were clamoring to be heard, and writers and producers were determined they were going to tell their story the way they wanted, given the kind of change that was taking place in the country.

Then in April 1966, the Supreme Court handed down a decision in the *Dallas Classification* case. The Court did two things. One, they enunciated what the lawyers called the doctrine of variable obscenity.

Ms. Fenwick: Of what?

Mr. Valenti: Variable obscenity. It is a nice logical Platonian word and I will try to tell you what they meant by it. They said there were movies that were appropriate or at least reasonable

Mr. Valenti: (cont.) for adults to see, but not for children. That is variable obscenity.

They also said that it was legally permissible for local communities and States to create their own classification and rating boards.

This decision was something that we had to take into consideration, because, while censorship always lurks as a grim shadow in the background, nonetheless, the first amendment remains a pretty good barrier against it. But now we faced the possibility of States and local communities doing their own ratings.

I have long held the view that the movies was an area that the government ought not invade. Motion pictures are under the canopy of the first amendment; like books, and magazines, and television, movies are in a creative area that the government ought to stay out of.

From this Court decision came the idea of the rating system, and it came from Chief Justice Earl Warren, who, from the bench, remonstrating with one of counsel said in effect, "The best way to handle these matters is for the film industry to protect children. Now, if you do that, I think you have taken care of this situation."

That was the genesis of the rating system. I formulated a plan for a rating system. I spent over 100 hours in meetings with theaterowners, independent producers, critics, religious organizations, motion picture directors, writers, Actors Guild. Anyone I could coax into listening to me for 2 minutes.

After long discussions with the independent distribution organizations' theaters, and others, the rating system was formed.

Let me tell you that the linchpin of this rating system was the interlinking of essential ingredients. First, the system must have integrity, must have probity. It must be proof against pressure from all sides, majors and independents, from anyone who has a personal economic stake, or anyone who may assume they have an economic stake, in the outcome of the ratings.

So we had to make this system proof against those pressures.

Second, we had to have a partnership of everybody

involved in films, the retailer, the theaterowner who exhibits the film, the independent director and producer, and the major director and producer.

These elements were essential to this partnership.

Third, a policy mechanism had to be created so that if someone felt aggrieved by a rating, he had a place to go. You can't have a czar or a dictator saying, "This is it, and no more."

Four, and this is the crux of the system, it really had to perform a service for parents. Otherwise, the ratings had no meaning.

Those were the four indispensable elements that formed the recipe for the rating system.

Now, I sincerely believe all these goals were met and are being met, more than 8½ years after the rating system was born in November 1968.

The rating plan is voluntary. Nobody has to get into it if they don't want to. That is very important to understand. It is voluntary. However, I will tell you this: Because of public pressure, because the parents and neighborhoods want to know what a rating is, very few theaters will play a picture without a rating, not because there are sanctions against them, but because Mr. and Mrs. Parent want to know beforehand, "What is the rating on this picture." So the public makes the system work.

I think about 99 percent of all the responsible producers in this country submit their films for ratings.

Hardcore pornographic films are another kind of business. Put them aside. They are not involved in the rating system.

There are four rating categories. I had a card made up so that you can see what we are talking about. Let me tell you what these ratings mean. G means all ages admitted. What that says to a parent is, "Look, Mr. and Mrs. Parent, we don't believe there is anything in this film that you as a parent would find offensive if your younger children saw this film."

This doesn't mean that it is a certificate of approval for a children's film. For instance, "A Man for All Seasons" is a profound film, but it was a G-rated film. Some snippets

Mr. Valenti:
(cont.)

of conversation in a G film might go beyond what we call politeness. I have seen a G film—I trust you will pardon the candor, Mr. Chairman—but in a John Wayne western he said, "Fill your hand, you son-of-a-bitch."

The rating board decided that they ought not to make that film a PG simply because of that one piece of language so they let it go by, and I must say, we did hear some criticism about that. Otherwise, there was nothing in the film that would warrant a different rating.

Now this [pointing to the card] is the category of PG. It is probably the most criticized, and the one we have the most difficulty with, because it is very difficult to draw these lines with precision.

We say to parents, "Look, we don't know what your particular concern may be. It may be language, violence, or sensuality, but please inquire about this film before you let your children see it. Call your neighbor, read reviews, call the theater, but do not willy-nilly, allow your child to see it without first making advance inquiry. That is very essential in this rating. We warn parents, "Don't send your child to see this film without looking at it or finding out about it."

There may be profanity in a PG film, but it is not hard, tough, mean, brutal language. If it has sexually connotive words, it could go into the R rating. There may be violence in a PG picture, though we don't deem it strong enough to go to an R rating. The toughest thing we must deal with, as I will tell you later, is "What is too much violence? How do you gage it?"

We have a difficult time with violence. There is no accumulative horror or violence in a PG film, although that may be subject to disagreement from time to time. There is no explicit sex in PG; brief nudity may appear, but it is not explicit sex.

The PG line is difficult to draw. It is a category that is most susceptible to criticism. How do you make a judgment for 200 million people that everyone is going to agree with? However, as long as the parent understands that he must inquire, he must ask, he must find out, I think we are somewhat safer on the PG.

Now, for the R picture, we are saying to parents,

"Look, this film contains adultery. If your child is under 17, he or she is required to be accompanied by a parent or an adult guardian. I don't know how much more you can tell a parent than to say, "Look, involved here is adultery, and please don't take your child unless you find out more about the picture." In an R picture the language can be rough, the violence could be hard, and included could be what we call explicit sex—we use shorthand expressions—but everyone in the motion picture business knows what we mean. I don't want to offend you Mr. Chairman but we seem to slide into the patois of the motion picture industry.

Mr. Russo: Being a young man of tender sensibility, I can understand it.

Ms. Fenwick: PG for you. [Laughter.]

Mr. Valenti: An X-rated picture is patently an adult film; children are barred. But X under the rating system doesn't necessarily mean pornographic or obscene. Those are legal terms. We are not lawyers and we don't pretend to make judgments about what is legally obscene. There could be a picture such as "Clockwork Orange," which got an X because of violence.

The reason why children aren't admitted to an X film is because we feel that there is an accumulation sometimes of brutality and perhaps sadistic violence on the screen and the kids ought not to see it.

An adult can attend if he or she wants to. Nobody puts a gun at their backs or subpenas them to go to this film. They make this judgment themselves.

That is essentially what the ratings are. What does all this mean?

I will come back to what I said. What is too much of something? Where do you draw the line between PG and R; between R and X?

The rating system has problems with violence. Take a classic Army movie. The Marines storm Iwo Jima and kill 2,000 Japanese. That is one kind of violence. Some of us were brought up on war movies.

Are the sheriff and the cattle rustler dueling in the muddy western streets violence? You hit somebody in a fight with your hand, or with a bat? How does that

Mr. Valenti:
(cont.)

become violent? Is violence one strangling, or two stab-bings? How do you handle this? Is the spilling of blood violence?

That is the problem we have in a subjectively organized system like this. The same vexing doubts occur in sex scenes, or even where language rises on the Richter scale. The result is controversy. It is inevitable, it is inexorable.

But what these raters in California try to do is simply try to estimate what a parent feels, what a parent wants to know about what a film is all about. That is the most that they can do.

They are not rating for Ph. D.'s, or psychiatrists, or even congressional committee chairmen. They are rating for the parent in New Jersey, or in Illinois, or in Califor-nia, or wherever ordinary people who want to know what kind of films their children ought to see. That is who we are rating for, and we hope we do a good job of it.

I have given you the meaning of the system. Let me tell you now how the system works.

We have set up in California a seven-person rating board. The board has women, blacks; we go through the usual cross section of trying to get the soul and heart of America.

Mr. Russo: Do you have any Italians on the board?

Mr. Valenti: I serve as honorary Italian, Mr. Chairman. You will be pleased and delighted to know that. [Laughter.]

I, and I alone, appoint the chairman. Nobody in the industry, no matter how powerful, or rich or successful can do anything with the chairman of the rating board. I stand, I hope, as Horatio at the bridge fighting off all attackers. No one can do anything with that, or intrude on it, and nobody has tried. No company can intrude on it.

The chairman of the board is insulated against the malevolent pressures that operate in the marketplace sometimes, and such pressures exist. But I make certain there are no politics, because I am going to shield the board chairman.

He may make some mistakes, but they are not because

of pressure. I have here the biographies of these people on the rating board, and if you would like to have them, I will give them to the subcommittee.

Mr. Chairman, I will tell you that in the almost 9 years of operation of this rating system, no one to this hour has come forward with the slightest jot or sliver of evidence that there has been any torturing, misshaping of any kind of the duties and the responsibilities of the people on that rating board.

If anybody ever comes to me with the slightest sign that these duties have been neglected, I will take instant action, because I know that this rating system rests on one rostrum, and one alone—integrity, honesty of purpose. If that ever erodes or collapses, the rating system will be washed away like a fiber house in a dam break. I know that.

Let me explain to you the journey of a film through the rating system. Let's suppose that you are a producer, you have a film, and you have just finished it. The film goes to California, where, in a screening room, the rating board views the film. The members ballot on language, sensuality, and violence, and, then, a final rating. They may see the film once, twice, or three times. They discuss among themselves privately and, then, they come to a decision of a rating. Let's say they gave the film an R rating because of violence.

They then call the producer and say, "Mr. Producer, your film has been rated R for violence."

He says, "That is crazy, that is a PG film. I want to talk to you."

Fine. My doors swing open on easy hinges.

The producer asks, "Why did my film get R?" And they will go through a litany of why.

The producer has three options. He can say, "You are wrong but I will take my film to market," and he can. Or he can edit his film to excise some of the offending parts. Or, he can say, "I am not going to cut this film," but asks "I wish you would look at this film again."

Many times a rating board will look at a film three, or four, or even five or six times. If the producer edits the film, and it is still R, he can edit it again and again if he

Mr. Valenti:
(cont.)

wants to, and the rating board will review it again and again and work with him.

Suppose the producer says, "I am not going to cut it. I am going to the appeals board to ask a review of your rating."

Since the inception of the rating board, a policy review committee was created. It consists of myself, the president of the National Association of Theater Owners, a representative of the Internal Film Importers, and a representative of the directors association, consisting of 51 independent companies. This is the partnership, the troika, if you please, that manages the system.

Under this management group is an appeals board on which sit nine representatives of MPAA, eight representatives of the Theater Owners of America, four representatives of the independent producers and myself as chairman.

There are 22 votes on the appeals board. Very early on a simple majority vote could overturn the rating board's original rating. I decided after a picture named "Ryan's Daughter" came along on appeal that the voting percentage had to be changed. I think that was one of the tarnishing marks of the rating system. It caused me great concern, because I think political pressure had been brought to bear on the appeals board.

So in 1971, at my urging, new rules were established. First, no one who has a case before the appeals board can talk to an appeals board member and if anyone brings me evidence of that, I can cancel the appeal without further recourse.

Second, a two-thirds voting rule was instituted. I said, "It takes two-thirds of those voting to overturn a rating board ruling." That diminishes the chances of different groups getting together on appeals. I think these rule changes have worked well.

A word on how an appeal is handled. We convene the appeals board and they watch the picture in a screening room in New York City. When the picture is over, a representative of the rating board, usually the chairman, comes forward and the producer and/or anybody he chooses, and they both stand up before this appeals board.

First, the producer tells why he thinks the rating board was abysmally wrong, and why the picture should get a different rating. Then, the rating board representative tells the appeals board why the rating board rated this picture how it did. After he is finished, questions develop, dialog goes on. It is a quasi-judicial hearing.

When the dialog and the questions are done, the producer and the rating board representative are asked to leave the room, and now the appeals board meets in private, except there is always present, to sort of monitor, a representative of the Catholic Office on Film and Broadcasting and a representative of the Protestant organization on film and broadcasting, and we invite the similar Jewish organization representative to sit, too. They sit through all this as monitors, as observers.

The appeals board members discuss the issues openly and freely among themselves. They discuss dialog and scenes. Finally I hit the gavel and say, "All right, gentlemen, we will now vote."

Ballots are passed out. This is a secret ballot. No one knows how the other votes. That is so integral to the whole mechanism of this integrity that I stress it. No one knows how other members vote.

The vote is taken, I call two people up, usually a theater-owner and usually a director, to act as tellers, and in full view of everyone, we count the votes: "I vote to sustain," "I vote to overrule," "I vote to sustain," "I vote to overrule."

If two-thirds of those voting vote to overrule, the producer has won his appeal. If less than two-thirds, he has lost his appeal.

Since November 9, 1968, we have heard 84 appeals; 71 percent of those who appeal have lost their case; 29 percent have won a different rating.

That is a brief capsule of how an appeal works.

Do we make errors? Of course we do. I think we probably have erred, because the people who operate the rating board are human beings, and we are dealing with a tormentingly difficult situation of making subjective judgments where the criteria are at best fuzzy, and sometimes obscure. The lines are dimly marked. The alleyways

Mr. Valenti:
(cont.)

we walk through are very poorly illuminated. The people who serve on the board love films, they are intelligent people, but they are neither gods, nor fools, and they make errors.

Not, however, as many as you might suspect. Mr. Louis Nizer, MPAA's general counsel, pointed something out to me the other day that is illuminating. "Do you realize," he said, "that the Supreme Court of the United States has reversed itself, admitting error, probably more often than the rating board has made errors." In the past 8½ years the board has rated 4,108 films, and out of that number, only a handful, maybe two dozen, have created what I would call substantial criticism, where people say, "That is an outrage, how could you have missed that one."

So, sure, we make errors, but we rate a lot of films. We rated 486 films last year. So we are bound to make errors, but on whatever errors we make we have critics. The major directors raise hell with us. The independents think the majors dominate the ratings and they give us a bad time. The conservatives think we are too liberal, and the liberals think we are too conservative. Sometimes I think I am back in the White House.

Mr. Russo: You sound like a Member of Congress.

Mr. Valenti: And the middle-of-the-roaders thinks we are both ways. But whatever errors we have made, I stand here to tell you they are errors of judgment, not errors of deliberate distortion of somebody's viewpoint. As I said, it is so difficult to draw this precise line, and I think sometimes in my own mind I see every now and then a rating that I think I might have done differently.

One final note, and then I am going to stop and let you ask questions. Many producers gripe about the ratings. Why?

I like to think I am in a creative industry, but I am also in a business. It is an economic marketplace, and it is a veritable jungle out there, everyone trying to fasten on to the consciousness and attraction of the audience.

Many producers, in order to widen their audience, mistakenly, in my judgment, think if they get a less severe rating that their pictures have a better chance in the marketplace. When they get a rating they don't like, they are immersed in the notion that the rating will affect their box office.

I will cite Valenti's law, not to be confused with Boyle's law of gases, but in its own modest way, I think it has vivid truth:

If you make a picture that many people want to see, no rating is going to hurt you.

If you make a picture that few people want to see, no rating is going to help you.

There have been many films G rated, notably from Disney. There have been some great PG pictures, "The Sting," "Rocky," "All the President's Men," that have done tremendously well. And such R pictures as "Godfathers I and II," and "The Exorcist." One of the great box office hits was "One Flew Over the Cuckoo's Nest."

The secret is the film itself, that is the real gage. It is the only gage by which the audience measures the movie.

Great films emerge from this mysterious source of talent, this perplexing chemical of talent. Nobody in the business knows what a picture is going to do until the audience collides with it and sparks fly up. But I have never seen a lousy picture made good by any rating or a great picture reduced by any rating. It simply can't be done.

I could go on, Mr. Chairman, hopefully to be even more humorous, and probably with some minor eloquence, but I am going to stop right now and let the subcommittee ask questions.

Mr. Russo: Mr. Valenti, on behalf of the subcommittee, we certainly appreciate your taking the time out to testify today. You have certainly lived up to the reputation that is given about you and your eloquence in delivering a statement. Ms. Fenwick?

Ms. Fenwick: Have you given guidelines, when you say rating members are a wide spectrum?

Mr. Valenti: It is difficult at best, Ms. Fenwick, and I am not sure we do it the right way. Two of the seven board members are fellows, interns if you will. We try to bring on young

Mr. Valenti: (cont.)

people who stay on 1 year or a bit more, and then move on, but who bring a fresh, new viewpoint to the board.

Of the seven people, six are parents, three are women, one is a black. All of them have one thing in common. They love movies. You couldn't watch this many movies if you didn't like movies. That is paramount.

Second, I don't want psychologists, psychiatrists, Ph. D.'s, novelists. I don't want people out of the mainstream or the main stratum of American society. I want people who can relate to others. The mother in Dubuque who has four children. We try to do that.

Ms. Fenwick:

I have a suggestion about violence. I don't think I will have a better opportunity to say something about it. I think the worst kind of violence is the careless, lazy violence, "boom, boom, and they are dead."

You know, someone falls dead from the gun you pull out. I think they ought to brood about it. I think it ought to be a torment before you kill somebody. I think that torment should be visible on the screen. I think it should be a climax of a terrible problem, if you see what I mean.

We have got to take it seriously. Somehow we have allowed movies on TV to convey a kind of a mindless violence, "toss it over your shoulder, it isn't really that big a deal."

I think if we could somehow bring—sometimes these terrible things happen, but what does it cost this man or woman to kill another human being? Do you see?

Then it wouldn't be so objectionable, the violence, because it would be—Dostoevski's "Crime and Punishment," for example. The torment that you go through, or should, and the anguish that allow man being—anyway, you get it.

Mr. Valenti:

Raskolnikov in "Crime and Punishment." That is a good example of a tortured man, and I might add that Dostoevski was one of the greater writers of terror and passion that the world has known but without actually depicting violence. I keep pointing that out to some of my creative friends.

I share what you said, Ms. Fenwick. But remember, I live in a creative world, with writers and producers and directors who want to tell the story the way they want to tell it. I am unable, nor should I be able to say, "That is not the way you should do that."

I may be put off by what they write. Maybe it is meretricious, tawdry, and repellant and repugnant to me. But I cannot tell them how to write.

Ms. Fenwick: And you shouldn't, but I am suggesting that would be a reason for R rather than PG. I can perceive of a G that might portray a death. You couldn't start censorship, of course.

Mr. Valenti: I couldn't agree with you more. You are asking to bring out a deeper and more sensitive view of violence other than if bullets go into a man and how much blood is spilled. We have discussed that many times, what we call contextual violence.

Ms. Fenwick: If one of these creative geniuses wants to portray the mindless violence which does exist, that would put it into another rating.

Mr. Valenti: That is true. We have over the last several years been more severe on portrayals of violence. Our rating system is like the society. We move through social pendulums. The pendulum is going this way on violence and then it is going this way on something else. Over the last several years we have recognized that the American public has become more troubled and anxious about violence. When they see on the evening television news a man with a wire around his neck and a shotgun attached to it and some wild-eyed man walking him around the streets, it is a terrifying situation. We must relate what is on the news to what is in the movies to make judgments.

Ms. Fenwick: I will try to be brief, but I have one more question.

Have you ever thought, or have the directors or the movie theaterowners ever thought of maybe raising the 12-year limit to 16 to the point of view of reduced costs to the children?

Mr. Valenti: Oh, for admission?

Ms. Fenwick: Yes, because children can't work, and I think 16—

Mr. Valenti: I can answer very precisely. The movie producers have nothing to do with the price at the box office. That is the total province of the theaterowner.

Ms. Fenwick: Have you gotten any feedback from them on such a thought? No? OK.

Mr. Valenti: The answer is, honestly, "No," because there is a wide variety of opinion among theaterowners.

Ms. Fenwick: You said pornography is a separate business. What does that mean?

Mr. Valenti: It means no responsible movie producer is involved in hardcore pornography. Such pictures are made in the loft of a building. They may cost as little as $10,000. They pay the leading actor $100. Unfortunately, there is a market cut there for it. There are enough persons who want to pay $5 or $6 to see this pornographic garbage, but the responsible industry is not involved in it in any way.

Ms. Fenwick: Do they make a lot of money?

Mr. Valenti: The return on the investment is high. "Deep Throat" cost $25,000, and grossed perhaps $15 million. So you can see the return on investment is very high in a picture like that, but that is a freak.

. . .

Mr. Russo: Let me ask you this: We have had hearings on sex and violence in the Communications Subcommittee, on which I also serve. We spent the entire day talking about violence, with very little discussion about the problem of sex. Basically, when you make these ratings, is there any particular provision of the four categories you mentioned that have a heavier weight on getting one of those ratings, whether it be sex or violence, or are they all treated equally?

Mr. Valenti: They are all treated equally, Mr. Chairman. I might add somewhat gratuitously that in the whole area of sex and violence, the movie industry is the only communications-entertainment business in the land that turns business away at the box office because of a self-imposed rating system. Books, and magazines, and television, none of them are doing that. I am not saying we have a halo, or are showing our piety. I point out that while others talk about this, we have done something about it.

Mr. Russo: Do you believe the rating system has cut back on the amount of violence shown in movies?

Mr. Valenti: I don't think there is any doubt about it, Mr. Chairman. The producers usually want a PG rating. I don't think it makes a difference, but they think it does. They are willing to cut their films. Many of these PG films began as R's; and they have been edited to conform.

Mr. Russo: How much editing did you do in "Jaws"? Because it got a PG rating, I understand.

Mr. Valenti: I think there was some editing in "Jaws," but I don't know how much. Let me discuss "Jaws" from the violence standpoint. There are some kinds of violence that I happen to go along with Ms. Fenwick and her definition of what is the sinister aspect of violence, and its wantonness.

"Jaws" had to do with a shark, a fish. No one can duplicate or imitate a shark. We think man-to-man violence, or woman-to-woman violence, or person-to-person violence is the meanest kind of violence. Natural violence, earthquakes, apes, sharks, lions, we don't find that is terrifying. Not until such natural violence goes beyond whatever fuzzy boundaries we have outlined is it likely to fall into an R rating.

In my view the natural disaster, or the natural violence, is quite different than person-to-person violence.

Ms. Fenwick: There is nothing saying "You could do it, too."

Mr. Valenti: That is right. It is different when one sees a film about a hostage; one can go out and hold hostages. But when a shark eats a person, it is difficult to put yourself in the place of a shark.

Mr. Russo: What is your assessment of the U.S. Catholic rating system?

Mr. Valenti: I am a Catholic, but I am opposed to my priest telling me what movies I ought to see. I am against indexing. I am against prescribing or proscribing. I am a flat-out first amendment man, whether it involves my church, or anything else.

I have no objection to the church examining films and giving information. Indeed we ask people when they are looking for more information to read the Catholic newsletters and the Protestant newsletters, as well as their reviews. But I do not subscribe to some of the things they say, because it is funded by and founded on church dogma and canon law, rather than on the current mores of society.

But I have no quarrel with them, and as a matter of fact

Mr. Valenti:
(cont.)   I consult with them very frequently in trying to help us develop a consensus.

   . . .

Mr. Kildee: Mr. Chairman, I have a question.

Just to back up a bit, in your response to Chairman Russo's question on the role of the Catholic conference, do you have any objection to the Catholic conference advising its willing and receptive members as to their opinion?

Mr. Valenti: Absolutely not. I must say, Mr. Congressman, I was speaking, I guess, as an individual Catholic. I just don't enjoy anyone trying to tell me what to read or what to see. I don't mind them sending me a newsletter, but I want to make my own judgments about that.

Mr. Kildee: But as far as giving advice to their willing and receptive members?

Mr. Valenti: No difficulty about that. Father Sullivan is a receptive man. We meet with him two or three times a year, and we listen to him; and he has been very useful in helping us improve the rating system.

Ms. Fenwick: Is that the sociologist, Father Sullivan?

Mr. Valenti: No, it is Patrick Sullivan.

In some of the literature we issue, we urge the people to read the Catholic and Protestant bulletins on film, as well as Parents' magazine, as well as reviews in newspapers, as a source of information about the content of the film. Indeed we try to publicize what the Protestants and the Catholics say about content of the film.

   . . .

Mr. Corman: I assume, as you say, that on the great bulk of pictures, there is no controversy, because the producer very probably knows what he is going to get, particularly if he is an experienced producer; and he isn't going to fuss about it. The controversy is where he disagrees, and it is at that point, I take it, that all the board members review it again?

Mr. Valenti: There are two levels to the word "controversy." At the rating boad level, if it is not a G film it is going to be in the PG and possibly in the R category. Then there is a film where there are shadings of difference, and they all look at it.

On the other hand, you are correct about what you say, Congressman Corman. Most producers really know the kind of film that they have made. They may protest, and they may scream, and they may try to intimidate the board, but they know the kind of film they have made, although I have to say that there are some films where the dividing line between PG and R is so dimly lit that there is significant anxiety on the part of the producer—very much so.

Mr. Corman: Thank you, Mr. Chairman.

Mr. Russo: One other question.

First, Mr. Lynch?

Mr. Lynch: Exactly how do you make sure exhibitors enforce your rating?

Mr. Valenti: That is a very good question. I have no authority over exhibitors. We are allies and partners and colleagues in the marketplace, but I have to say the National Association of Theater Owners has done a splendid job in trying to get theaters to go along. They have estimated in various surveys that about 85 percent of the theaters in this country are participating in the rating system. There is about a 15-percent leakage. I find it astonishingly good to have a voluntary program that has that kind of acceptance. I find that rather salutary.

But we do have some problems in that area. I point out that we have narcotics laws, and people violate them, and we have all kinds of rules and laws that people violate. To have this kind of acceptance in a voluntary plan I think is pretty good. But it is a problem, and I would be the last one to gainsay it.

. . .

Testimony of Stephen Farber, Film Critic and Contributing Editor, New West Magazine, Los Angeles, Calif

Mr. Farber: Stephen Farber. I'm a film critic and a contributing editor for the New West magazine in Los Angeles.

Mr. Russo: Would you proceed, Mr. Farber.

Mr. Farber: I was a member of the rating board for a period of 6 months in 1970. I want to make it clear, first of all, that

Mr. Farber:
(cont.)
the inside information that I have from that period—obviously, some things have changed since then. I can't speak with any absolute certainty as to what goes on in the board at the moment. I can only say that I follow it as closely as I can from a distance.

My conclusions are, that, although there are some changes in the basic policy that I observed, they haven't changed significantly, so let me go into some points that I observed, and some criticisms that were in the rating system that I have.

I think, although the rating system has been in operation for over 8 years, most people still have very little understanding of how the system works, and that is because of the secrecy that still surrounds the rating process, so I think that it's important for this subcommittee to get as much information as possible from the inside. I think most of the public has very little idea of it.

There are some points about the procedure—when I was on the board, the motion picture companies, in many cases, submitted scripts to the rating office before the shooting of the film even began, and one board member would be assigned to read the script, and would advise the studio of the rating they could expect, and also list changes that would need to be made in the script in order to secure a less restictive rating.

What I observed is that in many cases the board actually encouraged the studio to revise the script by providing unsolicited lists of details, page by page, of what would have to be changed or cut out to change the rating of the film from X to R, or R to PG.

I've been told that in terms of the number of scripts submitted—that there are not nearly as many of them read by the rating board presently as there were in the past. I hope that's true, and I'm encouraged if it is.

The fact is, over the years a great many films have been censored in advance of shooting because of these script letters from people on the rating board.

Then when the film is completed, then it is screened generally for the entire board and there's a brief discussion, and the members of the board will vote on the rating.

Outsiders often ask about the board's rating criteria, and again, I will tell what I observed.

Since there are no reliable psychological studies regarding the effects of films on children the board doesn't really pretend to make any kind of a value judgment about whether a particular film is or is not suitable for children.

Instead, the board really tries to gage what public reaction to a particular film will be, what a majority of parents throughout the country would feel about a film, whether they would or would not want their children to see it.

So in other words, the real concern of the board in ratings is what then would disturb adults rather than children. It's an interesting point that I don't think a lot of outsiders really realize, that the board's concern is whether they would get complaints from adults, so they are considering the sensitivities of the parents, even though—I think it's worth pointing out—they've never, to my knowledge, taken surveys of public attitudes as to what the issues are, that parents are sensitive about. They see films by themselves and not with audiences, but they're really very much guessing, I think, as to what the sensitivities of the public are.

I think the standards of the board are troubling to a lot of people. They range from being infuriatingly literal minded to extremely vague. There are a few rigid, arbitrary rules, particularly in regard to language and nudity that will change over the years, but they seem to be in effect now; there are certain words that cannot be heard in PG films, and there is no nudity that can be shown unless it's from the side or back, I believe. They have some ridiculous rules.

But in other cases it's very vague. For instance, in regard to film violence—this is a question that has often troubled people—the distinction—how do you decide that one film is too violent for PG, but another film should fit perfectly well into that category.

I think the inconsistencies in the categories are what have inspired a lot of complaints from producers; they don't understand why their film had a PG while another

Mr. Farber:
(cont.)

did not. It is very subjective on the part of the board, and it's very difficult to define these distinctions.

Now, when the rating has been assigned, it is not, in many cases, the end of the process, as the people have testified. A dissatisfied producer can take his case to the appeals board. A number of them have had their ratings changed on appeal.

In many cases a producer will reedit the film before it— without taking it to an appeal in order to win the rating that he wants, and although—I don't know the figures that are kept on this—when I was on the board, at least for the first few years, approximately one-third of all films that were screened were reedited to some degree before they were released. Sometimes the cuts were quite extensive, and in other cases they might have been only a few shots, running like 15 or 20 or 30 seconds.

I found that these editing discussions—would be very hypocritical and very distasteful, and also pointless in the end, because in many cases the cuts didn't really alter the impact of the film for people who hadn't seen it.

I found that a lot of the complaints from parents on ratings being too lenient were on films that had been cut, so the board thought—the impact had been altered, but the people who hadn't seen the original films still thought them too strong.

Yet, at the same time, it is distasteful to see the board members telling filmmakers what has to be cut out of their movies. I found that the board enjoyed its power over filmmakers in this area, even if it was only very minor cutting. It would hurt the artistry, I felt, in many cases, even though it didn't solve the problem that they were ostensibly working to solve, which was to mute the impact of the film.

This is why I've always objected to the statement that the board is not a censor board. Considering that the board has been involved in a great deal of editing of both scripts and films, I think all moviegoers are affected by what the board does, in the sense that they don't see the films that the writers and directors originally intended to make.

Also, a troubling point is that most directors are now

required by contract with their studio to bring in a film with a particular rating. Usually, that means it must not have an X rating. It is required to be an R rating or less restrictive; although, I've seen some contracts where even a PG is required in advance, so this does place constraints on filmmakers that they are very aware of while they're shooting.

In particular, the X rating is used to force changes in films, and this is because most studios won't realease X-rated films, many theater chains, as we've heard, won't play them, many major newspapers won't advertise them. Even the Los Angeles Times segregates all ads for X-rated films into a separate porno-film column, so it discriminates against seriously intended films like "Last Tango In Paris," for instance, which are rated X, but which are consigned to this porno category.

And this, because filmmakers are aware that they can't go beyond the R category, does place limits on what they can film. Again, it's a form of censorship in advance. I also think the X category is troubling in theory, because it prohibits a parent from taking his own child to a film that has been deemed out of bounds by the board.

Another question is the severity of the age restriction for the R category, no one under 17 admitted without a parent. I think people have acknowledged that this places a 6- or 7-year-old child in the same category as a 15- or 16-year-old. In many cases it is really not fair. It doesn't give those two groups of children—they really don't belong in the same category.

To the specific question that this subcommittee is investigating, whether the rating board has different standards for major studio films than independent films, it's difficult to give a clear cut answer one way or the other. I can only say what I observed when I was on the board, that the board members were frequently harsher in rating independent films.

Now, this doesn't mean necessarily that a lot of independent films got stricter ratings, because the board always felt that a film—not always, but in most cases—felt that a film producer could get whatever rating he wanted as long as he was willing to cut the film.

Mr. Farber:
(cont.)   Well, what it did mean, I found, is that the independent filmmakers often had to do more extensive cutting to get their film changed from an X to an R. There were cases where independent ones were cut by as much as 10 or 15 minutes to change their category; whereas, the big-studio films might also have to be cut, but the cutting is much more insignificant, sort of token cutting because board members were a little bit more afraid of tangling with the major studio on expensive films. So I think this was one area where there was a distinction made.

And finally, just one final point which has been raised by the chairman, which I agree with, that the purpose of the rating system ostensibly is to give information to the public, to the parents, but I always felt that the rating itself, G, PG, R, or X, does not really give much information, it doesn't explain what the reasons are for the restriction on the film.

I would prefer to see the board, rather than be involved in this kind of restrictive classification system, and involved in all the editing that they do, that they instead should simply disseminate information about the content of the film, with a simple recommendation as to whether the film is suitable for family viewing, for adults, or whatever.

I think that this would really be a way of giving information to the public. I question how much information is given by the present rating system.

Mr. Russo: I'm reading your book, "The Movie Rating Game." When the time comes I'm going to ask you a few questions about the comments you've made.

The gentleman from California.

Mr. Corman: I can understand your feeling about censorship, but I'm sure I understand how it would be different if the board just expanded upon a simple letter rating.

Mr. Farber: Well, that in itself doesn't necessarily—I would just prefer to see this present rating system as it exists—really done away with in the sense of enforced age restriction.

What I ultimately would like is none of the categories, an R, an X, PG, so the films have to have certain limits to fit within that category. I would rather see just information that it is recommended for adults because of sex or violence, and then leave it to the theaters—in some cases if they wanted to enforce their own age restriction.

I've thought about it a lot, and this kind of voluntary system would be the only way of doing away with a lot of the problems in terms of the censorship that I found.

Mr. Corman: Your primary concern is about the R rating and the youngster under 16, I take it?

Mr. Farber: Right; right.

. . .

Mr. Farber: It's impossible, I think, to really be objective, ultimately, which is why I'm not sure that the system can really function in an objective way, which it pretends to do in these categories of sort of mathematical symbols.

The presumption is that we know exactly what a PG film is, and what an R film is, and what an X film is, but no one knows if it's truely subjective.

Mr. Russo: Well, you do have some good things to say about the rating system anyway.

You mentioned that the existing rating system may have helped in encouraging maturity in many American movies, so it has helped the creativity, the freedom that's needed in the film industry.

Mr. Farber: I think, again, at the time it was introduced—

Mr. Russo: Do you still feel the same about that statement as you did then?

Mr. Farber: Well, I don't know. I think that these changes would have come into films simply because the filmmakers were insisting on it. The code simply was not going to be able to regulate the content of films indefinitely. It might have taken a little bit longer. The thing has sort of retreated a little in the last couple of years. During the first couple of years of the rating system there was a real surge of much franker adult films for a while. I think it's sort of gone backward. People have gotten frightened again, partly because they feel the audiences are tired of it.

I think the rating system had a positive effect. I think it had a lot of negative effects, too.

Mr. Corman: I want to be sure we don't get the wrong impression. We couldn't say that you could look at a film and there—

Mr. Farber: There what?

Mr. Corman: If it's a shlock film, we know it's an independent, and if

Mr. Corman: (cont.)	it's a good film we know it's a major studio; that's not fair.
Mr. Farber:	No; no; certainly not.
Mr. Russo:	Thank you very much.
	. . .

CHAPTER 22

Boogie Nights: Pornography

22.1 ATTORNEY GENERAL'S COMMISSION ON PORNOGRAPHY [ALSO KNOWN AS "THE MEESE REPORT"], JULY, 1989 [EXCERPT]

The Meese Report is the result of a commission ordered by President Ronald Reagan in 1986 to investigate the pornography industry. It is sometimes called the Meese Report for then U.S. Attorney General Edwin Meese. Excerpted below, this report discusses the history of pornography, the extent of the First Amendment protections for pornography, and what it concluded were the harmful effects of pornography, especially on women.

Descriptions of sex are as old as sex itself. There can be little doubt that talking about sex has been around as long as talking, that writing about sex has been around as long as writing, and that pictures of sex have been around as long as pictures. In this sense it is odd that historical treatments of pornography turn out to be historical treatments of the *regulation*, governmental or otherwise, of pornography. To understand the phenomenon of pornography it is necessary to look at the history of the phenomenon itself, prior to or at least distinct from the investigation of the practice of restricting it. Some works on the history of sexual behavior, eroticism, or erotic art help to serve this goal, but the history of pornography still remains to be written. Commissioning independent historical research was far beyond our mandate, our budget, and our time constraints, yet we do not wish to ignore history entirely. We feel it appropriate to offer the briefest overview here, but we urge as well that more comprehensive historical study be undertaken.

. . .

When earlier social inhibitions about public descriptions and depictions of sexuality and sexual practices came to be enforced by law, it was largely in the context of religious rather than secular concerns. Moreover, the earliest enforcement efforts were directed not against descriptions or depictions of sex itself, but only against such depictions when combined with attacks on religion or religious authorities.

. . .

3.1 The Presumptive Relevance of the First Amendment

The subject of pornography is not coextensive with the subject of sex. Definitionally, pornography requires a portrayal, whether spoken, written, printed, photographed, sculpted, or drawn, and this essential feature of pornography necessarily implicates constitutional concerns that would not otherwise exist. The First Amendment to the Constitution of the United States provides quite simply that "Congress shall make no law . . . abridging the freedom of speech, or of the press." Longstanding judicial interpretations make it now clear that this mandate is, because of the Fourteenth Amendment, applicable to the states as well,[1] and make it equally clear that the restrictions of the First Amendment are applicable to any form of governmental action, and not merely to statutes enacted by a legislative body.[2]

To the extent, therefore, that regulation of pornography constitutes an abridgment of the freedom of speech, or an abridgment of the freedom of the press, it is at least presumptively unconstitutional. And even if some or all forms of regulation of pornography are seen ultimately not to constitute abridgments of the freedom of speech or the freedom of the press, the fact remains that the Constitution treats speaking and printing as special, and thus the regulation of anything spoken or printed must be examined with extraordinary care. For even when some forms of regulation of what is spoken or printed are not abridgments of the freedom of speech, or abridgments of the freedom of the press, such regulations are closer to constituting abridgments than other forms of governmental action. If nothing else, the barriers between permissible restrictions on what is said or printed and unconstitutional abridgments must be scrupulously guarded.

Thus, we start with the presumption that the First Amendment is germane to our inquiry, and we start as well with the presumption that, both

---

[1] *Gitlow v. New York*, 268 U.S. 652 (1925).

[2] *E.g.*, *Bantam Books, Inc. v. Sullivan*, 372 U.S. 58 (1963); *Organization for a Better Austin v. Keefe*, 402 U.S. 415 (1971).

as citizens and as governmental officials who have sworn an oath to uphold and defend the Constitution, we have independent responsibilities to consider constitutional issues in our deliberations and in our conclusions.

. . .

3.2 The First Amendment, The Supreme Court, and the Regulation of Obscenity

Although both speaking and printing are what the First Amendment is all about, closer examination reveals that the First Amendment cannot plausibly be taken to protect, or even to be relevant to, every act of speaking or writing. Government may plainly sanction the written acts of writing checks backed by insufficient funds, filing income tax returns that understate income or overstate deductions, and describing securities or consumer products in false or misleading terms. In none of these cases would First Amendment defenses even be taken seriously. The same can be said about sanctions against spoken acts such as lying while under oath, or committing most acts of criminal conspiracy. Although urging the public to rise up and overthrow the government is protected by the First Amendment, urging your brother to kill your father so that you can split the insurance money has never been considered the kind of spoken activity with which the First Amendment is concerned. Providing information to the public about the misdeeds of their political leaders is central to the First Amendment, but providing information to one's friends about the combination to the vault at the local bank is not a First Amendment matter at all.

The regulation of pornography in light of the constraints of the First Amendment must thus be considered against this background—that not every use of words, pictures, or a printing press automatically triggers protection by the First Amendment.

. . .

But it should be plain both from the law, and from inspection of the kinds of material that the law has allowed to be prosecuted, that only the most thoroughly explicit materials, overwhelmingly devoted to patently offensive and explicit representations, and unmitigated by any significant amount of anything else, can be and are in fact determined to be legally obscene.

3.3 Is the Supreme Court Right?

. . .

With dissent existing even within the Supreme Court, and with disagreement with the Supreme Court majority's approach predominant among legal scholars, we could hardly ignore the possibility that the Supreme Court might be wrong on this issue, and that we would wish to find protected that which the Supreme Court found unprotected.

There are both less and more plausible challenges to the Supreme Court's approach to obscenity. Among the least plausible, and usually more rhetorical device than serious argument, is the view that the First Amendment is in some way an "absolute," protecting, quite simply, all speech. Even Justices Black and Douglas, commonly taken to be "absolutists," would hardly have protected all spoken or written acts under the First Amendment, and on closer inspection all those accused of or confessing to "absolutism" would at the very least apply their absolutism to a range of spoken or written acts smaller than the universe of all spoken, written, or pictorial acts. This is not to deny that under the views of many, including Black and Douglas, what is now considered obscene should be within the universe of what is absolutely protected. But "absolutism" in unadulterated form seems largely a strawman, and we see no need to use it as a way of avoiding difficult questions.

Much more plausible is the view not that the First Amendment protects all spoken, written, or pictorial acts, but that all spoken, written, or pictorial acts are at least in some way covered, even if not ultimately protected, by the First Amendment. That is, even if the government may regulate some such acts, it may never do so unless it has a reason substantially better than the reasons that normally are sufficient to justify governmental action. Whether this heightened standard of justification is described as a "clear and present danger," or "compelling interest," or some standard less stringent than those, the view is still that regulating any spoken, written, or pictorial acts requires a particularly good reason. And when applied to the regulation of obscenity, so the argument goes, the reasons supplied and the empirical evidence offered remain too speculative to meet this especially high burden of justification.

Other views accept the fact that not all spoken, written, or pictorial acts need meet this especially high burden of justification. Only those acts that in some way relate to the purposes or principles of the First Amendment are covered, but, it is argued, even the hardest-core pornographic item is within the First Amendment's coverage. To some this is because both the distribution and use of such items are significant aspects of self-expression. And while not all acts of self-expression are covered by the First Amendment, acts of self-expression that take the form of books, magazines, and films are, according to the argument, so covered. These, it is argued, are the traditional media of communication, and when those media are used to express a different world view, or even merely to achieve sexual satisfaction, they remain the kinds of things towards which the First Amendment is directed. As a result, regulation of the process by which an alternative sexual vision is communicated, or regulation of the process by which people use the traditional media of communication to experience and to understand a different sexual vision, is as much a part of the First Amendment as communicating and experiencing different visions about, for example, politics or morals.

. . .

Like any other act, the act of making, distributing, and using pornographic items contains and sends messages. For government to act against some of these items on account of the messages involved may appear as problematic under the First Amendment, but to hold that such governmental action violates the First Amendment is to preclude government from taking action in every case in which government fears that the restricted action will be copied, or proliferate because of its acceptance.

. . .

4.1.1 The Motion Picture Industry

With few exceptions, what might be called the "mainstream" or "legitimate" or "Hollywood" motion picture industry does not produce the kinds of films that would commonly be made available in "adults only" outlets. The films shown in such establishments, the ones containing little if any plot, unalloyed explicitness, and little other than an intent to arouse, are not the products of the motion picture industry with which most people are familiar. Nevertheless, sexuality, in varying degrees of explicitness or, to many, offensiveness, is a significant part of many mainstream motion pictures. One result of this phenomenon has been the rating system of the MPAA.

. . .

Most germane to this Report are the ratings of "R" and "X." An "R" rating indicates a restricted film, and those under the age of seventeen are admitted only if accompanied by a parent or guardian. Motion pictures with this rating may be somewhat, substantially, or exclusively devoted to themes of sex or violence. They may contain harsh language, sexual activity, and nudity. Films with this rating, however, do not contain explicit sexual activity. If a film contains explicit sexual activity, or if, in some cases, it contains particularly extreme quantities and varieties of violence, it is rated "X," and no one under the age of seventeen may be admitted.

Only in rare cases will anything resembling standard pornographic fare be submitted to the MPAA for a rating. More often such material will have a self-rated "X" designation, or will have no rating, or will have some unofficial promotional rating such as "XXX." It is important to recognize, however, that although no motion picture not submitted to the MPAA can have any rating other than "X," and that although standard pornographic items would unquestionably receive an "X" rating if submitted, not all, and indeed, not many *officially* "X" rated motion pictures would commonly be considered to be pornographic. Although the nature of what kind of content will get what rating will change with the times, it remains the case that the "X" rating, especially when applied to the small number of mainstream films that officially receive that rating after submission to the MPAA, is not in every case synonymous with what most people would consider pornography.

. . .

5.1 Matters of Method

5.1.1 Harm and Regulation—The Scope of Our Inquiry

A central part of our mission has been to examine the question whether pornography is harmful.

. . .

Most importantly, . . . we categorically reject the idea that material cannot be constitutionally protected, and properly so, while still being harmful. All of us, for example, feel that the inflammatory utterances of Nazis, the Ku Klux Klan, and racists of other varieties are harmful both to the individuals to whom their epithets are directed as well as to society as a whole. Yet all of us acknowledge and most of us support the fact that the harmful speeches of these people are nevertheless constitutionally protected. That the same may hold true with respect to some sexually explicit materials was at least our working assumption in deciding to look at a range of materials broader than the legally obscene. There is no reason whatsoever to suppose that such material is necessarily harmless just because it is and should remain protected by the First

Amendment. As a result, we reject the notion that an investigation of the question of harm must be restricted to material unprotected by the Constitution.

. . .

In thinking about harms, it is useful to draw a rough distinction between primary and secondary harms. Primary harms are those in which the alleged harm is commonly taken to be intrinsically harmful, even though the precise way in which the harm is harmful might yet be further explored. Nevertheless, murder, rape, assault, and discrimination on the basis of race and gender are all examples of primary harms in this sense. We treat these acts as harms not because of where they will lead, but simply because of what they are.

In other instances, however, the alleged harm is secondary, not in the sense that it is in any way less important, but in the sense that the concern is not with what the act *is*, but where it will lead. Curfews are occasionally imposed not because there is anything wrong with people being out at night, but because in some circumstances it is thought that being out at night in large groups may cause people to commit other crimes. Possession of "burglar tools" is often prohibited because of what those tools may be used for. Thus, when it is urged that pornography is harmful because it causes some people to commit acts of sexual violence, because it causes promiscuity, because it encourages sexual relations outside of marriage, because it promotes so-called "unnatural" sexual practices, or because it leads men to treat women as existing solely for the sexual satisfaction of men, the alleged harms are secondary, again not in any sense suggesting that the harms are less important. The harms are secondary here because the allegation of harm presupposes a causal link between the act and the harm, a causal link that is superfluous if, as in the case of primary harms, the act quite simply *is* the harm.

Thus we think it important, with respect to every area of possible harm, to focus on whether the allegation relates to a harm that comes from the sexually explicit material itself, or whether it occurs *as a result* of something the material does.

. . .

5.2.1 Sexually Violent Material

The category of material on which most of the evidence has focused is the category of material featuring actual or unmistakably simulated or unmistakably threatened violence presented in sexually explicit fashion with a predominant focus on the sexually explicit violence. Increasingly, the most prevalent forms of pornography, as well as an increasingly prevalent body of less sexually explicit material, fit this description. Some of this material involves sado-masochistic themes, with the standard accoutrements of the genre, including whips, chains, devices of torture, and so on. But another theme of some of this material is not sado-masochistic, but involves instead the recurrent theme of a man making some sort of sexual advance to a woman, being rebuffed, and then raping the woman or in some other way violently forcing himself on the woman. In almost all of this material, whether in magazine or motion picture form, the woman eventually becomes aroused and ecstatic about the initially forced sexual activity, and usually is portrayed as begging for more. There is also a large body of material, more "mainstream" in its availability, that portrays sexual activity or sexually suggestive nudity coupled with extreme violence, such as disfigurement or murder. The so-called "slasher" films fit this description, as does some material, both in films and in magazines, that is less or more sexually explicit than the prototypical "slasher" film.

It is with respect to material of this variety that the scientific findings and ultimate conclusions of the 1970 Commission are least reliable for today, precisely because material of this variety was largely absent from that Commission's inquiries. It is not, however, absent from the contemporary world, and it is hardly surprising that conclusions about this material differ from conclusions about material not including violent themes.

When clinical and experimental research has focused particularly on sexually violent material, the conclusions have been virtually unanimous. In both clinical and experimental settings, exposure to sexually violent materials has indicated an increase in the likelihood of aggression. More specifically, the research, which is described in much detail later in this Report, shows a causal relationship between exposure to material of this type and aggressive behavior towards women.

. . .

An enormous amount of the most sexually explicit material available, as well as much of the material that is somewhat less sexually explicit, is material that we would characterize as "degrading," the term we use to encompass the undeniably linked characteristics of degradation, domination, subordination, and humiliation. The degradation we refer to is degradation of people, most often women, and here we are referring to material that, although not violent, depicts[3] people, usually women, as existing solely for the sexual satisfaction of others, usually men, or that depicts people, usually women, in decidedly subordinate roles in their sexual relations with others, or that depicts people engaged in sexual practices that would to most people be considered humiliating. Indeed, forms of degradation represent the largely predominant proportion of commercially available pornography.

With respect to material of this variety, our conclusions are substantially similar to those with respect to violent material, although we make them with somewhat less confidence and our making of them requires more in the way of assumption than was the case with respect to violent material. The evidence, scientific and otherwise, is more tentative, but supports the conclusion that the material we describe as degrading bears some causal relationship to the attitudinal changes we have previously identified. That is, substantial exposure to material of this variety is likely to increase the extent to which those exposed will view rape or other forms of sexual violence as less serious than they otherwise would have, will view the victims of rape and other forms of sexual violence as significantly more responsible, and will view the offenders as significantly less responsible. We also conclude that the evidence supports the conclusion that substantial exposure to material of this type will increase acceptance of the proposition that women like to be forced into sexual practices, and, once again, that the woman who says "no" really means "yes."

. . .

5.2.3 Non-Violent and Non-Degrading Materials

Our most controversial category has been the category of sexually explicit materials that are not violent and are not degrading as we have used that

---

[3] We restrict our analysis in large part to degradation that is in fact depicted in the material. It may very well be that degradation led to a woman being willing to pose for a picture of a certain variety, or to engage in what appears to be a non-degrading sexual act. It may be that coercion caused the picture to exist. And it may very well be that the existing disparity in the economic status of men and women is such that any sexually explicit depiction of a woman is at least suspect on account of the possibility that the economic desparity is what caused the woman to pose for a picture that most people in this society would find embarrassing. We do not deny any of these possibilities, and we do not deny the importance of considering as pervasively as possible the status of women in contemporary America, including the effects of their current status and what might be done to change some of the detrimental consequences of that status. But without engaging in an inquiry of that breadth, we must generally, absent more specific evidence to the contrary, assume that a picture represents what it depicts.

term. They are materials in which the participants appear to be fully willing participants occupying substantially equal roles in a setting devoid of actual or apparent violence or pain. This category is in fact quite small in terms of currently available materials. There is some, to be sure, and the amount may increase as the division between the degrading and the non-degrading becomes more accepted, but we are convinced that only a small amount of currently available highly sexually explicit material is neither violent nor degrading. We thus talk about a small category, but one that should not be ignored.

We have disagreed substantially about the effects of such materials, and that should come as no surprise. We are dealing in this category with "pure" sex, as to which there are widely divergent views in this society. That we have disagreed among ourselves does little more than reflect the extent to which we are representative of the population as a whole.

. . .

A larger issue is the very question of promiscuity. Even to the extent that the behavior depicted is not inherently condemned by some or any of us, the manner of presentation almost necessarily suggests that the activities are taking place outside of the context of marriage, love, commitment, or even affection. Again, it is far from implausible to hypothesize that materials depicting sexual activity without marriage, love, commitment, or affection bear some causal relationship to sexual activity without marriage, love, commitment, or affection. There are undoubtedly many causes for what used to be called the "sexual revolution," but it is absurd to suppose that depictions or descriptions of uncommitted sexuality were not among them.[4] Thus, once again our disagreements reflect disagreements in society at large, although not to as great an extent. Although there are many members of this society who can and have made affirmative cases for uncommitted sexuality, none of us believes it to be a good thing. A number of us, however, believe that the level of commitment in sexuality is a matter of choice among those who voluntarily engage in the activity. Others of us believe that uncommitted sexual activity is wrong for the individuals involved and harmful to society to the extent of its prevalence. Our view of the ultimate harmfulness of much of this material, therefore, is reflective of our individual views about the extent to whether sexual commitment is purely a matter of individual choice.

. . .

---

[4] Nor, of course, do we deny the extent that the phenomenon, in part, also goes the other way. Sexually explicit materials in most cases seem both to reflect and to cause demand.

A number of witnesses have testified about the effects on their own sexual relations, usually with their spouses, of the depiction on the screen and in magazines of sexual practices in which they had not previously engaged. A number of these witnesses, *all women*, have testified that men in their lives have used such material to strongly encourage, or coerce, them into engaging in sexual practices in which they do not choose to engage. To the extent that such implicit or explicit coercion takes place as a result of these materials, we all agree that it is a harm. There has been other evidence, however, about the extent to which such material might for some be a way of revitalizing their sex lives, or, more commonly, simply constituting a part of a mutually pleasurable sexual experience for both partners. On this we could not agree. For reasons relating largely to the question of publicness in the first sense discussed above, some saw this kind of use as primarily harmful. Others saw it as harmless and possibly beneficial in contexts such as this. Some professional testimony supported this latter view, but we have little doubt that professional opinion is also divided on the issue.

Perhaps the most significant potential harm in this category exists with respect to children. We all agree that at least much, probably most, and maybe even all material in this category, regardless of whether it is harmful when used by adults only, is harmful when it falls into the hands of children. Exposure to sexuality is commonly taken, and properly so, to be primarily the responsibility of the family. Even those who would disagree with this statement would still prefer to have early exposure to sexuality be in the hands of a responsible professional in a controlled and guided setting. We have no hesitancy in concluding that learning about sexuality from most of the material in this category is not the best way for children to learn about the subject. There are harms both to the children themselves and to notions of family control over a child's introduction to sexuality if children learn about sex from the kinds of sexually explicit materials that constitute the bulk of this category of materials.

. . .

6.2 Should Pornography Be Regulated By Law?

6.2.1 *The Question is Deregulation*

Numerous witnesses at our public hearings, as well as many others in written evidence or in various publications, have urged upon us the view that pornography should not be regulated by law. Because such arguments have been around for some time, and because such arguments were substantially accepted by the 1970 Commission, we have very seriously considered them. To a significant extent, however, the arguments remain unpersuasive.

Many of the arguments against regulation, both those made currently and those made earlier, rest on claims of harmlessness that, as we have explained in Chapter 5 of this Part, are simply erroneous with respect to much of this material. Some of these claims of harmlessness tend either to ignore much of the evidence, or to extrapolate from plausible conclusions about the most innocuous material to conclusions about an entire class. Others start with the assumption that no finding of harm can be accepted unless it meets some extraordinarily high burden of proof, a burden of proof whose rigor often seems premised on an *a priori* assertion that the material being discussed ought not to be regulated.

In addition to erroneous or skewed claims of harmlessness, many of the arguments against regulation depend on claims of unconstitutionality that would require for their acceptance a view of the law strikingly different from that long accepted by the Supreme Court in its rulings on obscenity. As we discuss in Chapter 3 of this Part, we accept the Supreme Court's basic approach to the constitutional question. To the extent that claims for non-regulation thus rest on constitutional arguments with which neither we nor the Supreme Court accept, we reject those arguments for non-regulation.

To the extent that arguments for non-regulation do not depend on implausible claims of harmlessness or rejected claims of unconstitutionality, however, they deserve to be taken even more seriously. As questions of policy in particular areas or the appropriateness of governmental action in general, serious arguments have been made that go to the most fundamental questions of what governmental action is designed to achieve.

. . .

[W]e take the question of the governmental regulation of the legally obscene not to be whether if we did not have obscenity laws would we want them, but whether given that we have obscenity laws do we want to abandon them. In many areas the issues before us are not close, and how the question is put does not determine the outcome. But in many other areas the questions are indeed difficult, and how the questions are cast, and where the burden of proof lies, do make a difference. With reference to criminal sanctions against the legally obscene, for example, the burden must be on those who would have us or society make the specially strong statement implicit in the act of repeal. But with reference to certain forms of regulation that do not now exist, the burden is similarly on those who would have us or society make the specially strong statement implicit in urging the totally new.

. . .

Although once again we have been urged to recommend new laws that are substantially more encompassing than the existing definition of the legally obscene, we find such approaches both unnecessary and undesirable. The vast bulk of this material seems to us well within the *Miller* definition, and thus could be prosecuted in accordance with the concerns and the priorities we have urged here. In light of that, we see few advantages and substantial risks in going further. But we also urge that there be laws allowing the prosecution of such legally obscene material, and we urge as well that such laws be enforced. There seems now to be little enforcement, and in light of the frequency with which this material is used by minors, we deplore the failure to have and to enforce obscenity laws with respect to material of this type.

. . .

Citizen interest in pornography control is a vital component of any local law enforcement program. Since one aspect of the constitutional test for obscenity is the notion of contemporary community standards, this is an area of the law which presents significant opportunity for public input.

Citizens concerned about pornography in their community should initially determine the nature and availability of pornographic materials in their community, existing prosecution policies, law enforcement practices and judicial attitudes in the community. They should inquire whether these enforcement mechanisms are adequately utilized. They should determine whether the official perception of the current community standards is truly a reflection of public opinion. If enforcement mechanisms appear inadequate or ineffective, if legislative change is necessary to enhance the effectiveness of the criminal justice system, or if the volume of pornography or offensive material is a particular problem in the community, citizens should consider developing a community action program.

A successful community action program should contain the following components:

1. Sincere citizen interest in controlling the proliferation of pornographic material in their community;
2. A police department that is willing to allocate a reasonable portion of its resources to obscenity enforcement;
3. A prosecutor who, in keeping with his or her oath of office, will

aggressively pursue violations of obscenity statutes with due regard for the right to distribute constitutionally protected material;

4. A judiciary that is responsive to obscenity violations and will sentence offenders appropriately.

Additional methods by which community action organizations can express their concern about pornography in their community include:

1. Citizen involvement in educating legislators, law enforcement officials and the public at large as to the impact of pornography on their particular community;
2. Citizen action in the area of lawful economic boycotts and picketing of establishments which produce, distribute or sell sexually explicit materials in the community;
3. If the techniques of anti-display and nuisance laws as well as zoning ordinances are determined to be appropriately tailored to the pornography problem in their community, citizens are encouraged to advocate measures to their local legislators; and
4. A business community that exercises sound judgement as to the effect on the community they serve of material offered in their establishment.

In the area of pornography regulation it is important that the above items be seriously addressed and effectively coordinated. The best written laws will be ineffective if prosecutors do not enforce them or if judges fail to recognize the extent of citizen concern when sentencing offenders. The goals of the community effort against pornography should be to establish constitutionally sound obscenity laws that meet their particular needs, to encourage adequate enforcement of these laws and to use private action to curb the flow of pornography and obscenity in their community.

At the same time, citizens should be aware of the risks of an overzealous approach. First, citizens should recognize that there are a diversity of views as to what, if any, regulations should be imposed on pornographic material. The United States Supreme Court has established definitional guidelines for obscenity, which are discussed elsewhere in the Report, but not without considerable division of opinion. Undoubtedly, diversity of views regarding regulations, enforcement priorities and appropriate community action will exist to varying degrees in each community. These views should be recognized and addressed by citizen advocates.

In maintaining a balanced approach, citizens should be aware of the legal criteria for distinguishing material which is obscene from that which is merely distasteful to some. However citizen groups may wish to focus on materials which are not legally obscene and which are constitutionally protected from government regulation. Citizens may pursue a variety of private actions with respect to this non-obscene but offensive pornographic material.

It is also important for citizen activists to recognize the rights of other individuals' and organizations' when exercising their own. Advocates of strict enforcement of pornography laws should recognize the rights of individuals within opposing views. Moreover, while citizens have every right to picket, the pickets should not preclude others from entering or leaving business premises.

Finally, community action groups should guard against taking extreme or legally unsound, positions or actions, such as unfounded attacks on the content of school reading lists, library shelves and general discussions of sex-related topics. With respect to their communications with a public official, members of citizen action groups should also be aware that such official keep duty bound to determine the legality of material without regard to that official's personal opinion.

The decision to form or support a citizen action group is one that must be made by each community and participating individuals. If a decision is reached to establish such a group, its members should become involved in advocating, establishing and maintaining community standards related to pornography. The following discussion highlights ways in which citizens can maximize their efforts in this regard while recognizing competing constitutionally protected interests. The suggestions which have been developed were prompted by hundreds of telephone calls and tens of thousands of letters from concerned citizens seeking advice on how to address the pornography issue.

22.2 POSITION STATEMENT OF THE FREE SPEECH COALITION, 1991

The Free Speech Coalition formed in 1991 in response to what it considered "numerous government attacks." As it explains in its "history" and its "mission statement" reprinted below, the Coalition's goal is to not only protect the pornography industry (by way of the First Amendment) but to "mainstream" pornography, as well. While pornography is an issue very few prominent

Hollywood celebrities campaign for or against, a number of porn stars have successfully made the switch to mainstream productions and the adult entertainment industry has been explored by such popular vehicles as *The People v. Larry Flynt* (1996) and *Boogie Nights* (1997).

History

The Free Speech Coalition was founded in 1991 as a result of numerous government attacks against producers and retailers of adult products. But its roots are embedded deep within the birth and development of adult entertainment in the United States.

The concept of an organization as a rallying point for those who believe in the free expression of adult-themed works began as early as 1970. The first truly national group to emerge was the Adult Film Association of America (AFAA). At that time, adult entertainment was only available in adult theaters and bookstores so early members were largely theatrical exhibitors. With the advent of inexpensive home videos, the AFAA morphed into the Adult Film and Video Association of America (AFVAA).

The next significant event that galvanized the AFVAA was the arrest of Hal Freeman for pandering. Prosecutors wanted to establish once and for all that paying performers to have sex in a film was an act of prostitution. Freeman won that legal battle, which redefined the use of the pandering laws relative to providers of adult product. As video productions became the dominant factor in the marketplace, theatrical exhibition diminished. Video chains and many independent stores in suburbs and smaller cities started carrying adult fare. Overzealous law enforcement officials subjected more and more retailers to "obscenity" charges. Then in 1990, under the first Bush administration, the Federal government attacked most of the major manufacturers of adult video with a sting operation designed to destroy the industry. In response, the Free Speech Legal Defense Fund (FSLDF) was formed by industry leaders to protect the rights of members in all areas of adult entertainment.

In 1992, as the government attack was blunted, the FSLDF decided to select a name more reflective of its broadened role in the adult community and the Free Speech Coalition (FSC) was born.

During the Clinton Administration, there were few obscenity prosecutions. Then-Attorney General Janet Reno seemed to see "obscenity" as a victimless crime. She also realized that in many areas community standards had changed and "obscenity" convictions were becoming more difficult to sustain.

In 1997 FSC retained Kat Sunlove as California lobbyist to represent its legislative interests in the state. Efforts to make adult industry views heard and to build relationships in the State Capitol have been very successful. Sunlove introduced an annual lobbying training program for FSC members entitled Celebrate Free Speech Lobbying Days, and FSC has produced that event each year since to high acclaim.

In 1999 FSC hired its first full-time Executive Director and began to gain a nationally recognized reputation as a defender of First and Fourth Amendment rights. FSC has formed alliances with other organizations whose missions are compatible with our own.

In 2002, FSC views were upheld in the U.S. Supreme Court in Ashcroft v. Free Speech Coalition, the so-called VIRTUAL CHILD PORN case, which has been described by no less than the ACLU as "the most important victory for the First Amendment in decades."

We welcome your ideas and energy as we continue to work for YOUR rights to produce, perform and consume adult entertainment.

Mission Statement

The Free Speech Coalition's mission is to:

Lead, protect and support the growth and wellbeing of the adult entertainment community. As the trade association for the adult entertainment we do this by:

- Being the legislative watchdog for the industry
- Lobbying
- Public education and communication
- Member education and communication
- As a last resort, litigation

Vision Statement

We envision a national association that helps limit the legal risks of being an adult business, increases the profitability of its members, promotes the acceptance of the industry in America's business community, and supports greater public tolerance for freedom of sexual speech.

Free Speech 2007–2009 Strategic Plan

Public Relations

FSC will be widely recognized and easily identified as the adult entertainment industry's trade association. It will do so though the development and/or enhancement of:

1. Brand Identity—Development of a clear look, message and content.
2. Internal and External Communications Plan—Identification of audiences (industry, members, media, legislators, etc), development of methods and materials to reach those audiences and the planning and implementation of message dissemination.
3. Code of Ethics & Best Practices—by 3rd quarter 2008, review, revision and endorsement of Code of Ethics & Best Practices by the membership. Development of message materials for general public by the end of the 4th quarter, 2008.
4. Communication Infrastructure—Develop and implement plan for annual review, revision and update of current methods of communication (website, publications, etc).

Membership

Bearing in mind all segments of the industry (novelties, talent, webmasters, producers, distributors etc.), FSC will cultivate and maintain a vital membership base that understands and values the benefits of being an FSC member. Membership enhancement will be accomplished through:

1. Membership Survey—Develop and implement a bi-annual membership survey—the first survey to be completed by the end of the second quarter 2007.
2. Benefits & Services—Utilize information gathered from the membership surveys and build on existing member benefit and services program with annual goals and evaluation.
3. Retention & Recruitment—Create a process for data tracking and analysis to monitor trends in new memberships and member retention. Develop a membership monitoring program that addresses lapsed members, membership retention and member recruitment. Program developed in 2007 with membership goals for 2008 and 2009.

4. Meetings, Seminars and Trade Shows—Utilize information gathered from the membership surveys and develop and implement an annual calendar of membership meetings and seminars that are of interest to our members. Also determine a schedule of trade shows in which FSC should have a presence and determine what level. Review FSC activity through participant evaluations at each event.

5. Publications—Maintain strong lines of communication with membership through FSC website and publications (Xpress, Free Speaker e-mail blasts, etc.). Utilize membership survey to determine a publication's value to membership as well opportunities for publication enhancement.

Organizational Development

FSC will apply systems, processes and oversight to promote solid business practices and long-term sustainability.

1. Diversification of Funding—Develop an annual schedule of member fundraisers. Create sponsorships opportunities and recruit sponsor for FSC publications and program activity. Solicit donations for FSC litigation and programs. Schedule and implement fundraising events. Coordinate these efforts to reduce dependence on membership dues by 25%.

2. 501(c)3—Develop a 501(c)3 nonprofit to provide community education about freedom of speech and freedom of expression and the adult entertainment industry. Papers filed by the end of the 2nd quarter 2007.

3. Oversight—Develop policy and process for comprehensive Executive Director Evaluation and fiscal oversight. Process in place by the end of the 2nd quarter 2007. Executive Director evaluated annually, fiscal reports reviewed bimonthly with audits performed annually.

4. Board Development—Review and revise board committee structure and participation (by end of 2nd quarter 2007) and the board nomination and election process (by 3rd quarter 2007). Develop and implement annual board work plans.

5. Chapter Development—Develop a structure, guidelines, and support network for state and/or regional chapters to address issues at a local level and broaden the scope of our membership.

Government

FSC will continue to be the watchdog for the adult entertainment industry, working to prevent legislation that is harmful to the industry and FSC members. FSC will guard against harmful legislation by:

1. Legislative Tracking—Track legislation throughout the 50 states and develop a vehicle for member information and alerts.
2. Message Development—Develop white papers and talking points for use in lobbying and media inquiries.
3. Federal and California Lobbying—Continue FSC presence at the California state capital and our Nation's capital. Create support materials about the industry that will be useful to our lobbyists. Develop a network of industry spokespeople ready, willing and able to testify, lobby or be interviewed at a moment's notice.
4. Grassroots Organizing—Develop and implement a plan to organize and activate industry members and the industry's consumer base.

Litigation

When appropriate, FSC will continue to protect its members through the oversight and coordination of litigation. FSC will provide appropriate litigation selection and oversight through:

1. Litigation Criteria and Approval Process—FSC will develop written criteria and an approval process that potential litigation must pass prior to being brought before the board for a vote.
2. Budget—FSC will develop litigation budgetary guidelines for future litigation proposals.
3. Attorney Selection—FSC will develop a process for attorney selection and oversight.
4. Litigation Updates—FSC will develop and implement a process for regularly updating our membership on current litigation.

FSC 2007 Annual Report

Dear FSC Member,

I am pleased to present to you FSC's 2007 Annual Report in the link below. Included in this report is a brief overview of FSC's accomplishments for the year as well as some of FSC's plans for 2008. This report is especially significant not only because it is the first of its kind for FSC, but also because it includes FSC's audited financials. Your membership is important to FSC and we want you to know how your membership dollars are invested.

While this is the first of its kind, FSC's commitment to you is that it will not be the last. We will continue to provide this report to our members each and every year from this point forward. Feel free to contact me, personally, if you have any questions or comments at 818-348-9373 or diane@freespeechcoalition.com.

Thank you so much for your membership and your support. We are proud to be your trade association and will continue to serve the adult entertainment industry with dedication and commitment.

Sincerely,
Diane Duke
FSC Executive Director

CHAPTER 23

Home Alone: Family Values in the 1990s

23.1 1996 TELECOMMUNICATIONS REFORM ACT, FEDERAL COMMUNICATIONS COMMISSION [EXCERPT]

During the 1992 election, "family values" became a hot political topic, and a bipartisan effort emerged to force the same kind of self-censorship of television programs that the film industry had adopted. Senator Joe Lieberman (then a Democrat, now an Independent from Connecticut) and former Secretary of Education William Bennett led the charge in this campaign, and Lieberman cosponsored the Telecommunications Reform Act, which became law in February 1996. Below are excerpts from the legislation which, among other things, set up a Parental Ratings System for programs and required all television receivers to possess a "V chip," a device that allows parents to block programs based on their ratings.

In the Telecommunications Act of 1996, Public Law 104–104, effective February 8, 1996, in Section 551, "Parental Choice in Television Programming," Congress enacted the following;

- *passed "findings" on the subject*, Section (a)
- *prescribed procedures for Establishment of a Television Rating Code*, (Sections (b) and (e)(1); and
- *prescribed procedures for newly manufactured television sets* to include a mechanism to block programs, referred to popularly as the V-Chip (Sections (c), (d) and (e)(2)

The following is the text of these provisions.

I Findings

(Sec. 551. Parental Choice in Television Programming.)

(a) *Findings*

The Congress makes the following findings:

(1) Television influences children's perception of the values and behavior that are common and acceptable in society.

(2) Television station operators, cable television system operators, and video programmers should follow practices in connection with video programming that take into consideration that television broadcast and cable programming has established a uniquely pervasive presence in the lives of American children.

(3) The average American child is exposed to 25 hours of television each week and some children are exposed to as much as 11 hours of television a day.

(4) Studies have shown that children exposed to violent video programming at a young age have a higher tendency for violent and aggressive behavior later in life than children not so exposed, and that children exposed to violent video programming are prone to assume that acts of violence are acceptable behavior.

(5) Children in the United States are, on average, exposed to an estimated 8,000 murders and 100,000 acts of violence on television by the time the child completes elementary school.

(6) Studies indicate that children are affected by the pervasiveness and casual treatment of sexual material on television, eroding the ability of parents to develop responsible attitudes and behavior in their children.

(7) Parents express grave concern over violent and sexual video programming and strongly support technology that would give them greater control to block video programming in the home that they consider harmful to their children.

(8) There is a compelling governmental interest in empowering parents to limit the negative influences of video programming that is harmful to children.

(9) Providing parents with timely information about the nature of upcoming video programming and with the technological tools that allow them easily to block violent, sexual, or other programming that they believe harmful to their children is a nonintrusive and

narrowly tailored means of achieving that compelling governmental interest.

II Ratings

(Sec. 551. Parental Choice in Television Programming.)

(b) Establishment of Television Rating Code

(1) Amendment

Section 303 (47 U.S.C. 303) is amended by adding at the end the following:

(w) Prescribe—

(1) on the basis of recommendations from an advisory committee established by the Commission in accordance with section 551(b)(2) of the Telecommunications Act of 1996, guidelines and recommended procedures for the identification and rating of video programming that contains sexual, violent, or other indecent material about which parents should be informed before it is displayed to children: Provided, That nothing in this paragraph shall be construed to authorize any rating of video programming on the basis of its political or religious content; and

(2) with respect to any video programming that has been rated, and in consultation with the television industry, rules requiring distributors of such video programming to transmit such rating to permit parents to block the display of video programming that they have determined is inappropriate for their children.

(2) Advisory Committee Requirements

In establishing an advisory committee for purposes of the amendment made by paragraph (1) of this subsection, the Commission shall—

(A) ensure that such committee is composed of parents, television broadcasters, television programming producers, cable operators, appropriate public interest groups, and other interested individuals from the private sector and is fairly balanced in terms of political affiliation, the points of view represented, and the functions to be performed by the committee;

(B) provide to the committee such staff and resources as may be necessary to permit it to perform its functions efficiently and promptly; and

(C) require the committee to submit a final report of its recommendations within one year after the date of the appointment of the initial members.

(3) Applicability and Effective Dates

(1) APPLICABILITY OF RATING PROVISION- The amendment made by subsection (b) [*ed. note: printed below*] of this section shall take effect 1 year after the date of enactment of this Act, but only if the Commission determines, in consultation with appropriate public interest groups and interested individuals from the private sector, that distributors of video programming have not, by such date—

(A) established voluntary rules for rating video programming that contains sexual, violent, or other indecent material about which parents should be informed before it is displayed to children, and such rules are acceptable to the Commission; and

(B) agreed voluntarily to broadcast signals that contain ratings of such programming.

III V-Chip

(Sec. 551. Parental Choice in Television Programming.)

(c) Requirement for Manufacture of Televisions that Block Programs

Section 303 (47 U.S.C. 303), as amended by subsection (a), is further amended by adding at the end the following:

(x) Require, in the case of an apparatus designed to receive television signals that are shipped in interstate commerce or manufactured in the United States and that have a picture screen 13 inches or greater in size (measured diagonally), that such apparatus be equipped with a feature designed to enable viewers to block display of all programs with a common rating, except as otherwise permitted by regulations pursuant to section 330(c)(4).

(d) Shipping of Televisions that Block Programs

Section 330 (47 U.S.C. 330) is amended—

(A) by redesignating subsection (c) as subsection (d); and
(B) by adding after subsection (b) the following new subsection (c):

"(c)

(1) Except as provided in paragraph (2), no person shall ship in inter-state commerce or manufacture in the United States any apparatus described in section 303(x) of this Act except in accordance with rules prescribed by the Commission pursuant to the authority granted by that section.

(2) This subsection shall not apply to carriers transporting apparatus referred to in paragraph (1) without trading in it.

(3) The rules prescribed by the Commission under this subsection shall provide for the oversight by the Commission of the adoption of standards by industry for blocking technology. Such rules shall require that all such apparatus be able to receive the rating signals which have been transmitted by way of line 21 of the vertical blank-ing interval and which conform to the signal and blocking specifica-tions established by industry under the supervision of the Commission.

(4) As new video technology is developed, the Commission shall take such action as the Commission determines appropriate to ensure. If the Commission determines that an alternative blocking technology exists that—

(A) enables parents to block programming based on identifying programs without ratings,

(B) is available to consumers at a cost which is comparable to the cost of technology that allows parents to block programming based on common ratings, and

(C) will allow parents to block a broad range of programs on a multichannel system as effectively and as easily as technology that allows parents to block programming based on common ratings, the Commission shall amend the rules prescribed pur-suant to section 303(x) to require that the apparatus described in such section be equipped with either the blocking technology described in such section or the alternative blocking technology described in this paragraph."

(e) Applicability and Effective Dates

(2) Effective Date of Manufacturing Provision

In prescribing regulations to implement the amendment made by subsection (c), the Federal Communications Commission shall, after consultation with the television manufacturing industry, specify the effective date for the applicability of the requirement to the apparatus covered by such amendment, which date shall not be less than two years after the date of enactment of this Act.

23.2 JOE LIEBERMAN, "WHY PARENTS HATE TV"

Even after the "V-chip legislation" became law, critics of the television industry continued to bemoan its programming. As Senator Joe Lieberman explains in "Why Parents Hate TV," the V chip was merely a "surrogate for their anger at the entertainment industry." Particularly targeting daytime talk shows, Lieberman calls on the entertainment industry to commit to producing "high-quality family-friendly" material.

Over the past few months, the V-chip has quickly become the most celebrated piece of computer circuitry in America. In swift succession, President Clinton championed this little byte of technology in his State of the Union address, Congress passed legislation mandating its use, and the major networks grumbled loudly about challenging the law in court. The drama finally culminated in February at a summit at the White House, where the TV industry's chieftains grudgingly accepted the president's challenge to do more for America's parents and create a ratings system compatible with the V-chip.

The story of the V-chip unfolded so fast, and its potential impact is so great, that the media has spent most of its time struggling to answer a host of basic questions: How does this signal-blocking technology work? When will it be available? How much will it cost? Will it live up to its billing? Some are still not even sure what the "V" actually stands for. (It originally stood for "violence," but it seems everyone has their own interpretation. I hope it comes to mean "values.")

As a Senate cosponsor of the V-chip bill along with Democrat Kent Conrad, I know these details matter, but I also believe the media's focus on them has obscured a larger point. Far more important than what the "V" stands for is what the coming of the V-chip tells us about the public's plummeting regard for the product that television delivers to our homes. Although this invention may merely be an irritant to those in the television business, to millions of Americans the V-chip is a surrogate for their anger at the entertainment industry for degrading our culture and our society.

That anger is clearly reflected in any number of public opinion polls, which uniformly show that the public is fed up with the rising tide of sex, violence, and vulgarity in the entertainment media. These surveys are useful, but based on my conversations with people in diners, schools, and small businesses back in Connecticut, I believe they barely begin to measure the public's intense feelings toward television.

My experience tells me that beneath the surface of the Telecommunications Revolution bubbles a revolution of another kind—a "Revolt of the Revolted," as William Bennett and I have taken to calling it. It is being fueled by a growing sense that our culture is not only out of touch with the values of mainstream America, but out of control as well. Many people believe that there are no standards that television will not violate, no lines television will not cross. Broadcasters may see the V-chip as a threat to their independence and financial well-being, but many average citizens see television as a threat to their children and their country. In the V-chip, they perceive a modicum of protection for their families.

Why are people afraid of television? Much of the news media has focused on the violence, but that is only part of the problem. Millions of Americans are fed up with explicit sex scenes and crude language during prime time and with the pornographic content of those abysmal talk shows and soap operas during the day. They feel television is not only offensive, but on the offensive, assaulting the values they and most of their neighbors share.

People are angry because they cannot sit down to watch TV with their children without fearing they will be embarrassed or demeaned. And they are angry because they feel our culture has been hijacked and replaced with something alien to their lives, something that openly rejects rather than reflects the values they try to instill in their families. In the world they see on TV, sex is a recreational pastime, indecency is a cause for laughter, and humans are killed as casually and senselessly as bugs. It is a coarse caricature of the America they love.

David Levy, the executive producer of the Caucus for Producers, Writers, and Directors, aptly describes this situation as "television without representation." Some critics tell me that, in the zealous pursuit of the prized demographic cohort of young adults, the industry has shut out the rest of the public, and let the tastes of a few dictate the menu for all.

Average viewers may not be aware of market dynamics at work, but they certainly understand the consequences. They have a growing sense that the anything-goes mentality permeating our electronic culture contributes to the moral crisis facing America. I believe this notion—that the contemporary entertainment culture is affecting our values in a deeply troubling way—is at the core of the brewing cultural rebellion.

This is a very anxious time in our history. The bonds of trust that people once took for granted in their neighborhoods and schools and workplaces are withering, and the social order that once anchored their lives and their communities is breaking apart. Stability is giving way to an increasingly chaotic and threatening world in which a snowball fight can quickly escalate into fatal shotgun blasts, as happened recently on a major thoroughfare in the city of Hartford.

The source of this social breakdown, many people believe, is the collapse of fundamental values. A critical connection exists between the erosion of morals and the explosion of social pathologies around us— brutal violence committed more and more often by strangers, the disintegration of the family, the epidemic of illegitimacy. In much the same way, many of us see a critical link between this erosion of values and the plummeting standards of decency on television and in our culture.

Some in the entertainment industry continue to argue that they are merely holding up a mirror to our culture, and scoff at the notion that the entertainment culture is responsible for all our social ills. The time has come to take a torch to this straw man. Neither President Clinton nor William Bennett nor I nor anyone I know is suggesting that any individual entertainment product, or even the whole of the entertainment industry, has single-handedly caused the rise in juvenile violence or illegitimacy. We are saying that the entertainment culture is immensely powerful, more powerful than any lawmaker in Washington, and that this power is wielded in ways that make our country's problems worse, not better.

Consider a few facts. There are 95 million households in America with televisions, which means more households own TV sets than telephones. Sixty-five percent of those homes have at least two TVs, which on average are turned on seven hours a day. The typical child watches 25 hours of television every week. That is more time than most of them spend attending religious services, talking to their parents, reading books, or even listening to their teachers. Many kids spend more time watching television than any other activity except sleeping.

No one can seriously deny the potential influence that kind of constant exposure carries with it. And because of that power, those responsible for television programming do not just mirror, but also mold, attitudes and behaviors. Whether they want the responsibility or not, they are influencing our values. And whenever they air degrading programs, they contribute to—not cause, but contribute to—the moral and social breakdown we are suffering.

So many studies have documented the threat posed by steady exposure to violence on television that the point should not even be subject to debate. But to add yet another voice to the mix, consider this passage from a stunning article Adam Walinsky wrote last year in the Atlantic Monthly, in which he warned of a coming generation of "superfelons" who when they mature will likely make the cities of today look peaceful:

> These young people have been raised in the glare of ceaseless media violence and incitement to every depravity of act and spirit. Movies may feature scores of killings in two hours time, vying to show methods ever more horrific. . . . Major corporations make and sell records exhorting their listeners to brutalize Koreans, rob store owners, rape women, kill police. . . . These lessons are being taught to millions of children as I write and you read.

The media's messages are not transforming these young people into killers, Walinsky says, but they are feeding into a cycle of violence that is getting harder and harder to break and that has dire repercussions for our country. Much the same could be said about the effect of sexual messages sent to our children. No single show is corrupting America's youth, or creating the epidemic of teen pregnancy or sexually transmitted diseases. But television as a whole says over and over to our children that sex is as devoid of consequences as a game of charades, and they are missing out on something great if they don't have sex right away. It is hardly surprising, then, that a recent poll of kids aged 10 to 16 found that nearly two-thirds believe TV encourages them to become sexually active too soon.

If you still doubt the influence that television wields, just listen to America's parents. I cannot tell you how many times I've heard mothers and fathers say that they feel locked in a struggle with the powerful forces of the electronic culture to shape their children's values—and that they're losing. They feel that television and the culture undermine their fundamental duty as a parent—teaching right and wrong, instilling a sense of discipline—and that their kids' lives are increasingly controlled by careless strangers a world away.

This is why the concept of the V-chip is so appealing to parents. It offers them a silicon hard hat to protect their kids from television's falling standards. The implications of the V-chip's popularity are remarkable.

The public feels so strongly that their children need to be shielded from words and images in the entertainment media that they are turning to the government for help—not censorship, but help. Considering the low esteem with which Americans today regard Washington, this should tell us something about the public's faith and trust in the TV industry.

The public's fear and anger is understandable when you consider the industry's thoughtless response to its concerns. For instance, after hearing a growing chorus of complaints last year about the quality of prime-time programming, capped by last summer's debate in Congress over the V-chip, the major networks reacted by unleashing what critics widely assailed as the crudest, rudest new fall season in history. All too typical were scenes like the one from *Bless This House* on CBS, broadcast during the old Family Hour, when a female character said she was so sex-starved that she wanted to "do it on the coffee table." To that another character responded, "Don't you ever get your period?"

This rash of vulgarity is only the latest step down in an ongoing trend. A study done by a research team at Southern Illinois University recently found that the frequency of indecent and profane language during prime time had increased 45 percent from 1990 to 1994.

But the most disturbing thing about this fall's "slow slide into the gutter," as the *Hartford Courant*'s TV critic called it, was that much of it was happening in the 8 p.m. time slot when millions of children are watching. As the Media Research Center documented in a recent report, this crossover marked the death knell of the traditional Family Hour. Among other things, this study found that in 117 hours of programming reviewed over a recent four-week period, 72 curse words were used, including 29 uses of the word "ass," 13 uses of "bitch" and 10 uses of "bastard."

If these developments are not enough to drive parents to embrace the V-chip, then consider how several network executives responded recently to criticism of the decline in prime-time standards. One top official's justification was that "sexual innuendoes are part of life." Another said, "Society has become crasser, and we move with that." And yet another said, "It is not the role of network TV to program for the children of America."

After hearing these comments, I can't help but ask how these industry leaders would feel if I came into their home and used some of this kind of foul language in front of their children. I doubt they would stand for it. But why then do they feel it is perfectly acceptable and appropriate to use that kind of language in my home, in front of my child? That is essentially what is happening when they decide to send these shows into my living room—they are speaking to me and my family, which includes my eight-year-old daughter.

The same question could be asked of the major syndicators who produce and distribute the daytime "trash TV" talk shows. I recently joined William Bennett and Sam Nunn in a public campaign to focus attention on these degrading, offensive, and exploitative programs. The point we are trying to make is there are some things that are so morally repugnant that they should not be broadcast for mass consumption, least of all by the eight million children who watch these shows regularly. The examples we cite, such as the teenage girl who slept with more than a hundred men, or women who marry their rapists, were unequivocally beyond the pale.

Yet, although we have received comprehensive public support for our efforts, not one of the major communications companies that own the shows we raised concerns about—such as Gannett, Tribune, Sony, Time Warner, Viacom—would publicly acknowledge that their products were problematic in any way. Nor, to our disappointment, has the leadership of the broadcasting industry stepped forward to talk about this genre's excesses.

Those same corporate leaders tried to kill the V-chip in its legislative crib, and for a long time they seemed prepared to pursue a court challenge at all costs. But to their credit, the networks and the National Association of Broadcasters dropped their opposition following the president's appeal in his State of the Union address and agreed (albeit reluctantly) to create a comprehensive, self-enforced rating system. Regardless of how it came to pass, this was a historic breakthrough. The tools offered by the V-chip and a ratings system will go a long way toward empowering parents to keep overly violent and offensive programs out of their homes and out of reach of their children.

But the industry must realize that these tools will not eliminate the fundamental problem that is fueling the deep-seated anger felt by so many Americans: the deterioration of the industry's programming standards. The V-chip is no panacea; the harmful messages abounding on television are still going to reach many young kids. Moreover, the V-chip is no substitute for network responsibility, for recognizing that the programming they send into our homes carries with it enormous influence. Simply put, the American public wants more from television than just good warnings on bad programming.

There is some reason for hope. A growing chorus of voices within the industry is calling for fundamental changes in the way television does business. For instance, in a recent high-profile speech, Richard Frank, the president of the Academy of Television Arts and Sciences, recently said,

"Why do you think people such as C. Delores Tucker, William Bennett, Tipper Gore, Reed Hundt and many others are attacking music and the media? Because *the reality is frightening*" (emphasis added). Frank went on to urge the industry to use the enormous power at its disposal to take some risks and set higher standards. "We cannot and will not ignore the important issues facing television," he said. "We must deal with them responsibly."

One of the most important steps the industry can take now to address the concerns we have raised, and to begin to restore public confidence in its programming, would be to adopt once again a voluntary code of conduct. I know that some in the creative community will charge that such a code is an attempt to chill their free speech, but the truth is that self-regulation is common sense, not censorship.

The time has come to recognize that not every aberrant behavior or hostile voice has the right to be featured on television on a daily basis, especially at times when large numbers of children are watching. That means asking the industry to draw some lines which programmers cannot and will not cross, something Court TV has already done by adopting a code of ethics for its own programming.

I hope that the industry will include in any voluntary code they develop a commitment to bring back the Family Hour and to recreate a safe haven for children during prime time. The major broadcast networks would not only be helping parents by taking this step, they would also be helping themselves. There clearly is a market for high-quality, family-friendly material, as evidenced by the fact that Nickelodeon was the top-rated cable network in the nation last year. This channel has viewers that ABC, NBC, CBS, and Fox could win back.

Lastly, we must not just focus on what is bad about television, we must also talk about what could be good and even great about television. One of the most revealing studies I've come across recently showed that at-risk children who watch *Sesame Street* score significantly higher on math and verbal tests than peers who do not. Just imagine what we could do for the nation's children if there were 20 variations of *Sesame Street* to choose from after school instead of 20 *Jerry Springers*. While that is not likely to happen any time soon, it's a safe bet that the president and many others will continue to push the industry to increase the amount of quality educational programming for kids.

These are just a few suggestions. The devil here is not in the details but in the big picture—or rather, in all the troubling pictures and words the TV industry is pumping into our homes, and in the damage that the sum of those messages inflicts upon our society. The people who run television have a choice before them: Respond to this Revolt of the Revolted, or face the Sentinels of Censorship. The last thing I want is the government setting standards, but I fear the public will soon turn again to Congress to take stronger actions if the TV industry continues on its path downward.

We must avoid that outcome at all costs. To do so, the TV industry must see the V-chip for the powerful symbol of discontent it is, and treat it as a beginning and not an end. More and more these days television is becoming a pariah in America's living rooms, and no slice of silicon can block out that reality.

Joseph Lieberman, a Democratic U.S. senator from Connecticut, is the chairman of the Democratic Leadership Council.

Talkin' Trash

Democratic senators Joseph Lieberman of Connecticut and Sam Nunn of Georgia have joined Heritage Foundation fellow William J. Bennett in urging producers, broadcasters, and advertisers to scale back their support of talk-show sleaze. *Policy Review* offers these descriptions of actual topics discussed on daytime television talk shows.

Jenny Jones (**Warner Bros. Television**). Guests have included: a woman who said she got pregnant while making a pornographic movie; a husband who had been seeing a prostitute for two years and whose wife confronted him on the show. *Selected show titles*: "A Mother Who Ran off with Her Daughter's Fiancé," "Women Discuss Their Sex Lives with Their Mothers."

Sally Jessy Raphael (**Multimedia Entertainment**). Guests have included: a 13-year-old girl who was urged to share her sexual experiences, beginning at age 10; a person who claimed to have slept with over 200 sexual partners; a man who appeared on stage with roses for the daughter he had sexually molested, and revealed that he had been molested when he was five. *Selected show titles*: "Sex Caught on Tape," "My Daughter Is Living as a Boy," "Wives of Rapists," "I'm Marrying a 14-year-old Boy."

Jerry Springer (**Multimedia Entertainment**). Guests have included: a man who admitted to sleeping with his girlfriend's mother; a 16-year-old girl (wearing sunglasses to disguise her identity) who said she buried her newborn baby alive in her backyard; a 17-year-old who had married her 71-year-old foster father (with whom she first had sex when she was 14) and had borne four children by him; a husband who revealed to his wife on the show that he was having an affair, after which the mistress emerged, kissed the husband, and told the wife that she loved them both.

Montel Williams (**Paramount**). Guests have included: a pregnant woman who boasted of having eight sexual partners during her first two trimesters; a 17-year-old girl who boasted of having slept with more than a hundred men; a man claiming to be an HIV-positive serial rapist of prostitutes. *Selected show titles*: "Married Men Who Have Relationships with the Next-Door Neighbor," "Promiscuous Teenage Girls."

Maury Povich (**Paramount**). Guests have included: a young mother who had no qualms about leaving her sons in the care of her father, a convicted child molester, because the father had only molested girls.

Geraldo (**Tribune Entertainment**). Guests have included: a gold-chained pimp who threatened to "leave my [expletive] ring print" on the forehead of an audience member, while scantily clad prostitutes sat next to him. *Selected show titles*: "Men Who Sell Themselves to Women for a Living," "Mothers Try To Save Their Daughters from Teen-age Prostitution," "Women Who Marry Their Rapists."

Richard Bey (**All American Television**). Guests have included: a woman who said her 16-year-old sister had slept with 15 men; two sisters who hate each other and who mudwrestled while the show played pig noises; a man who wanted to have sex with his girlfriend's sister before he and his girlfriend got married. Selected show title: "Housewives vs. Strippers."

Ricki Lake (**Columbia Tri-star Television**). Guests have included: a woman who boasted she once pulled a gun on her boyfriend's wife; a man who explained to his surprised roommate that he had revealed the roommate's homosexuality to the roommate's mother. *Selected show titles*: "Women Confront Exes Who Cheated and Then Warn New Girlfriends," "Now That I've Slept with Him, He Treats Me Like Dirt!"

Rolanda (**King World**). Guests have included: a woman who revealed her love for her female roommate, whose response was, "Now I know why she comes in the bathroom every time I take a shower"; a woman serving as maid of honor to her best friend who alleged that she had slept with the groom a week before the wedding. *Selected show titles*: "I Use Sex To Get What I Want," "Get Bigger Breasts or Else."

CHAPTER 24

The Last Temptation: Religion in Hollywood

24.1 PAT SAJAK, "THE DISCONNECT BETWEEN HOLLYWOOD AND AMERICA"

Seventy years after Hollywood won the nickname "Sin City," critics continued to complain that Hollywood was not only promoting immorality but that it was anti-religious. In the article "The Disconnect between Hollywood and America" by Pat Sajak, the popular game show host explains that he works in Hollywood but lives in Maryland, because he cannot abide the hypocrisy in Tinseltown. For example, Sajak finds it ironic that filmmakers tolerate and even promote "disrespect toward Christianity" but want to censor smoking.

Because Hollywood is so big and so powerful, so great and so well-known, it has an exaggerated view of its significance. Not Hollywood, the town. Not much Show Business actually goes on there. Most of the studios are spread around other Southern California communities, like Culver City or Burbank. But I mean Hollywood, the Entertainment Mecca—which includes parts of Southern California and New York City, and, because news has become entertainment, some of Washington, D.C., as well.

While I work in Hollywood, I live elsewhere. My family and I live in a quiet suburb of Annapolis, Maryland. The kids go to school there. They live near their grandparents—my in-laws—and most of my neighbors care very little about overnight ratings, box office grosses and sweep weeks. We don't hate L.A. In fact, we like it, and we spend a great deal of time there. But I happen to have a job that allows me a great deal of flexibility, and that gives me the luxury of living a *real* life in addition to my fake one.

You see, one of the dangers of my business is that it has the potential to fill you with a distorted view of life and your importance in it. And it's understandable in a way. If you are part of a successful enterprise, people treat you very well. They pretend the most outlandish or inane things you might say are important and quotable. Drugs? Adultery? Alcoholism? Deviant behavior? Don't worry. You go on *Oprah*. . .you cry. . .people call you heroic for being so open. . .and your career soars to new heights.

You're treated importantly, so you must be important. Suddenly your views are not just your own private opinions; they become part of a public record. They quote you on *Entertainment Tonight* and in *People* magazine. You can endorse a candidate, fight for a cause, call people names—it's pretty heady stuff. The world waits breathlessly for your next pronouncement.

Rosie O'Donnell—a daytime talk show host—goes public with her sexual preference, and she is lauded as brave. What exactly is brave about that? First of all, who cares? And what's brave about getting the chance to be interviewed by ABC and landing on magazine covers? I characterize it as bravery-as-a-career-move.

I don't mean to pick on Ms. O'Donnell, but it's just another example of the self-importance that Show Business can bestow on you—the idea that your sexual preference matters to anyone other than your immediate family and your partner, or partners, seems rather silly to me.

Speaking of silly, Alec Baldwin, an actor, recently compared the election of George W. Bush to the terrorist attacks of last September. This is the same Baldwin brother who promised to leave the country if Bush were elected. Sadly, he reneged on that one. Baldwin also went on Conan O'Brien's late-night show during the Clinton impeachment to say that Illinois Republican Congressman Henry Hyde should be shot—along with his family.

Do remarks like that get you chastised in Hollywood? Ostracized? Marginalized? No, it's Alec Baldwin. He's an actor. He's in Show Business. He's important.

The silliness and outrageousness that emanates from Hollywood comes from non-performers as well. Ted Turner once mocked his employees who had ashes on their foreheads for Ash Wednesday as "Jesus Freaks." Mr. Turner, a self-proclaimed protector of human rights, apparently has his limits.

Filmmaker Rob Reiner—a cofounder of Castle Rock Entertainment—is reportedly upset by what he sees in many films these days, and he plans to do something about it. In fact, he's so upset about this thing, anyone who wants to depict it in a Castle Rock film must meet with Reiner first in order to justify its inclusion.

So what's got Rob so upset? Gratuitous violence? Casual sex? Disrespect toward Christianity? Bias against Big Business? Is that what he wants to cut down or eliminate? No, of course not. That would be censorship. He wants to get rid of smoking. There's too much smoking in movies.

To quote Mr. Reiner, "Movies are basically advertising cigarettes to kids." No knock on Rob. In fact, I agree with him. But why is smoking open to censorship and not these other issues? And what happened to Hollywood's argument that movies and TV shows don't *cause* bad behavior, they just reflect it? Or is it merely a health issue? But surely, health is involved when it comes to violence and casual sex. The answer is, there is no answer. It's just Hollywood being Hollywood. It's monumental hypocrisy. Kids can't pick up bad habits from what they watch. . .oh, except for smoking.

You see, if *you* complain about what you see as excesses on the screen, you are a book-burning prude who wants to tell everyone else how to live. You are a censor. You have no right. That is a right saved for the wise. They know better. They are important.

It's the same kind of nonsense that brings celebrities to "Save the Earth" benefits in eight-mile-per-gallon limos. Or that allows them to make a public service announcement urging recycling—filmed at their 20,000 square foot homes. They can lecture to you and you should listen, even if they don't because. . .well, because they're celebrities. They're from Hollywood, for goodness sake. . .and you live in Michigan (or wherever)!

I could go on with a laundry list of silly and hypocritical things said and done by some of my fellow Show Business luminaries, but the point here is not to make them look silly. They're perfectly capable of doing that without my help. The larger point is the disconnect between the realities of this nation and its people, and the perceived realities of many in the entertainment community.

I don't mean to sound too harsh—or hypocritical. After all, I seem perfectly happy to have cashed my checks for the more than 30 years I've been in television. And I'm not exactly working on the Dead Sea Scrolls. I *do* make a living by selling vowels and spinning a giant multicolored wheel! So who am I to be pointing fingers? Well, I'm just someone who wants to feel prouder than he does—as proud as he once was—about what goes on in his industry. And that's why I spend only part of my time around it. I need to step back occasionally. I think it does help me see the world more clearly.

And that's the irony of it all. Most of you, in a very real way, are more aware of what this nation and this world are about than the supposedly well-connected and in-tune people who inhabit our media culture.

Former *CBS* newsman Bernard Goldberg has written a best-selling book called *Bias*, in which he maintains that the real problem with the media is not a bias based on liberal vs. conservative or Republican vs. Democrat. It is a bias based on the sameness of worldview caused by social, intellectual, educational and professional inbreeding. These are folks who travel in the same circles, go to the same parties, talk to the same people, compare their ideas, and develop a standard view on issues that makes any deviation from them seen somehow marginal, or even weird.

They think they have diversity in their midst because they take pains to hire a representative mix of gender and race. But there is no diversity of *thought*. On the great social issues of our time, there is an alarmingly monolithic view held by what has become known as the "media elite." You can bet that the *New York Times* is careful about how many women it hires, but you can also bet that it is *not* very careful that these women hold diverse views on issues they'll be writing about, such as the environment, gun control or abortion. My guess it that a pro-life view within the wall of the *Times* is a pretty rare one. And the same holds true on the entertainment side.

It is just assumed that "right thinking people" hold certain views. If you *don't*. . . well there's the problem. How can you portray people fairly in film or on TV if you think their attitudes are so foreign?

How can you write about people fairly if they seem so out of touch with that you are used to in your everyday life? That might help explain why religion is rarely depicted as a natural part of life in the average sitcom or drama series, despite the fact that tens of millions of Americans say that it is important to them.

At a dinner party in Los Angeles recently, our hostess was about to say some grudgingly kind words about President Bush and the way he was handling the War on Terror. She prefaced her remarks by saying, "Now I know everyone at this table voted for Al Gore, but. . ." Well, she knew no such thing. She just presumed it. It's what "right-thinking" people did. This "false reality" is a phenomenon that permeates media circles.

It's the phenomenon that caused Pauline Kael, former film critic for *The New Yorker*, to remark after Richard Nixon's election sweep in 1972, "I can't believe it! I don't know a single person who voted for him." This was a man who won in 49 out of 50 states and she didn't know *one* person who voted for him. And I don't think she was dealing in hyperbole. She simply had never met those people. She couldn't believe they really existed.

It's the phenomenon that allows the media to "rediscover" patriotism and heroism in the wake of September 11, when millions of others in St. Louis, Cleveland, Salem, Phoenix, Cheyenne, and a thousand other cities and small towns, know that those traits never went away.

It's the phenomenon that explains Hollywood's disdain for Big Business. You read about it in the newsmagazines and see it in the movies. Big Business is bad. The people who run these businesses are heartless, often criminal, brutes. There is no regard for the little guy. Thousands are laid off while the greedy business executives reap windfall profits. Never mind that some of the biggest and least-competitive businesses are in entertainment. They merge, they lay off thousands, while stock options accrue to the top executives. Top talent at networks and in movies get tens—even hundreds—of millions while so many of their co-workers lose their jobs. They simply don't see the contradiction. They are above it.

And, perhaps worst of all, it's the phenomenon that allows movie studios and television networks to program with an utter disregard for your kids and your communities. It's not that they're evil people. *They* have kids, and they care about them. But they see no connection between what they do and the results of what they do. And, besides, you're not really families and communities. You're ratings, demographics and sales.

You see, they are—for the most part—clueless. Clueless about this country and its people. Clueless about you. And they are afraid. They are afraid of the new technologies. . . afraid of the dwindling numbers of viewers or readers or listeners. . . afraid for their very existence. So, don't you see, they have to do what it takes to survive. They must survive. They are important. Who do you people out here—the ones they fly over on their way to the other Coast for meetings—who do you think you are?

Well, you are this country. You are its future. And I think that's a very good thing to be.

24.2 JAKE TAPPER, INTERVIEW WITH MATT STONE AND TREY PARKER, *NIGHTLINE*, 2006 [EXCERPT]

Trey Parker and Matt Stone, the creators of Comedy Central's animated television show *South Park*, are often criticized for the rude and crude material on their program. In the *Nightline* interview below, Parker and Stone admit that they understand why some viewers may be offended by their show and even say that they have some regret for their portrayals of Jesus, especially when they have been prevented from making fun of the prophet Mohammed. Nevertheless, they assert their desire to satirize everyone and everything.

Nightline: How does the process work? Just let me tell you probably how I picture the process. You guys sleep in, maybe like . . . 2 p.m. You roll into the writers' room, you do huge bong hits—

Matt Stone: That's what people think!

Nightline: You and all your college friends. You order pizzas. Then you just, like, start watching cable tv and throwing crap on the wall.

Matt Stone: That's what people think.

Trey Parker: We do order pizzas.

. . . [Nightline explains the creative process, which is actually a grueling, 6-day turnaround, and shows excerpts of *South Park*, including an episode about Paris Hilton] . . .

Trey Parker: One day I walked into Guess Jeans, and there she [Paris Hilton] is modeling Guess clothing and these little 12 and 13 year-old girls looking up at it. That's the worst thing you can say to a little girl: is this is great . . . I don't care what anyone says about what we have done. We have never done anything that can mess up a kid as much as that does. So that was the point of that episode.

Nightline: A point many social conservatives would applaud as some of them have. There's even a book called *South Park Conservatives*.

Matt Stone: We love to think that we could control a group of people and take over the country with a new political party.

Nightline: You're the new soccer moms.

Matt Stone: [laughing] Yeah.

Nightline: What are your politics?

Trey Parker: They're *South Park*. We're the only "South Park Conservatives," actually.

Nightline: South Park and their 2004 *Team America World Police* constantly take on liberal celebrities. Parker and Stone say they're not really conservatives as it's just more rebellious to lean right in the liberal enclave of Los Angeles. So who did they vote for in 2004, Bush or Kerry?

Trey Parker: There's a show called "Giant Douche vs. Turd Sandwich," right, and that came out right before the election . . . it's like: "Watch that episode. You'll know exactly who we voted for." 'Cause they're told you have to choose between the Giant Douche and the Turd Sandwich [for the new school mascot]. And Stan says well you know what, if I have to pick between a Giant Douche and a Turd Sandwich, I'm not gonna vote. Everyone is like, you're what? You're not gonna—how dare you! Even his father is like, how dare you, you need to vote, you know people died for your right to vote. You need to pick between the Giant Douche and the Turd Sandwich.

. . .

Trey Parker: This is how little kids talk. This is what four little boys do when left alone. It's just an honest portrayal. There's the *Peanuts* [comic strip] and that's nice and cute and everything, but here's how kids really are.

. . .

Matt Stone: They're selfish. They're little bastards. And society makes them better. It's not, "society corrupts them." I think that's where people see there's a conservative thing.

Nightline: But this year, events had them wondering if maybe the world had become so oversensitive, it was time for the show to end.

Trey Parker: The thing we've stood behind for ten years is it's gotta all be ok or none of it is. Because as soon as you start picking, well ok, we won't do this, then all of a sudden the ones you did about that shouldn't be ok either. So we were starting to say, I don't know that this is a world, you know, *South Park* can live in.

Nightline: After all, in the fictional town of South Park, Colorado everything is fair game. Everything and everybody. Even the prophet Mohammad appeared in an episode in July 2001. But this year when Stone & Parker wanted to put Mohammad in an episode, it was after Muslims worldwide had rioted over cartoons of Mohammad in a Dutch newspaper. And Comedy Central told them not to do it.

Trey Parker: If we were going to say, ok then we won't do that, then you shouldn't be able to do that to Jesus, you shouldn't be able to do it to Buddha—

Nightline: Well, it is a weird standard because in that same episode don't you have Jesus defecating on George Bush?

Matt Stone: Yeah, that was the end point, and that's where we kinda agree with some of the people who've criticized our show because it really is open season on Jesus. We can do whatever we want to Jesus and we have. We've had him say bad words, we've had him shoot a gun, we've had him kill people, and we can do whatever we want, but Mohammad we couldn't just show a simple image.

Trey Parker: But that was so funny, too, because so many people stood behind—actually, to Comedy Central's credit, they didn't do this—but so many people were saying, well, we're not going to do anything with Mohammad because we're religiously tolerant. No you're not, you're afraid of getting blown up!

Matt Stone: Finally, Comedy Central copped to that.

Trey Parker: Yeah, "we're afraid of getting blown up." Well, ok, we can't really argue with that.

Nightline: *South Park's* roots are in mocking that which is held most sacred. It began as this short film, "The Spirit of Christmas," featuring Jesus and Santa Claus fighting. They've stayed true to the spirit of that film, taking on, last season, Tom Cruise [for his unwillingness to "come out of the closet"] and Cruise's religious beliefs, the powerful and very litigious Church of Scientology.

Nightline: Why weren't you allowed to rebroadcast that episode? I know eventually they decided you could because the bad press was so much it didn't make any sense . . .

Matt Stone: We were told that the people involved in *Mission Impossible III* demanded that the show be pulled off the air, and it was.

Nightline: Media behemoth Viacom owns not only Comedy Central but Paramount, the studio that at the time needed Cruise to promote *Mission Impossible III*. For one second, pretend I'm Tom Cruise. Tom Cruise might say, "I'm not gay, and you're implying that I'm gay and I'm living a lie."

Trey Parker: No, we implied that you were in a closet, and you wouldn't come out of it. [shrugs] That's all we implied.

Nightline: Does he have no reason to be offended?

Matt Stone: Oh, he's got total reason to be offended. The thing is, is that he's sued people for implying that he's gay, right,

South Park creators Matt Stone and Trey Parker with cutouts of two of their animated show's characters on November 5, 1997, at their studio in Westwood, California. "Equal opportunity offenders," Stone and Parker used sarcasm and parody to explore a number of social and cultural issues, including celebrities and politics. AP Images.

Matt Stone: **(cont.)**	which is funny. You know people have implied that we're gay, and we haven't sued anybody. I don't give a shit if somebody says I'm gay. That's the difference. That's super funny.
Nightline:	Are either of you religious at all?
Matt Stone:	No.
Trey Parker:	Yeah, I consider myself religious but it would take me a long time to explain it to you.
Matt Stone:	He's been explaining it to me for a while.

Trey Parker:	And he still doesn't get it.
Nightline:	Do you believe in God?
Trey Parker:	Yeah.
Matt Stone:	I'm on tv, yeah.
Trey Parker:	I believe there's something going on that we don't know. That's as far as I can go.
Matt Stone:	Recently, atheists and people who hate religion have really glommed on to our show, because we make fun of a lot of religion, we've made fun of everything. But neither one of us is anti-religious at all. I mean, I'm fascinated by religion.
Trey Parker:	Cause all the religions are super funny to me. The story of Jesus, it makes no sense to me, like, God sent his only son. Why can God only have one son? And why would he have to die? It's like the whole story doesn't . . . it's just bad writing, really, and it's really terrible in about the second act, but basically out of all of the ridiculous religion stories, which are greatly, wonderfully ridiculous, the silliest one I've ever heard is, yeah, there's this big, giant universe, it's expanding, it's all gonna collapse on itself and we're all here, just 'cause. Just 'cause. That, to me, is the most ridiculous explanation ever. I think we have a big atheism show coming up.
Matt Stone:	Just this morning we were talking about an atheism show we could do. We could make fun of atheism.

PERMISSIONS ACKNOWLEDGMENTS

Every effort has been made to cite completely the original source material for each document and article used in this collection. In the event that something has been inadvertently been used or cited incorrectly, every effort will be made in subsequent editions to rectify the error. We offer our sincere thanks to all of the sources that were courteous enough to help us reproduce the contents of this volume.

Part I *Mr. Smith Goes to Washington* (1939) Columbia Pictures, d. Frank Capra. Poster from the author's collection

Chapter 1

1.1 "DeMille Backs Merriam, Saying Films Threatened," *Los Angeles Times*, September 16, 1934, p. 5

1.2 Richard Sheridan Ames, "The Screen Enters Politics: Will Hollywood Produce More Propaganda?" *Harper's Monthly Magazine* March 1935, pp. 473–82. Copyright © 1935 Harper's Magazine. All rights reserved. Reproduced from the March issue by special permission

Chapter 2

2.1 George Murphy with Victor Lasky, *Say . . . Didn't You Used to Be George Murphy?*, New York: Bartholomew House, 1970

2.2 Letter from Dore Schary to Adlai Stevenson, December 2, 1955, Dore Schary Papers, Wisconsin State Historical Society

Chapter 3

3.1 Don Hewitt Oral History, October 8, 2002, John F. Kennedy Presidential Library

Chapter 4

4.1 Ronald Reagan, "A Time for Choosing," October 27, 1964, Public Papers of Ronald Wilson Reagan

4.2 Memo from Bess Abell to Lyndon Johnson, November 23, 1964, Lyndon Baines Johnson Presidential Library

Chapter 5

5.1 Stanley Plog Oral History, "More Than Just an Actor: The Early Campaigns of Ronald Reagan," 1981, UCLA Oral History Program, UCLA Special Collections

5.2 Ronald Reagan Inaugural Address, January 5, 1967, Public Papers of Ronald Wilson Reagan

Part II *Dirty Harry* (1971) Warner Brothers Pictures, d. Don Siegel. Poster from the author's collection

Chapter 6

6.1 Memos from Liz Carpenter and Joe Califano to Lyndon Johnson, June 11, 1968 and June 20, 1968, Lyndon Baines Johnson Presidential Library

6.2 Beau Bridges and Charlton Heston, "Guns: Open Season or Cease-Fire?" *Elle Magazine*, February 1993, pp. 58 and 60

6.3 Transcript from The Rosie O'Donnell show, on which Tom Selleck was a guest, May 19, 1999

6.4 "I'm the NRA" advertisement with Tom Selleck, 1999, NRA Archives

Chapter 7

7.1 Transcript from Nuclear Freeze Debate between Charlton Heston and Paul Newman on ABC's *The Last Word*, October 30, 1982

Chapter 8

8.1 Army Archerd "Twenty Years with AIDS and H'w'D," *Variety*, June 4, 2001

8.2 Ronald Reagan, "Remarks at the American Foundation for AIDS Research Awards Dinner," May 31, 1987, Public Papers of Ronald Wilson Reagan

Chapter 9

9.1 Norman Lear, "From the Desk of Norman Lear," the Environmental Media Association

9.2 Ann Coulter, "Let Them Eat Tofu!" February 28, 2007, Universal Press Syndicate

Part III *Full Metal Jacket* (1987) Warner Brothers Pictures, d. Stanley Kubrick. Poster from the author's collection

Chapter 10

10.1 Testimony of Darryl F. Zanuck, U.S. Congress Senate Subcommittee of the Committee on Interstate Commerce, Hearings Regarding Moving Picture Screen and Radio Propaganda, September 1941, Congressional Record

10.2 Recommendation for Award of the Silver Star Medal to Captain John Hamilton [Sterling Hayden] from Hans V. Tofte to the Director of the Strategic Services Unit, February 28, 1946, Records of the Office of Strategic Services, Box 108, "Hamilton, John," National Archives and Records Administration

Chapter 11

11.1 "Statement of Principles," Motion Picture Alliance for the Preservation of American Ideals, 1944

11.2 Testimony of Walt Disney, U.S. Congress House Un-American Activities Committee, Hearings Regarding the Communist Infiltration of the Motion Picture Industry, October 24, 1947, Congressional Record

11.3 Testimony of Ring Lardner, Jr., U.S. Congress House Un-American Activities Committee, Hearings Regarding the Communist Infiltration of the Motion Picture Industry, October 29, 1947, Congressional Record

11.4 Waldorf Declaration, 1947, Courtesy of Larry Ceplair

Chapter 12

12.1 Picture of John Wayne, Courtesy National Archives, photo no. NWDNS-127-N-A187201

12.2 Transcript of Jane Fonda's Radio Hanoi Broadcast, U.S. Congress House Committee on Internal Security, Travel to Hostile Areas, HR 16742, 19–25 September, 1972

Chapter 13

13.1 Petition Letter from Artists for Winning Without War, 2003, Courtesy of Moveon.org

13.2 Rich Lowry, "Love Your Country," May 2, 2003, http://www.Townhall.com (accessed November 20, 2008)

Chapter 14

14.1 "Statement of Conscience," Not in Our Name

14.2 Remarks by Ron Silver as Prepared for Delivery at the 2004 Republican National Convention, August 30, 2004

Part IV *Adam's Rib* (1949) Metro–Goldwyn–Mayer Inc., d. George Cukor. Poster from the author's collection

Chapter 15

15.1 Letter from David O. Selznick to Walter White, Executive Secretary of NAACP, 4/2/40, Papers of the National Association for the Advancement of Colored People, Collections of the Manuscript Division, Library of Congress

15.2 "Fundraising Notes," August 1965, New York Friends of SNCC, Reel, Student Nonviolent Coordinating Committee, Microform, Reel 27

15.3 "Blacks vs. Shaft," *Newsweek*, August 28, 1972, p. 88

Chapter 16

16.1 Speech by Sacheen Littlefeather at the Academy Awards, 1973, Mason Wiley and Damien Bona, *Inside Oscar: The Unofficial History of the Academy Awards*, New York: Ballantine Books, 1996

16.2 Robert E. Thompson, "Brando's Rejection of Oscar Scored," *L.A. Herald Examiner*, April 1, 1973, E7

Chapter 17

17.1 Mike Lawrence, "Senators M*A*S*H 'Hawkeye'" *Quad City Times*, May 15, 1975, Phyllis Schlafly Papers, Eagle Forum Archives, Clayton, Missouri

Chapter 18

18.1 Position Statement of the National Italian American Foundation, "Focus: Image & Identity Report"

18.2 David Rensin, "*Playboy* Interview: Martin Scorsese," *Playboy* April, 1991, reprinted with permission. All rights reserved

Chapter 19

19.1 George Clooney, Best Supporting Actor Acceptance Speech, 2006 Academy Awards, March 5, 2006

19.2 Jonah Goldberg, "Hollywood's Eye Contact with Social Issues," March 8, 2006, http://www.Townhall.com (accessed November 20, 2008)

Part V *Some Like It Hot* (1959) United Artists, d. Billy Wilder. Poster from the author's collection

Chapter 20
20.1 Hays Code, 1934
20.2 Motion Pictures Classified by National Legion of Decency: February, 1936–November, 1950

Chapter 21
21.1 *Joseph Burstyn, Inc. v. Wilson*, 343 U.S. 495 (1952)
21.2 Testimonies of Jack Valenti and Stephen Farber, "Movie Ratings and the Independent Producer," Hearings before the Subcommittee on Special Small Business Problems of the Committee on Small Business, House of Representatives, Ninety-Fifth Congress, First Session, March 24, 1977 and April 14, 1977

Chapter 22
22.1 Attorney General's Commission on Pornography [also known as "The Meese Report"] U.S. Department of Justice, July 1989
22.2 Position statement of the Free Speech Coalition, 1991

Chapter 23
23.1 1996 Telecommunications Reform Act, Federal Communications Commission
23.2 Joe Lieberman, "Why Parents Hate TV," *Policy Review* no. 77, May/June 1996

Chapter 24
24.1 "The Disconnect between Hollywood and America" by Pat Sajak, 2002, reprinted by permission of *Imprimis*, a publication of Hillsdale College
24.2 Interview with Matt Stone and Trey Parker on *Nightline*, September 22, 2006, reprinted by permission of ABC News and *Nightline*

INDEX

Related titles from Routledge

History Goes to the Movies
Studying History on Film
By Marnie Hughes-Warrington

Can films be used as historical evidence? Do historical films make good or bad history? Are documentaries more useful to historians than historical drama?

Written from an international perspective, this book offers a lucid introduction to the ways films are made and used, cumulating with the exploration of the fundamental question: What is history and what is it for?

Incorporating film analysis, advertisements, merchandise and internet forums, and ranging from late-nineteenth century short films to twenty-first century DVD "special editions," this survey evaluates the varied ways in which filmmakers, promoters, viewers, and scholars understand film as history. From *Saving Private Ryan* to *Picnic at Hanging Rock* to *Pocahontas*, *History Goes to the Movies* considers that history is not simply to be found in films, but in the perceptions and arguments of those who make and view them.

This helpful introductory text blends historical and methodological issues with real examples to create a systematic guide to issues involved in using historical film in the study of history.

History Goes to the Movies is a much-needed overview of an increasingly popular subject.

ISBN 10: 0–415–32827–6 (hbk)
ISBN 10: 0–415–32828–4 (pbk)
ISBN 10: 0–203–39094–6 (ebk)

ISBN 13: 978–0–415–32827–2 (hbk)
ISBN 13: 978–0–415–32828–9 (pbk)
ISBN 13: 978–0–203–39094–8 (ebk)

Available at all good bookshops
For ordering and further information please visit:
www.routledge.com

Related titles from Routledge

A Knight at the Movies
Medieval History on Film
By John Aberth

"This is an ambitious and exciting book. The author combines very up-to-date historiography—some of it controversial but all of it interesting—with a sensitive and deep appreciation of the art of the films. Any teacher of film or medieval studies should make use of this valuable resource."—*Jeremy duQuesnay Adams, Southern Methodist University*

Long before *Monty Python and the Holy Grail*, Hollywood's version of the Middle Ages had sometimes been laughable. Who could resist chuckling at *The Black Knight* (1954), in which Arthurian warriors ride across a plain complete with telephone poles in the background? Or *The Black Shield of Falworth* (1954), in which Tony Curtis, in his best medieval Bronx accent, utters the immortal line, "Yonda is the castle of my fodda"? These films may not be paragons of historical accuracy, but much of what we know—or think we know—about the Middle Ages has been dictated by what we've seen on the movie screen.

In this entertaining and deeply informative book, John Aberth, author of *From the Brink of the Apocalypse*, assesses the historical accuracy of well-known cinematic interpretations of the *Middle Ages*. Separating fact from fiction in more than fifty films from the silent era to today, including *Camelot, Excalibur, Braveheart*, and *The Adventures of Robin Hood*, Aberth shows how narrative license routinely makes the distant era familiar by projecting contemporary obsessions and fears onto the past. These stock images of knights in shining armor and damsels in distress rarely sum up real life in the Middle Ages. Instead, the best and most thought-provoking works—like Ingmar Bergman's *The Seventh Seal*—revel in the differences between those times and our own, drawing us into another world in order to understand and appreciate the differences. With provocative insight into the blurred lines between medieval fact and fiction, both history buffs and film aficionados will find much food for thought here.

ISBN 10: 0–415–93885–3 (hbk)
ISBN 10: 0–415–93886–4 (pbk)
ISBN 10: 0–203–87356–4 (ebk)

ISBN 13: 978–0–415–93885–3 (hbk)
ISBN 13: 978–0–415–93886–0 (pbk)
ISBN 13: 978–0–203–87356–4 (ebk)

Available at all good bookshops
For ordering and further information please visit:
www.routledge.com

Related titles from Routledge

Screened Out
Playing Gay in Hollywood from Edison to Stonewall
By Richard Barrios

"A finely nuanced analysis of how gays and lesbians were presented on screen from the 1920s through the 1970s."—*G.M. Kramer, Lambda Book Report*

"Building on the legacy of *The Celluloid Closet*, Barrios manages to be both encyclopedic and breezy; taking the reader on a comfortable and well-documented tour of 20th century American screen images of homosexuality. *Screened Out* is a must-have for film buffs and queer buffs and will be the standard reference work and source for all future work in this area."—*Esther Newton, author of Margaret Mead Made Me Gay*

"A comprehensive and lucidly written contribution to the history of queer images in Hollywood films, rich in sharp analysis and fresh perspectives. It is also a must-read for anyone trying to make sense of the cultural climate leading up to the Stonewall riots, which ushered in the modern gay rights movement. An important book and a terrific resource."—*Michelangelo Signorile, author of Queen in America*

Rapacious dykes, self-loathing closet cases, hustlers, ambiguous sophisticates, and sadomasochistic rich kids: most of what America thought it knew about gay people it learned at the movies. A fresh and revelatory look at sexuality in the Great Age of movie making, *Screened Out* shows how much gay and lesbian lives have shaped the Big Screen. Spanning popular American cinema from the 1900s until today, distinguished film historian Richard Barrios presents a rich, compulsively readable analysis of how Hollywood has used and depicted gays and the mixed signals it has given us.

Mining studio records, scripts, drafts (including cut scenes), censor notes, reviews, and recollections of viewers, Barrios paints our fullest picture yet of how gays and lesbians were portrayed by the dream factory, warning that we shouldn't congratulate ourselves quite so much on the progress movies—and the real world—have made since Stonewall.

Captivating, myth-breaking, and funny, *Screened Out* is for all film aficionados and for anyone who has sat in a dark movie theater and drawn strength and a sense of identity from what they saw on screen, no matter how fleeting or coded.

ISBN 10: 0–415–92328–X (hbk)
ISBN 10: 0–415–92329–8 (pbk)

ISBN 13: 978–0–415–92328–6 (hbk)
ISBN 13: 978–0–415–92329–3 (pbk)

Available at all good bookshops
For ordering and further information please visit:
www.routledge.com